Praise for *Sins of the System*

"In *Sins of the System*, Regina courageously shares her family's heart-wrenching story of generational trauma, mental health struggles and gun violence with grace, honesty and compassion. Her journey from grieving aunt to passionate advocate is truly inspiring. Regina is working to ensure no other family has to endure the pain that hers has, and through her words, she offers hope for a brighter future, even among the many challenges some families and children in our country face."
    —Shannon Watts, founder of Moms Demand Action

"In this thorough and moving account of a tragedy so stark it takes our breath away, Regina manages to convey both the brokenness of a system that shattered a family and the power of love to lift and mend the most seemingly hopeless conditions. Regina's steadfast dedication to the goodness that shines through the darkest nights of our collective soul render this book much more than a gripping memoir: it is a powerful prayer."
    —Mirabai Starr, Author of *Caravan of No Despair* and *Wild Mercy*

"In *Sins of the System*, Dr. Griego offers an intimate window into the heartbreaking tragedy of youth violence, and an inspiring vision of the healing we can experience when we do not settle for mere retribution, but instead engage in the redemptive work of nurturing compassion, even for children who have caused great harm."
    —Preston Shipp, Senior Policy Counsel, Campaign
        for the Fair Sentencing of Youth (CFSY)

"Dr. Griego has written a searing personal account of what it has been like to see her traumatized nephew thrust into a world of national publicity, the courts, and our juvenile justice system. She is to be applauded for sharing publicly the details of her private experience. This is an important book which is accessible beyond those involved in our criminal justice system."
    —NM State Senator Bill O'Neill, novelist, poet and playwright

SINS
OF THE
SYSTEM

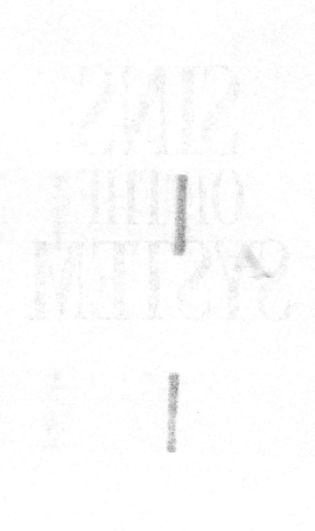

SINS
OF THE
SYSTEM

TRAUMA, GUNS,
TRAGEDY,
AND THE
BETRAYAL
OF OUR CHILDREN

REGINA M. GRIEGO, PhD

Published by Transcending Futures, LLC
www.Transcending-Futures.com

ISBN (paperback): 979-8-9857105-0-2
ISBN (ebook): 979-8-9857105-1-9

Edited by Valerie Costa, Costacreativeservices.com
Book design by Christy Day, www.constellatiobookservices.com

Printed in the United States of America

for all children in tough situations

CONTENTS

AUTHOR'S NOTE

This book was written based on the author's personal journals, extensive notes taken during hearings and meetings with professionals (i.e., attorneys, medical professionals, educational specialist, and others), e-mails exchanged during the course of events, recorded phone messages, newspaper articles, personal letters, copies of legal documents, photographs, and video recordings. The author consulted with several of the people who are mentioned or are a part of the book for their accounts and recollections. The author's own memory of these events were also a source for this memoir. Although many of the events recounted in the book were public at the time to one degree or another, the names of most but not all of the individuals mentioned have been changed to protect people's privacy or safety. Occasionally people or events were omitted for the same reason, but only when that omission had no impact on either the veracity or the substance of the story.

This memoir has stories of trauma that might trigger people who are dealing with trauma. If you feel triggered as you read this book, please seek professional support.

PROLOGUE

A storm was brewing that would ravage our lives again. There was no hint before our flight, but our return had a very, very hard landing. My husband, Mark and I returned from our vacation a day early, on Saturday, January 9, 2016, instead of Sunday. It would give me a day to prepare for the next emotional week when I was scheduled to testify at the hearing for my nephew Ezekiel. In retrospect, I suppose I was naïve.

In a phone call the evening of my return, my brother Leo said, "Looks like a letter was written to the judge and the *Albuquerque Journal* from Jenny, Dad, and other family in California. They want Ezekiel to go to prison."

The next morning, the headline on the front page of the Sunday *Albuquerque Journal* shouted in bold print, "Teen Who Killed Family in Court This Week." The article continued: "*The tragedy has split much of his extended family. A local aunt and uncle support a juvenile sentence and treatment for Pacheco, but his grandfather, older sister and other family members are urging the judge to impose an adult prison sentence.*" It felt like a slap in the face. Who were these other family members?

It had been a shock to learn that Ezekiel killed his father (my brother), his mother, and his three young siblings three years prior to the upcoming hearing. Our family rallied behind Ezekiel and none of us saw anything that indicated that he could do such a thing.

Leo worked hard at keeping the family together including making sure that everyone was on-board with the plea agreement Ezekiel's attorneys negotiated that allowed him this hearing in the children's court. Now it seemed that we were no longer united as a family.

My grief and anxiety about the hearing starting the next day grew as I tossed and turned in my bed remembering all the conversations with Ezekiel's sisters. I took guardianship of Ezekiel because his sisters were living elsewhere and I felt like it was the right thing to do. Supporting him as his guardian while remaining sane had dominated my life and relationships over the course of the last three years.

This whole tragedy was a perfect storm and navigating the juvenile justice system and learning all that happened leading to the murders was like being in a small vessel in the middle of a hurricane. Many systems failed and led to what happened that fateful night when we lost five family members. Losing a sixth member—my brother's son— felt unbearable.

A week later I wrote this Journal entry.

January 18, 2016: My head, heart, and stomach are a jumble. I know I am exhausted. I want to be anonymous, to forget my own name. The swirl of last week, everything from being blindsided on Sunday by an article in the Albuquerque Journal, to some initial tense moments as the proceedings began as to whether I would be able to sit in the court-room for the week since I was a witness, to outbursts from Mark, to the fight we had after he got hurt when I told him that his outbursts were not helpful, to Ezekiel's half-sisters and other family members who we didn't expect turning up.

I'm strung out emotionally, on caffeine, and imbibing more wine each evening. All that I can think of is that it isn't over yet. There is follow-up testimony and rebuttal scheduled for February 10-12. The goal post has moved out again. Ezekiel's half-sister wants to rebut my testimony, but so far Ezekiel's attorney isn't concerned, as there is nothing to rebut.

His sisters haven't been around for over two years. My father, Ezekiel's other half-siblings, and all the other family haven't been around at all, except one visit by Ezekiel's maternal aunt in March of 2014.

I took sick leave this week; my name was all over the paper and in the network news last Friday. The network media did an incompetent and sensationalized job of reporting, no surprise. The Albuquerque Journal did better. After February 12th it could take up to thirty days before a sentencing hearing.

My brother Leo, who has been with me through this, is celebrating his fiftieth birthday on Saturday, January 23rd, the same day as Mark's birthday. Mark and I are going to Ojo Caliente near Taos tomorrow for a couple of days. I need to let myself go down, let go, rest, visit nature, and forget for a little while. Mark is anxious for things to get back to normal. I have forgotten what normal looks like.

My heart hurts. I know I need to continue to be present for Ezekiel and support the defense team and I will, but I do not have the capacity to worry about the California crowd and other family.

I visited my therapist today and then I wrote this in a coffee shop where I stared at the beautiful Sandia Mountains dusted with snow and vultures fighting over roadkill. I feel like roadkill right now.

The sense of betrayal and sadness I felt after the hearing settled in my being for months after but I continued in my commitment to Ezekiel. I thought we were on the home stretch of this unwelcomed journey. Little did I know it would be another four years before the outcome would be decided.

FOREWORD

"Every calculation based on experience elsewhere fails in New Mexico."
—Lew Wallace, Governor of the New Mexico Territory, 1878-1881

New Mexico is a bundle of contradictions and populated by a people living perpetually in-between and on the margins of mainstream U.S. culture. For example, we are a majority-minority state with very little in common with any of our neighbors, sandwiched between Arizona and Texas, with the Mexican state of Chihuahua to the south and Colorado to the north. We are a poor state, with the third lowest average income and a large portion of the population living below the poverty level. The state is the fifth largest in the U.S. by area, but 36th in population, and even lower, 47th, for population density. Based on the most recent census numbers, the population is approximately 48 percent Hispanic, which is an estimate at best because of the historical exclusion of "Hispanic" as a designated race; it often is instead included as an "ethnicity." The Hispanic population was expected to endorse "White" for race, and "Hispanic or Latino" for ethnicity. For generations the numbers of our Hispanic population were underestimated, due to our elders either submitting incomplete forms or, more likely, declining to respond entirely.

We are a unique, proud, stubborn people who often keep to ourselves. We are none of these things by accident. To understand us, it helps to go back to our historical and geographic roots. At first a land largely of ancestral Pueblo peoples, Spanish settlers colonized the region in the 16th century, christening the territory *Nuevo Mexico* after an Aztec valley of the same name. It is a long-running, if relatively obscure joke, that New Mexico predates Mexico by several hundred years. Part of New Spain until Mexican Independence in 1821, New Mexico became a region belonging to Mexico for a brief 27 years. With the end of the Mexican-American War in 1848, New Mexico became a U.S. territory and then the 47th state on January 6, 1912.

Our terrain is extremely diverse, with mountains, deserts, forests, plains, and the Rio Grande running down the center, north to south, like an ancient backbone. With mountains to the east of the river and volcanoes to the west, the life-sustaining floodplains of the Rio Grande suitable for early human habitation are located in a basin, a naturally-occurring hiding place, shielded by the surrounding harsher, higher grounds. In addition to this geography, one-third of the state is federally owned land, with Reservation land occupying another 10 percent. This constellation of factors left us isolated and largely forgotten by the rest of the world. We became somewhat insular, with our own flavors of food, culture, language, religion, and worldview. Our Spanish, for example, is often mocked by other Spanish-speakers from around the globe, as many of our words are different in pronunciation, meaning, or both. I recall an incident involving a conversation between my father, a native New Mexican who learned (our) Spanish as his first language, and a visitor from Spain. The Spanish gentleman used a word that New Mexicans found particularly vulgar. When my father explained this, the Spanish gentleman stated, with a note of condescension, "The rest of the world considers that word tame." My father replied, "New Mexico is not the rest of the world."

As a neuropsychologist, I routinely ask my patients which language they learned first and find I must include multiple follow-up questions when my elderly patients state, "English." Further probing often indicates Spanish as the first language learned, with English learned in school. This is not surprising to me, as often, we hesitate to reveal details about ourselves until directly asked. Many families speak our own brand of "Spanglish" with each other, and exclusively English with members from outside the community.

Our food is not Mexican, or "Tex-Mex," but something all our own. Our traditional art, architecture, and music are influenced by our Indigenous, Mexican, and Spanish ancestors. Even with increased access to the rest of the world, we have resisted mainstream acculturation.

Barelas, home to the family whose story you are reading, is the oldest neighborhood in Albuquerque, located near downtown and just along the Rio Grande. The neighborhood began as its own self-contained village, growing in population from a handful of families original to the area and eventually engulfed by the spread of the newer, growing city of Albuquerque. Even as a neighborhood within the city limits, it remained somewhat isolated and insular, resisting gentrification into the early 2000s. From the 1930s to the 1950s, when the American Dream was out of reach for most people of color, Barelas residents opened their own businesses and passed them down the family line so that some are still in existence. Invested in their children and community, residents worked with local organizations to build a community center, completed in 1942, that remains in operation to this day. Displaced and reduced by highway expansion and the declining railroad industry that together restructured the neighborhood and demolished hundred-year-old adobe houses, but never their community, Barelas stubbornly refused to vanish, digging its heels into Albuquerque's "South Valley" and becoming inseparable from it.

The poverty rate has historically been higher than the rest of the city, with a larger portion of the population remaining Hispanic, and it is not unusual for multiple generations to reside together under one roof. These characteristics gave rise to unflattering stereotypes, and again in the 1960s and '70s, *Bareleños* fought displacement. Despite the combination of neglect and persecution, of the years spent caught between history and the "progress" of outsiders, and the many times they have had to fight for the right to peacefully live their lives, residents of Barelas refused to let their community die. In addition to being unique, proud, and stubborn New Mexicans, residents of Barelas have the reputation among much of our larger Hispanic community of being a hard-working, resourceful people with open hearts and traditions that run deep. In many ways, they are the most New Mexican of us all.

Against this backdrop and within this context, then, we consider the field of psychology. Due to the characteristics and history of New Mexico, there are too few mental health providers and resources to go around, and most are concentrated in Albuquerque. Poverty on one side, and stigma on the other, are significant barriers to mental health care, and the vast expanses of wild land surrounding Albuquerque requiring sometimes three hours' drive makes accessing services prohibitively challenging for much of the state's population. In addition, the local Hispanic culture is often suspicious of services the mainstream has to offer, and dubious about the extent to which psychology can help them.

This is not an irrational hesitation, as psychology has historically been focused on the mainstream majority, with research, assessments, and treatment that often overlooked the Hispanic population. As the U.S. population has diversified, with a particular increase accounted for by Hispanic/Latino people, there has been a push to diversify the field of psychology and develop more culturally appropriate tools. However, this is a work in progress, and the progress is slower than the growing need. Psychology training programs have increasingly included a diversity requirement, but, with fewer psychologists of color available in leadership positions to contribute, we have been left with concrete, reductive, bumper-sticker-like adages such as, "Latinos value family." While it is true that our New Mexican sense of family often extends much farther than the nuclear, one size does not fit all, and the Hispanic world is anything but homogenous. Science has offered some support regarding the Hispanic sense of *family*, with consistent findings, for example, that Hispanic males with psychotic disorders have better outcomes when they have strong family support and heavy involvement in treatment. But this, too, fails to capture the "value" we place on family, and how it often innervates every aspect of our lives. The question remains in many hearts and minds: *what does the world of mental health have to offer communities like mine?*

In my specialty of psychology, neuropsychology, we face all the same issues, and then some. We evaluate cognitive functioning using standardized measures, developed largely based on a monolingual, English-speaking, mainstream U.S.-educated population. To make matters worse, our most recent self-evaluation, performed approximately every five to seven years, suggests the field of neuropsychology remains approximately 86 percent White. Between our limited tools and the lack of diversity among researchers, forensic experts, and clinical service providers, the chances that non-mainstream cultural, educational, and linguistic factors will be over-pathologized is high. Here in New Mexico, with few providers to manage the overwhelming need and a general neglect from the outside world, it is unfortunately too easy to receive substandard care—when one is able and willing to receive care at all. When I returned to New Mexico, a neuropsychologist colleague of mine from a faraway, densely populated, much wealthier state said to me, as if he understood my people better than I did, "The patient population here doesn't know good care from bad. You don't have to work very hard to be successful here." While there may be some truth to the first part of that statement, the attitude expressed in the second is disheartening. Not all health care providers in New Mexico share this attitude, of course, but conditions tend to, if not promote it, turn a blind eye to it.

I have heard the same story too many times to count: It begins with generational trauma borne from a combination of rural poverty, experiences of individual and systemic racism, unacknowledged and untreated mental illness (including PTSD), and lower quality education. This leads to high rates of substance abuse and various types of violence that often result in traumatic brain injury (TBI). Cognitively, this history is likely to result in reduced executive functioning, the suite of cognitive abilities that includes response inhibition, planning, organizing, emotion regulation, problem-solving, and applying reason to appreciate the consequences of hypothetical actions. Further reduce already impaired executive functioning with a substance like alcohol, or by exacerbating PTSD symptoms with actual or even suggested threat, and this is a recipe for impulsive, sometimes violent reactions.

This is often where psychology and the law intersect. It has largely been in my role as expert witness that I have heard this same story from all over the state. The question is often one of competence, either to stand trial or waive *Miranda*. While each examinee varies to some degree, many have undiagnosed learning disabilities, undiagnosed due to lower quality education and the stigma of such disorders within many families. On top of this, there is often some form of violence, though it is frequently minimized by the examinees themselves, revealing how "normal" it seems to them—as if everyone naturally gets hit in the head with tire irons or baseball bats until they lose consciousness. Many never receive medical evaluation or treatment for these kinds of "normal" head injuries. When assessed for PTSD, many will deny symptoms, particularly Hispanic New Mexican men. This population may be culturally reluctant to describe abuse from family members or report a personal or family history of mental illness. With a large military population in New Mexico, many examinees will state outright that they do *not* have PTSD, because they know what the disorder looks like in veterans and will often add they have not experienced anything like military trauma. All of these factors, and more, make these cases challenging. Many attorneys hire experts from out of state who often do not know much about our history or culture, and therefore could not possibly interpret test results within the appropriate context. While not all courts are the same, there are plenty that are just waiting to hear a racist story about a violent Hispanic male from Barelas who deserves to be convicted, and no scarcity of out-of-town experts willing to tell that story.

Why all this prologue? Because this story is one that is both uniquely New Mexican and one that strikes a universal chord in cities and towns across the United States. A family with generational trauma from a culture wary of outsiders and stigma against mental health treatment shattered by tragedy when the weight of all these factors became too much for the family system to bear. Widely available firearms and the lack of accessible mental health and educational services—even had they been desired—contributed to the hurricane that swept up this family into a legal system with a loose grasp of the psychology of abused children from this particular background. The available interventions, once so many systems have failed a child, are often more punishing than therapeutic, despite the fact that we no longer call correctional centers "penitentiaries." There are answers to the questions of how to "correct" many of the behaviors that result in incarceration, but in New Mexico there are few resources and, it seems, even less interest from those who benefit from the current systems in place, many of whom are not native New Mexicans themselves.

This background also serves to highlight that the author's journey mirrors that of Barelas, fighting to protect and hold a family together, and to have them seen publicly for their better attributes and within their context. It also mirrors that of New Mexico, persevering to maintain an identity despite the many pressures from outside forces. Above all, it is the story of a struggle to right generational wrongs, to make changes to multiple flawed systems to ensure our most vulnerable do not slip through the cracks. It is an example, in all its heartbreak and nuance and resilience, of what *family* means to the people of New Mexico.

Lynette M. Abrams-Silva, Ph.D., ABPP
Board Certified in Clinical Neuropsychology
Psychology Clinic Director
University of New Mexico

PART ONE

OUR
ORDINARY
WORLD

CHAPTER 1

THE FOUR OF US

It was always the four of us for as long as I can remember: Janice, Tom, Leo, and me. Janice, the eldest, is two years older than I. She was a *tomboy*, always had scraped knees, usually running at the nose but she could run like the wind. Her skin was dark with angular features framed by her black frizzy hair. She was often lost in the TV, unaware of anything but the television program she was watching. But sometimes she would come up with crazy ideas, like taking us to visit my Grandma Pacheco, my father's mother, when Tom was only three years old. At age seven, she put him in a red wagon with toys, and I walked behind while she pulled the wagon. When we arrived, Grandma Pacheco ran across the street screeching with a worried look on her face, "We were so scared, what are you doing here?" It was not her normal greeting of hugs and cookies that we were hoping for.

Tom was sixteen months younger than I. He and I would spar together, but he never hurt me. When he got older and could take me, I would feign injury, and he would let me go. Leo was the baby and was four years younger than Tom. He had light brown hair like my father, long eyelashes, and dimples. We all thought he was cute, and he was a character. He played off the attention he got. Mom's favorite without a doubt. He would sing into the mirror, holding a hairbrush as a microphone Paul Simon's song, *Loves Me Like a Rock*. He would really get into it because it was true for him.

Our parents had a volatile marriage for most of the ten years they were together. We lived in a nice three-bedroom house because my dad worked as a salesman for prefabricated homes, which was good considering he never graduated from high school. My bedroom was next to the living room, and the fighting was so intense, with Mom throwing lamps and other objects at my father when he came home drunk late at night. He, hitting Mom. Afraid they would kill each other, I would drift off to sleep at night praying that they would still be alive in the morning.

The last time I saw Mom and my father together I was seven and they were in their room. My siblings and I were so happy because he had been gone and we thought he wasn't coming back. Mom woke up that morning cheerful, and said, "Let's get ready for church." Excited, I put my prettiest pink, frilly dress on. Church was fun because I loved to sing. Mom came out in her spring green dress with a lacy overlay. We were all ready to go, except my father, who usually didn't attend church.

Suddenly, a loud knock came at the door, and Mom answered. Frightened and shocked, we heard a woman's voice say, "Frank, let's go! Frank, I know you're in there."

Mom screamed, "Get out of here *puta* (whore)!" Her face was bright red, and features scrunched up.

"Not without Frank. He has no business with you, bitch!" and they continued to argue into the street and to her car.

Without a parting word, not even a goodbye, my father got his things together and left. Mom and this woman were fighting out in front of the house, and we didn't know what to do. We were all crying and wondered who this woman was and why my father left. Mom returned with her face scratched up and drops of blood on her dress.

Through tears, I asked her, "Can I get you a rag to clean your dress?" Janice disappeared into her room with Tom. Leo, who was two, was wrapped around Mom's legs, crying, when she picked him up. Grandma Lucero (Mom's mother) rushed over with my aunt after Mom called them. We didn't go to church that day.

Our parents were never together again. The woman at the door was my father's former fiancée, who he had never stopped seeing after he married Mom. That day my father left and never came back to live with us. He visited a couple of times, but that didn't last for long. Soon, Mom was taking care of four children all by herself and my father had a new family, and he was living in California. We were sad and shellshocked by the divorce, eventually making two moves because our house was sold. Mom was extremely sad. She would make an effort to take us to the park, where we would play, but I often found her crying as she lay on the blanket in the grass. That's about the time I started sleepwalking.

We ended up in a house that Mom had bought before she married my father. At age nineteen she got into an automobile accident, and with the insurance money she got in the settlement she bought an old two-room adobe house next to Grandma Lucero. While married to my dad, they added two more rooms, including a bathroom, and rented it while they were married. After the divorce, the five of us lived in this four-room house. There was no heat in the only bedroom or the bathroom. Mom and my brothers slept in the living room, and Janice and me in the bedroom. It was very cold in the bedroom and bathroom during the winter. Tom would reluctantly shower in the winter and would run to the living room after a shower with his blanket over him. He would hug the heater that stood almost three feet tall with the vent leading to the ceiling as he dressed. One time we heard him yelp and realized he burned his butt as he was trying to put on his underwear under his blanket, and we all laughed.

Grandma Lucero lived next door to us. In the summer, the houses were so hot that most of the families, including Grandma Lucero and visiting family, would sit outside on summer evenings as the day got cooler. It was a great time to hang out in the front yard or play in the streets with our cousins. Since we lived next door, we weren't as special to Grandma Lucero. While she fed all the other cousins, aunts, and uncles, she would usually shoo us away. She sent the cousins to our house since it was usually messy and in need of repair. That way they wouldn't mess up her house.

My sensitive nature compelled me to attempt to keep Mom happy. That first night at the little house, I stayed up most of the night organizing our belongings, hoping that would help her mood. At night I often laid in bed praying or conversing with God or the angels about Mom and our family, hoping that someday we could have a nicer house and that Mom wouldn't be so sad. Janice never understood my sensitive, almost morose demeanor. When she saw me crying as I listened to sad songs, she would laugh and say, "What's the matter with you?" I could feel the pain of others even from listening to a song. Sometimes Janice and her friends would let me spend time with them, but often I stayed home.

Tom was also sensitive, and he cried easily when he was younger but grew to be more stoic as a teenager and man. He learned that it wasn't acceptable to cry, especially in the barrio where we lived. *Barelas* is one of the oldest barrios in Albuquerque, originally home to the railroad workers. We lived a block from the zoo and a block from the river. It wasn't a good idea to be out alone, especially at night, in the barrio. As Tom grew older, he suppressed his sensitive nature; otherwise, he was picked on and had to fight.

Tom somehow got the worst of Mom's anger. She called him lazy and threw things at him when she was mad. Now I wonder if his darker skin played a part in her animosity toward him. There is a dynamic with darker skin in Hispanic families because there was a time when the lighter-complected children could go into the stores and purchase essential goods for the family because they didn't look "Mexican." Lighter skin, or *huero* children, were usually treated better; given more food and the *good* clothes for that reason.

To anger Mom was worse than a volcano erupting or an earthquake. Janice had a knack for setting the volcano in motion, and she would also make herself scarce after she did. Janice and I got our share of beatings from Mom. She would drag us around by our hair and break brushes on us. My tactic was to do everything I could to keep her quiet; making her breakfast, keeping the house clean, and doing laundry at the coin-operated Washeteria with too few coins and too much attention from the *pendejos* (idiots) and vagrants who wandered downtown Albuquerque.

When I was in sixth grade, my older half-brother Vincent came home with his new wife, Amalia, a Cuban woman who spoke only Spanish. Vincent was eleven years older than me. Mom had him at age fifteen when she was forced to marry after becoming pregnant from an older man. The marriage lasted only a year and Mom managed to finish high school after they divorced. Vincent spent a lot of time with my Grandma Lucero. He joined the Air Force after high school and wasn't around much after I was six years old. We were always excited when he came home for a visit in his uniform. He was a quiet, soft-spoken man with a face pitted from acne. While stationed in Spain, Amalia, who was older, swept him off his feet.

By the end of their visit to Albuquerque, they decided that Tom and I would go live with them in Florida. At that time, Tom was ten and happily living with Grandma Pacheco, but Amalia convinced Mom that we would be better off with them. Mom was having health problems and needed surgery. Tom and I left Albuquerque with Vincent and Amalia so it would be easier for Mom with only Janice and Leo to watch over.

Amalia took a particular liking to me. She had to leave behind her only daughter in Cuba when she managed to escape. Still, she forced both of us to eat until we were sick because she thought we were too skinny. After we were in Florida, she developed an animosity toward Tom. He wet the bed on a regular basis. When he did, she would wake him up in the middle of the night and punish him by putting him in a bathtub with ice water or making him drink a concoction of vinegar and fish oil. She would say to him in broken English, "You pee, you drink your pee." One morning I awoke to her crazy screaming. She clutched Tom by the arm and led him out to the front yard. Her screaming drew the attention of neighbors and kids riding by on their bikes. The humiliation that happened next stayed with Tom and me forever, and the memory of it haunts me to this day. When we returned to Albuquerque and reunited with Mom, it was almost two years later, and we were beyond happy.

After graduating from high school, Tom joined the National Guard. They called his unit into the 1980 Santa Fe prison riot, the most violent prison riot in U.S. history. The inmates took complete control and took officers hostage. He saw the worst of humanity in that riot. Several inmates were killed by other prisoners, with some being tortured and mutilated because they were snitches.

Tom tried college for a while at a university in eastern New Mexico where Janice was attending nursing school. It was a small school and most males who attended were either jocks or farmers. Tom did not fit in at all. He was six foot, dark complected, and looked like a

Comanche Indian. Mom said we had Comanche blood; they were a warrior and horseman tribe with broad hips and square foreheads. Though Tom was intelligent enough to be there, he didn't last more than a year. He joined the Army 82nd Airborne, an elite unit that the military uses in first-encounter situations. He spent months in training, parachuting into areas where insects ate at his flesh, and he slept in mud and cold. He trained as a gunner and carried a large gun over his shoulder with him. He prided himself on how tough a *grunt* he was.

Janice, Leo, and I went off to college. Leo went to the same university that I attended, New Mexico State, but I had graduated and was in graduate school by then. Janice transferred to a school in Texas, where she graduated with a bachelor's in nursing and joined the Army as a nurse. Janice and I both got married after graduating from college and started our families. Leo went on to graduate school on the east coast and then started his career with a position at the Department of Labor. We all lived in different areas of the country, though Janice also lived in Japan and England.

CHAPTER 2

FAMILY TIME

Beginning in 2004, we all lived in Albuquerque again. We hadn't all lived in the same town together since Janice left for college in 1977. Even when we lived in different towns, we would gather for holidays and special events. We four siblings decided who would host family gatherings spontaneously, and as the 2012 holidays approached we were making plans as a family.

Janice the eldest had been married for twenty-nine years to John, a tall Anglo with blond hair, the kind of guy she always dated, and they had three grown daughters. She was a nurse and he was a navigator in the Air Force. For Mark and I, it was our second marriage. We had been married for four wonderful years, and we each had three grown children. Mark retired after thirty years in the insurance business when he moved to Albuquerque from San Antonio to be with me. In our wedding photos he towers over me with his broad German stature. I fell in love with his kind face and rugged features. We both have crooked smiles and share common spiritual beliefs.

We both grew up in the Catholic tradition and our faith brought us together. Our faith journey, especially since we had married, had become much more expansive and inclusive, and less based on the doctrine or mythology in the Catholic Church. We met at a drumming circle. We don't go to mass regularly, except for special celebrations. We enjoy various spiritual retreats on a regular basis.

Our brother Tom was married to Amy and they had five children together, with four living at home: Ezekiel, Malachi, Miriam, and the youngest, Grace. Their eldest daughter, Jenny, was married and living on her own. Having had relationships prior to his marriage to Amy, Tom also had five older children who were stepchildren to Amy.

Leo, our youngest brother, was married to Lily. They had a cute three-year-old son. Leo was forty-five years old when they married. Leo was a director for a nonprofit that did research on the status of children, but had recently lost a run for a national congressional seat. Lily was a special education administrator for the Albuquerque Public Schools. They lived in the house that we grew up in, which had been remodeled several times over the years. Lily is almost as tall as Leo, usually very cheerful with a twinkle in her green eyes, often with her blonde hair swept up into a ponytail. She was originally from New Jersey, and Leo would call her his *Jersey girl*. They both loved folk music, and she laughed easily at his almost constant jokes and wisecracks.

Celebrations were usually at Janice's, Leo's, or my house. I can't remember Tom hosting; this was one of those unspoken things. Tom struggled financially, and while he invited us to his house for occasions related to his children, we rarely gathered as a family for holidays at Tom's house. Mark and I volunteered to host Thanksgiving in 2012. We made the usual Thanksgiving dinner with New Mexican embellishments. There was turkey, homemade stuffing, mashed potatoes, plain whole pinto beans, roasted vegetables, and my famous caramel sweet potatoes.

We rarely bothered to make gravy, because New Mexican red chile was the *gravy* of choice. Chile is the cornerstone of New Mexican dishes; in fact, the state question is "red or green?" New Mexican chile is just chile peppers with a small amount of meat (optional), oil (lard), flour, garlic, and salt to taste. So, when we say chile, we are talking about the pepper, usually Anaheim or Big Jim varieties cultivated in New Mexico.

Learning how to cook New Mexican food was one of those unspoken expectations while growing up with my Grandma Lucero living next door, and Mom and her sisters were always competing for whose chile or enchiladas were better.

Both Mark and I had kids who were going to come for Thanksgiving that year and we were excited to see them. Four of the six were coming for the holiday. We found a place for all of them to sleep and everybody was pitching in and talking as we prepared for Thanksgiving guests. Tom and Amy arrived with their four youngest children.

Tom and Amy met in the summer of 1990 when she was eighteen years old and in her senior year of high school. Amy's sister egged her on when she noticed her interest in Tom, "You think you can make a catch like that?"

Tom started dating her and soon she was pregnant and dropped out of school. He didn't tell her that he had five children already and he also lied about his age. He was twenty-eight but told her he was twenty.

Tom met his first wife in 1981, when he was in the army. She was a homegirl (a girl from a Hispanic barrio) from California. He towered over her, and when I visited them at Fort Bragg, you could tell he had the whole macho, guy in charge persona to him and in that relationship. They had one child together before Tom was deployed as part of a peacekeeping mission in the Middle East, and his wife and child went to live with Mom in Albuquerque. His wife told him she was pregnant with their second while Tom was on deployment, and when he returned he went AWOL from his military post.

He left the military, initially under dishonorable circumstances, but later changed to an Honorable Discharge and they reunited. He decided to go to California to live with my father. Tom began questioning whether the second child was his. He started drinking and doing drugs, seeing other women, and became involved in gangs. They divorced and he started dating a second woman. She was a big and tough lady, as tall as Tom with her five-inch heels, heavy make-up, and sprayed hair that went straight up four inches. She hung out with the gangs in LA. I first met her at Leo's college graduation and said to myself, "Wow, I wouldn't mess with that woman."

His first wife, who remarried, wouldn't allow Tom to see the children because he did not support them financially and he was a bad influence. His ruca (slang for girlfriend) eventually had two children by Tom: Carla and Julie.

I got a call from Tom in the summer of 1986. At age twenty-six, I was pregnant with my third child and married to my first husband for three years. We were devout Catholics and unsuccessfully practicing natural family planning.

"You're going to have nieces," Tom reported with excitement.

"Nieces?" I said. "Do you have twins?"

He said, "No."

I was confused.

He continued, "Another woman I met is pregnant and so is my girlfriend."

"Who's the other woman?" I asked.

"A lady I met when I was drunk, and my girlfriend and I were in a fight."

He sounded so proud to be having more children, which normally I am happy to hear about, but it turns out these two nieces of mine were going to be born four months apart.

"My girlfriend is due around my birthday in December," he remarked with pride in his voice. "I hope she is born on my birthday."

"Congratulations, I'm due in December as well," I said with as much enthusiasm as I could, concerned about how he was going to care for the children. My husband and I were both engineers, and I was feeling overwhelmed with our growing family.

"Are you going to spend time with them both? I mean is the new woman going to let you be a part of the baby's life or will it be like it is with your older kids?"

He brushed me off and said, "I'll get to see the baby, but I'm living with my girlfriend. I'll help when I can."

I had worried about Tom since he went AWOL. When I learned about his gang activity, I was afraid that someday I would get a call informing me that he was dead. Every time I talked to him I just couldn't tell if he would be OK. Helpless to do anything about it since I was starting my engineering career and we had three little ones, I wrote and sent cards of encouragement regularly and we would talk on the phone. When he seemed to be doing well in his job, it made me happy, but I was unable to visit much so I really didn't know what was going on in his life.

The call about the pregnancies was difficult for me. Raised by a single mother working as a secretary, we were so poor. We got most of our meals through the free meal program at school and didn't have good clothes, shoes, or coats. It was hard to believe he was repeating behavior that would create the same circumstance for his own children. He went on to have another child with his girlfriend, which made a total of five children by three women when he met Amy. We didn't see his eldest son and daughter from his first wife. The woman he had a fling with let her daughter visit Albuquerque occasionally when she was young, but then insisted on child support so we hadn't seen her in a while. His ruca let Carla and Julie visit in Albuquerque, so we knew them a little better.

Amy didn't learn the truth about Tom's age and his five children until months into her pregnancy, well after she felt able to back out of the relationship, and Jenny her eldest was born in June 1991.

In October 1992, Tom was in a California jail and up for fifteen years to life for a drive-by shooting which he was involved in. He had become the leader of a gang at age thirty. Most of the members of his gang were around sixteen years old. He was coaching wrestling, something he loved since high school, and recruited most of the boys, all from rough family situations, to join his gang.

No one from any of the other gangs came forward to testify against him after his arrest, so he was ultimately set free. He was convinced that God gave him a second chance and now he was going to serve Jesus; he was "born again." He cleaned up his act and returned to Albuquerque for a brief time to attend a ministry school and then returned to California. His son Ezekiel was born March of 1997, and shortly after, Tom, Amy, Jenny, and their infant son made a permanent move to Albuquerque and actively pursued the ministry. He would travel back to California once or twice a year to see our father and stepmother, Amy's family, and any of his children who he was able to see.

Tom and his family moved in with Mom at first when he returned to Albuquerque, and they had many disagreements. It was clear that Amy and Mom did not like each other. He eventually borrowed money from me, and probably others, to buy a small mobile home for his family of four. He earned a living working in a prison ministry with some side jobs. His family was active at Calvary, the largest evangelical church in Albuquerque, which was associated with a Calvary Church in California where he had committed his life to Jesus. After several years, Tom secured a position as a pastor at Calvary.

Tom and Amy went on to have a total of five children; two born in California and three in New Mexico. Tom was able to see Carla and Julie, two of his five children he had left in California, but the other two women refused to let him see his other three children until he paid child support. It took him several years and some creative financial maneuvers until he was able to pay negotiated back child support to all three women he left in California while he was raising children with Amy in New Mexico. The law had changed, and he couldn't get out of paying unless he wanted to be on the run, unlike my father, who never provided a dime of support other than a veteran's check of forty dollars a month that Mom had somehow found a way to claim.

Tom appeared to do well as a pastor, growing the prison ministry, which he was passionate about. His redemption story touched people. He also started a Spanish service and was able to use the Spanish he learned while living in Florida with Vincent and Amalia to give his sermon in Spanish. Seeing Tom doing well made me feel happy and relieved; much better than when he was in the gangs in California. Mark and I would take part when invited to special functions at Calvary, and I was proud that Tom had come so far.

Mark, our children, and I welcomed Tom and Amy, Ezekiel, Malachi, Miriam, and Grace to our Thanksgiving 2012 celebration. Jenny, their eldest, was married and celebrating with her in-laws. Tom picked biblical names for his children since he had been *born again*. Miriam was five years old; she was a little lover and liked people holding her, and we enjoyed giving her attention. Mark swooped her up at once and gave her a big hug. Grace was two and timid. She clung to her father as he went around greeting everyone. He lumbered forward when he walked since his wrestling accident, when he had a rod inserted where a bone snapped in two. Ezekiel and Malachi hugged everyone shyly and were smiling the whole time.

I was pulling the turkey apart and putting it on a serving tray. Miriam ran over to ask me for food, and Grace quickly followed. They devoured the chunks of turkey I handed them like they hadn't eaten in a while—which I worried was probably true. Tom's kids always seemed hungry. It was particularly noticeable this year. I wondered how Tom was managing since he had lost his job as a pastor at Calvary the previous April. Tom said it was a setup. The head pastor said Tom was spreading rumors about another assistant pastor who had arrived recently from California, but it was another pastor who started the rumors. Tom was very bitter about what had happened.

My kids helped serve drinks as we were finishing preparations when Leo, Lily, and their son arrived. Leo brought his guitar, which he often did. He knew my son would also have his guitar. Mark's youngest daughter had her djembe drum with her. We were all looking forward to hearing them jam later. Leo's son was excited to see all his cousins and everyone was excited to see him. He was a happy kid with blond locks of curls, dimples, and glasses.

Tom said a prayer before we all started eating, ending the prayer with "God's people say…" and expecting an "Amen" from everyone. Amy then immediately stood up to prepare a plate for Tom.

After we ate, the instruments came out. We had a couple of drums and Ezekiel, age fifteen, started playing one of them. He was an exceptional musician, and he played by ear. His brother Malachi, age nine, was learning and the two of them showed off for a while. Then Leo and my son pulled out the guitars and Leo even strapped on a harmonica. Everyone sat and listened or joined in singing the folk song *Home* by Edward Sharpe and the Magnetic Zeros.

Tom and his family had to leave early. He had a night job at a homeless shelter, something he started after he lost his position as a pastor at Calvary. In the kitchen before he left, he said, "There's a big homeless guy who keeps coming around causing trouble. I had to tell him to leave several times and I finally pushed him out and he tried to punch me." He seemed angry about it and continued, "He'd better watch out, I'm going to bring my gun and look for him outside." He seemed very agitated, and Mark and I noticed Ezekiel stopped playing, stood up and began paying close attention to Tom.

After listening for a while, I changed the subject. The conversation made me nervous, and I was concerned that Tom would revert to a more lawless existence. Not knowing how to respond to his story, I asked him, "How are things, are there any job prospects?" He talked about the possibility of a job with the Veterans Administration counseling vets with PTSD (post-traumatic stress disorder). I was happy to hear that, but I could tell the family was struggling.

Leo and his family lingered, and the music continued with his son joining in occasionally on a toy piano. Overall, our Thanksgiving celebration was a success and we took many photos and videos to remind us of that day.

Three weeks after Thanksgiving I was on a plane to Baltimore to attend my annual Georgetown Leadership Coaching Conference, which had been rescheduled due to Hurricane Sandy. It had been a year since I had seen my cohort and I was so excited to go. The six-month Leadership Coaching Certification Course at Georgetown was a very transformative experience. The people in the course grew remarkably close as we coached each other and talked about many of the details of our lives. Soon after I had graduated the previous December, I eagerly made plans to attend the conference.

Sally from Newtown, Connecticut, was my closest friend from the group. We hugged when we saw each other and it was as though no time had passed. She hugged Mark and we went to check in and made plans to meet for dinner; it was so good to see her. We hung out for most of the conference and caught up with all our friends and it was a delightful time. There were great speakers and various coaching workshops.

Toward the end of the conference, the televisions in the conference hotel became noticeably loud, as word of the mass shooting of children at a school in Newtown, Connecticut, spread. At first, we were confused about what was happening, involved in our conversations. As we started listening closer and scanning our phones, the horrifying news caused a silence to take over the room as everyone listened to the television. We were all stunned; it was a surreal transition from all this deep and lively conversation to something so horrific, and we could scarcely take it in.

The Georgetown leadership coaching approach is about changing leaders from the inside out; it is a deep and altruistic approach to transforming corporations and our culture. The news magnified the need for transformation.

On our way home Sally, Mary, another friend who lived nearby Newtown, and I were texting about the mass shooting. "This cannot happen in our country," I wrote.

The feelings of sadness and commitment to change our gun culture were so visceral for all three of us, and our conversations continued for weeks as Sally joined her community's efforts to heal. Watching the tears on President Obama's face, I prayed that this time our country would change its gun laws. It was inconceivable to me that Congress wouldn't act, with the slaughter of this many innocents at the hands of a clearly ill young man. Guns were a scourge on our society, and we were irresponsible as adults for allowing our children to die daily because guns were so readily available. Little did I know what the new year would bring.

CHAPTER 3

THE UNTHINKABLE

The call came on my cell phone at around 1:00 a.m. that mid-January morning, 2013. My cell phone was usually off at night, but I left it on unintentionally.

"Auntie Gina, is it true! Is my dad and the family dead?"

The words did not register, my mind could not take them in. Although familiar, at first, I didn't recognize the woman's voice on the other end of the line and what she was saying didn't fully sink into my sleepy brain.

"I haven't heard anything," I responded.

"Have you talked to Jenny?" she insisted.

I finally realized it was Carla, my brother Tom's second-eldest daughter who lived in California. Jenny, Tom and Amy's eldest, was her half-sister and lived in Albuquerque with her husband.

She continued, "I read on Facebook that my whole family was killed. They said it was a murder-suicide, but I know my dad wouldn't do anything like that, there's no way."

Finally I woke up enough to realize the gravity of what she was saying. Not knowing how to respond, I struggled through a response, "I will try to contact Jenny."

Hanging up the phone, my head and heart swelled to the point where sobs came out and I woke up Mark. Frantically I tried to call Jenny; my hands were shaking and at that moment she was calling me. She confirmed that her father, mother, and three of her younger siblings were dead. She and her husband were at the sheriff's building where they were holding her brother Ezekiel.

"I've been trying to contact Aunt Janice and Uncle Leo, but they didn't answer," she said and asked me to call them.

I was reeling as I tried calling my brother Leo, who did not answer so I left a cryptic message. Forgetting that Lily was out of town, I called her but she didn't answer either. Janice, my sister, didn't answer either. After trying other numbers for Janice, I called my niece, Janice's daughter.

Forcing the words out of my mouth I told her what I learned. "Tom, Amy, Malachi, Miriam, and Grace were killed in their house, we don't know anything else," sobbing and squeaking a bit as I tried to get the next sentence out. "I am trying to contact your mom; do you have any other numbers?"

"I'll find her, I can get a hold of her," she retorted in a very matter of fact way.

After hanging up I was unsure of what to do. Tears just kept streaming down my face and my heart was heavy. "This just can't be true," I thought to myself, my heart pounding, the adrenaline surging. Should I drive in the middle of the night to Leo's house, should I go to the sheriff's building? The shock and horror of the news left me disoriented.

Mark made coffee and as I was dressing my phone rang; it was Janice. She was dressing to go to Leo's house.

"I'll meet you there," I said.

We blubbered a bit about what happened, not knowing how to make sense of what our nieces had told us.

We drove the familiar streets to the house where I grew up and that Leo bought after Mom died. Leo wanted to live in the old Albuquerque neighborhood of *Barelas*. The night was dark at 1:40 a.m., and my head was racing with thoughts and questions as I stared out the car window. Mark and I arrived at Leo's house before Janice.

We rang the door a few times, aware that their three-year old was sleeping. When Leo answered the door, he was clearly half asleep. Throwing myself into his arms, he kept saying, "What happened? What happened?"

As best I could express through tears I told him what we had learned and gave him the few details that I pieced together from my brief conversations with Carla and Jenny. In a familiar way he pressed his hands to each side of his forehead, stroking his short kinky hair back on both sides.

He said, "Oh my God, oh my God, oh my God!" over and over again.

Crying, I studied my brother's reaction, his face was white, and a shocked gaze came over his eyes.

"I tried to call you and so did Jenny," I said.

He went for his cell. He started to question me, and I had few answers, then he started to scroll the messages on his phone.

"Janice is on her way," I told him.

Mark and I made our way inside and sat on the couch. Janice came with her husband, John, minutes later. She cried into Leo's arms, as well. We greeted each other with tears, and we all took our places in Leo's small living room in the familiar house. Janice gave the details she had, and Mark and I asked questions but there were few answers. Leo made coffee, called his wife, Lily, and told her what he knew of the situation. She had just left the morning before for a ladies weekend with longtime friends. Janice said her daughter was flying to Albuquerque right away. Leo offered coffee and anything he had in the kitchen.

We sat in the home we grew up in, waiting for divine revelation, not understanding or believing the situation. I gazed at the large painting on the wall; it overwhelmed the living room. Our cousin, a painter, sold it to Leo. I looked for the small image of my Grandma Pacheco; she was the size of a shoebox in the canvas of about six by eight feet. Our cousin wanted to reflect the time when my Grandpa Pacheco would leave my grandma alone in the middle of nowhere in the llano (the grassy treeless plains of the southwest). The homestead was between Santa Rosa and Albuquerque, and my grandma would spend months at a time with their ten children while he went into the nearest town to work. Sometimes he would take his oldest sons and leave her with seven or eight of the children, who had plenty of chores on the homestead.

I thought of Mom in this house; thank God she wasn't alive to hear this horrific news. We received a call from Jenny as she was leaving the sheriff's building.

"Can we go and talk to Ezekiel?" I asked.

"I don't think so," she said, "they wouldn't let me talk to him."

We made her commit to not leaving downtown until we went to see her. We climbed into Janice's truck and drove about a mile to the sheriff's building to meet with Jenny and her husband. Mark stayed with Leo's sleeping son.

On our way, I remembered the last time I saw Jenny when Tom turned fifty-one on December 8, 2012, just over a month earlier. Mark and I hosted his birthday. He was struggling more than usual emotionally as well as financially since he had lost his pastor position at Calvary.

The first guests to arrive were Jenny, Tom and Amy's oldest daughter, and her husband. Jenny is lighter-complected compared with her brothers; she looked a lot like her mother, with pale, flat features, and a resting scowl/sad face. She had dark penetrating eyes and long dark hair that she wore straight. She was shy, and she mumbled and spoke softly like her mother.

"I wasn't sure you were going to make it," I told her. I was surprised she was there, and she had gained a good amount of weight since the last time I had seen her. She had gotten married in the middle of May in 2011, while I was working in Washington, DC and we couldn't make it to her wedding. I sent a hefty check as a gift and as an apology for not being able to be at the wedding. Her mother and father were so proud. Amy emphasized, "She's wearing white."

Jenny was nineteen when she married, and I had heard stories from Ezekiel her brother of how before she was married, she couldn't go anywhere with her boyfriend alone. She would have to take one or both of her brothers along. It was a rule her parents imposed to maintain her purity. Marriage appeared to agree with her; she looked happier than I had ever seen her. She and her husband were going to move to Phoenix.

When Jenny lived with her parents, she was the nanny for her four siblings and fed and took care of them most of the time. She was very thin in an unhealthy way; now she looked good and healthy. Like the other children, Jenny was homeschooled, which always seemed a bit off to us since her mother never graduated from high school and had trouble enunciating her words. It took Jenny three tries, but she finally succeeded in getting her GED. Once Tom became a pastor, he didn't want the children to become corrupted with all of the teaching about science or to fall into the wrong circle of friends.

The next to arrive at Tom's birthday party was Leo and his family.

There were greetings all the way around, and Leo gregariously hugged Jenny and her husband.

"Looks like marriage agrees with you, you look great," Leo said. "I didn't expect to see you."

Jenny smiled a nervous smile.

Within a few short minutes Tom came with his family, but without Ezekiel, who was at the church practicing with the young adult music group. Tom went around greeting everyone and he was especially happy that Jenny was there.

At one point, Tom sat on the couch in the living room and I sat across from him. He asked me about my job. Tom didn't talk much when all the family was around. Janice had a propensity to dominate the conversation, and between her and Leo's political endeavors, which was another focus of conversation, it was rare for people to ask me about my job as an engineer.

Tom was reserved and often stayed quiet around us, except for laughing at Leo's jokes. Leo was quite witty and used humor since he was a child to make people laugh and relieve tension. He especially liked to make Tom laugh. Tom had a deep barking laugh and his face lit up with a goofy smile and he would mumble a funny comment under his breath that people rarely caught.

Tom talked about the lawsuit he was planning against Calvary for wrongful termination. He talked about Calvary firing him because he was Hispanic, and he was angry. He also seemed a bit lost; Calvary and his allegiance to the leader of the church had been Tom's whole life. Before Tom left the gathering that night, he got a phone call from Ezekiel, and he sounded very stern.

I looked at him after he said, "I'm coming to pick you up now!" and hung up.

He rolled his eyes and said, "We need to take off, I need to pick up Ezekiel."

We boxed up a bunch of leftovers, which was usual, and sent food home with him. As he was leaving, I again said, "Happy Birthday," and gave him a big hug goodbye. I was worried about him. Tom's redemption story was his identity, and he felt betrayed; probably betrayed by God. His anger seemed to bubble under the surface, and I hadn't seen him that bad since his gang days. I had no idea how he was going to recover from the blow of losing what was a prestigious and honorable position as a pastor at the largest Evangelical Church in New Mexico. The weight of his financial situation was apparent. He worked hard to make ends meet, but I didn't know how bad things were for him.

He left with his usual "I love you, and God bless you."

We arrived at the sheriff's building within two hours of the phone call when we learned our family members were dead, and Jenny and her husband were waiting for us. We asked her more questions, but she had little to say. She was swollen on one side of her face and in pain from an infected tooth. She told me that she had given my name and address to the officers holding Ezekiel and that they would call me when they were ready to release him.

"I don't think they'll let you see him now," she said.

We hugged her and said our goodbyes; she wanted to go home and clearly was distressed about everything. She agreed to talk with us the next day.

CHAPTER 4

A PAINFUL NEW REALITY

We decided we would try to get into the sheriff's building and walked up the steep steps and looked for a way in. There were giant doors at every entrance, but no clear doorbell or way of getting the attention of those inside. We knocked with our fists several times on the heavy wooden doors that were at least ten feet tall, but it was futile because they weren't receiving people at 3:00 in the morning. Crying and desperate to know something, I wondered why I couldn't talk to Ezekiel.

Distressed, Leo remarked, "He's a minor with no adult."

Confused and disoriented, we returned to Leo's house. As we settled in again on the couch, Leo offered us toast or a sandwich but none of us were hungry. We started to talk about what might have happened. We still didn't know much about the deaths. We had no idea if it was a murder or murder-suicide. We wondered if there was any chance that someone, possibly one of the ex-cons who Tom worked with and sometimes housed, could have possibly killed the family. Why was Ezekiel not killed as well?

We all dozed at Leo's house as the time went by slowly. At about 4:00 a.m. we decided to send John to Tom's house to see if it was possible to talk to anybody at the scene. He was in the military and probably could relate to the sheriff's deputies better. When he returned, he had a card with a number to call for information.

He described the scene like this, "The street to Tom's house is blocked off and there are a number of police cars and other vehicles."

Leo called the number on the card for the sheriff's information office. A receptionist answered and he left a message. We were hopeful that someone would be able to tell us what had happened. Part of me wanted to go to Tom's house and find that he was there and that somehow this was a hoax. As we waited for a call back, we continued to guess about what might have happened. Leo was the first one to suggest that Ezekiel might have killed them.

At one point, I blurted, "Tom would have never killed his baby girls, he loved them too much," remembering the last time I saw Tom almost one month before this black day for our family January 20, 2013.

The last time we saw Tom was at the Christmas family gathering at Janice's house on December 22, 2012. She made an abundance of food for our family celebration, as is usual in our family gatherings. Janice and John lived in a nearby mountain community, and we drove up the switchback road until we recognized the turn; luckily there was no snow. Once everyone arrived, including Leo and his family, Tom and his family, and Mark and I, Janice offered us all drinks and before long we were all shuffling about the kitchen and dining area filling our plates. Everyone was eager to try the green chile enchiladas, turkey, potatoes, red chile, vegetables, and several desserts. There was pecan, apple, and peach pie, biscochitos and other cookies, brownies of all kinds, and more.

We celebrated Christmas as we had many times before, with a gift exchange for the adults and the kids all got gifts from everyone. We bought clothes and toys for all the children, and when Miriam opened her present from us that included a frilly dress, necklace, tiara, and sparkly shoes, she ran back to her father excited.

Tom's face lit up and he said, "Show me your princess dress for such a beautiful princess."

It was so sweet. Little Grace was temperamental and didn't want to take part, so Tom held her on his lap most of the time. We gave Ezekiel a fifty dollar Apple gift card and shirts; we had been careful not to pick shirts that were too violent or goth, as he was only fifteen and a half years old. The previous year, Janice and I had gone in on an iPod, exactly like an iPhone without the phone, and with the gift card he could afford apps. Ezekiel seemed pleased with the gifts he got. Malachi got an iPod nano, which is what Tom told us he wanted. This year we got Leo's son a Thomas the Train set, which he opened and with help set up a train track immediately.

The adult gift exchange was entertaining. We followed the rules for white elephant gift exchanges, where you could select a yet-un-opened gift or take someone else's gift, with a prescribed number of times a gift could exchange hands. It was fun and the gifts were nice. After the gift exchange was over, everyone went for more dessert, coffee, or other drinks.

Before our gathering ended, Tom was sitting in a chair in the living room watching TV with only a couple of people in the room. Sitting down next to him, we talked a bit about how he was doing and I asked about his plan to go to California.

"Jenny will be with us," he shared with excitement. She hadn't gone with them the Christmas before, and I sensed that they were trying to work out how to do holidays with Jenny now that she was married.

The thought of his minivan filled with eight people, four adults and four children, sounded intense. He preferred to drive at night, which was always bothersome to me because of the possible dangers. It was a twelve-hour journey. It worried me especially after he told me of a hostile encounter he had with the police a couple of years earlier in Arizona. They treated him very poorly and thought he was an undocumented Mexican with his entire family in the minivan.

Tom cussed and blustered about that event and said, "I came close to pulling a gun on the cop because of the way he was treating me." When he told me, I was scared for him. I didn't know if it was just bravado, but I could tell he was indignant about the event.

Not really knowing if he had guns or how many, I thought, "God I wish these things wouldn't happen to him."

Tom then said, "I'll be staying with Dad as usual." My father's son (our half-brother) and his family had a sizable home in the inland area of Los Angeles. It was a custom-built home that they shared with our father and stepmother. He was forty years old when I met him; he was born about a year after my parents divorced. Three years prior I visited and stayed in their home with Mark after deciding to forgive our father and stepmother for what they did to Mom and us; seven years after Mom died.

As my conversation with Tom dwindled, I put one hundred dollars cash in his hands. "I'm sorry, this is all I have in cash with me now."

The cash was to help him with his trip to California, which I tried to give him each year. I felt bad because I usually tried to give him two or three hundred dollars, and I knew he probably needed it this year.

People slowly started saying their goodbyes and we exchanged hugs. Picking up each of the kids, I gave them all a big hug. Sometimes they would start with an almost hug or sideways hug, but I wouldn't settle for that. I liked to believe they enjoyed the hugs, but wondered if they would remember me as that crazy aunt who squeezed them to death with her hugs. Tom got an extra hug because I was worried about his travels and all that he was dealing with in his life.

Little did I know it would be the last time that I would see him and that the four of us would ever celebrate Christmas together. All the pictures over the years of the four of us flashed in my head, including the one that had the four of us on a couch at Grandma Lucero's house when Leo was a baby seated with Janice holding on to him. Leo enlarged the photo and framed it in a rustic wood frame and gave one to each of us for Christmas two years prior when we celebrated at his house.

As I thought about Ezekiel being held at the sheriff's building alone, I wondered if I would hear from him. The possibility that Ezekiel killed his family was hard to accept; he was a sweet and sensitive boy. Ezekiel had become sullen in the last year, as teenagers typically do, but we hadn't noticed anything that would alert us to real trouble.

We dozed in and out. Leo made coffee again, and turned on the only TV in the house, which was in his bedroom. He was listening for the top of the hour news clip. After more than an hour had passed, Leo called the sheriff's information office again just after 5:00 a.m. All of us were scanning the internet with our phones for any information in the press about our family.

Leo came back into the living room and said, "They are having a press conference at 7:00 a.m."

We still hadn't heard anything from the sheriff's office. Calling the sheriff's information number again with the press conference just over an hour away, I explained that we were the family, we called twice with no response, and they had scheduled a press conference. Within twenty minutes I got a call from the sheriff at the scene. After explaining who I was and what we knew, I fired several questions at him.

He was cautious as he explained, "Ma'am, I can't talk to you over the phone, I have no way of knowing who you are, but if you come to the scene and call me, I can verify your identity and answer your questions."

Janice, Leo, and I got into the large truck again, with John driving. We drove in silence; it was difficult to anticipate what we would learn, or if we would be able to go into the house, or if they would release Ezekiel. We simply didn't know. When we arrived, we talked to the officer near the car that was blocking the road to Tom's house. He was making people turn around and not allowing anyone to go down the street to Tom's house.

I got out of the truck; it was cool and still dark. I told the sheriff about the conversation I had with the lead deputy. "Can we go down the street to the residence?" I asked.

"No, I'll call, and he will come meet you. Stay in your vehicle," he said.

Returning to the truck, I was eager for the warmth, and we waited. When a sheriff's patrol car pulled in behind us, we all got out of the truck. I showed him my ID and my siblings fumbled as they all got their own IDs out, though he barely looked at them.

The sheriff began to tell us the story of what had happened. He started with the previous evening when a former police officer who worked as the Calvary security officer talked to Ezekiel because he had been at Calvary all day without his family, which was unusual. The officer explained that Ezekiel at first said that his family was in an automobile accident. After further questions, Ezekiel said that he came home after spending the night at his friend's house and found his family dead. He was not making sense.

The Calvary security officer got Ezekiel in his car and headed to

Tom's house. Having a bad feeling on his way, he pulled over, called the police and asked them to meet him at Tom's house. When the deputies got to the house, the door was locked. They went to the vehicle where Ezekiel sat and got the key and entered the house. That was when they found my brother Tom at the foot of the stairs. They went upstairs, and found the two girls, Miriam and Grace, their mother, Amy, and their brother, Malachi, all dead.

The deputies questioned Ezekiel at the sheriff's office, and they received a full confession.

As the sheriff told us everything he knew, we stood outside the truck. Then as we shivered, he invited us to return to our vehicle. He joined us in the back of the truck as he finished the story.

He told us they arrested Ezekiel and that he would go to the county juvenile detention facility. We asked questions and he gave us more details on the nature of the crimes and how they found things inside the house.

He asked us about Ezekiel's behavior. "How did your nephew seem the last time you saw him?" As he spoke, he seemed both angry and resentful at Ezekiel.

I told him, "I haven't seen him since around Christmas and he seemed normal, nothing unusual."

Stunned, I refused to believe what was happening, what had happened. The fog of guessing and not knowing had lifted, but in its wake was a stark and painful new reality, and I didn't know how to react. The officer finished speaking, got out of the truck, and walked away.

Janice and I cried as we took in the harshness of the situation. "This can't be happening," I said as I stared at my brother next to me and he put his hand over mine.

Leo's eyes were glistening as he said in a somber voice that was choking back tears, "It's going to be all over the news, we need to let the whole family know."

We agreed on a phone tree and on who would call whom. It was customary to call our closest family in this order: my father, Tom's remaining children and our children, then our close aunts, and let them call the other aunts or uncles, and each of the aunts usually would spread the news to their children; it was an efficient calling tree for our large family.

As we traveled home, I began to make calls, breaking the news to family. I cried each time. It was uncomfortable, almost embarrassing to speak the words to my aunts.

"Hello, this is Gina. Tom, my brother, Amy, his wife, Malachi, Miriam, and Grace were killed by Ezekiel, their fifteen-year-old son."

I listened as the news landed. Some would start crying, and most would say something to the effect of "Oh God" or "Dear Jesus."

"Go ahead and tell the family," I told them, knowing it would soon be all over the news.

"Thank you mija for calling, let us know what's going to happen next. God bless you," my aunts usually responded.

When we got to Leo's house, I jumped down from the truck and went to hug Mark and told him through tears what we had learned. He held me as I cried.

We all gathered around the TV in Leo's bedroom to watch the 7:00 a.m. news. We didn't learn anything new, but suddenly everything was real. When Leo's son woke up, he was surprised to see everybody so early in the day.

"Hey buddy, good morning. Everyone is here today because we got some bad news." We refrained from talking too much when he was in the room.

I wanted to see Ezekiel. It felt important to speak to him, to understand his state of mind, so I looked up the number of the county detention facility and called.

They gave me visiting hours and said I would need to show proof that I was his aunt.

We left Leo's house at about 8:30 a.m. to get food and rest, and we all agreed to come back later.

That afternoon, Mark and I went by the county detention facility before going back to Leo's house, but they would not let us see Ezekiel. There was a twenty-four-hour period after receiving a detainee before he could have visitors. It was the first time I had ever been to a place like this, and I looked around for information about the place, the rules, anything that could give me information on what we were facing, but I didn't find anything helpful.

CHAPTER 5

A FAMILY UNITED

By that evening, close family were arriving, Tom's daughters Carla and her sister Julie, Janice's daughter, and Lily. We gathered in Leo's living room again. Extended family had already been by dropping off food, and Lily madly tried to organize it all in her tiny kitchen.

"Does anybody want food?" Lily asked, trying to make space on the table-sized counter between the kitchen and living room. "There's some casserole here."

We huddled and talked about what happened. The speculation on why Ezekiel had done such a horrible thing began, and there seemed no reasonable explanation. The idea that Ezekiel *snapped* came up in the conversation, as well as lamenting the fact that Tom lost his pastoral position at Calvary in April and that meant they didn't spend as much time there anymore. We reviewed together our memories of the last time we saw or talked to the family and Ezekiel.

Leo said, "Amy and I were texting about meeting up to celebrate birthdays as a family." It was January 20th, Leo's birthday was January 22nd, Mark's was on January 23rd, and Amy's was on January 25th.

Leo was surprised because he hadn't heard back from Amy after he texted proposing a dinner at his house with Chinese takeout. "Amy is always responsive with texts. I sent that text late Friday." It was now Sunday afternoon.

We cried on and off again. Leo's son was in his bedroom with one of his cousins. He seemed happy to have all the company.

We began talking about the things that we needed to take care of in the aftermath of the family deaths. Extended family and friends started asking about the services for our deceased family. Tom's house was still a crime scene, and after talking to the sheriff's office we learned that they would not finish until Monday afternoon or evening. We asked Carla, Julie, and Jenny if they knew about a will, and they didn't. There was no word when we would be able to go into the house to look for documents and know what needed to be taken care of. We knew they were going to take the remains of the family, but we didn't know what would happen from there.

On Monday morning, I contacted my employer to tell them what had happened and that I would not be in that week. My manager didn't know how to respond. We had a Program Management Meeting that week in Las Vegas to review the milestones and plans for the year, and obviously I wouldn't be attending. "The team was prepared," I said, and apologized for not going.

Mark and I went to the county detention facility. This time they let me see Ezekiel. Visitors weren't allowed to see his holding cell or the conditions in which they kept him. Instead, we met in an open area with metal tables bolted to the floor like you might see at an outdoor venue or mall food court.

He looked strung out and had a strange, unsettled demeanor that was bordering on edgy. Eye contact was hard for him. He was not the same person as the kid we saw at Christmas.

A guard supervised us during the visit, and we had a stilted conversation.

Cuing into Ezekiel's nonverbal behavior to get a sense of how he was doing, it seemed that some kind of schism had occurred. Focusing on how he was doing, I did not probe him about what happened, but on how they were treating him.

"How are you doing?" I asked.

He gave me a glancing look, "I'm here."

He looked gaunt. "Are you eating?" I asked.

"Yeah, they don't let me use forks or spoons," he responded.

I learned that he was in the *bubble*, or the observation room, where they watched him from multiple angles. He was also under suicide watch, and he couldn't eat with utensils or have anything that he might use to harm himself. At night he slept in a *turtle suit* that secured his arms to his side and on a thin mattress with no bedding or blankets. The whole situation made me incredibly sad to see my fifteen-year-old nephew, who seemed so young, and was so small (he was barely 100 lbs. with a slight build) in this crazy place.

"Would you consider suicide?" I asked him.

"Nah, my father said only cowards killed themselves and you would go to hell for that," he said.

The incongruence struck me. Trying to reflect non-judgment while still absorbing the gravity of everything he had done, I nodded and gazed at him. Deep down I knew there were no easy answers. My goal was simply to let him know that I was here for him, and that the family would not abandon him.

We went from the county detention facility to Leo's house. Soon after we arrived at Leo's, we learned that the detectives would finish investigating the crime scene later that day, and we would still not be able to enter Tom's house. They said that biohazard remnants of the crimes would remain, and that we needed to arrange for special cleaning before we could go into the house. The thought of walking into the house with the blood of our family all over made me sick to my stomach. Mark volunteered to go in first and figure out how to contact the insurance company. He worked in the insurance business for thirty years and knew this would be an area that we needed the homeowner's insurance company to advise us on before we moved ahead.

The detective phoned us later that day to set up a time to review their initial findings. We tried to get our bearings on what the next steps were. We spent much of the day at Leo's house comforting each other and greeting family as they arrived. By late afternoon, we decided to go our separate ways and meet at my house at seven, and we called the detective back with the time and the address.

Just before 7:00 p.m., a circle of eleven of us joined in our living room. When the detective arrived, he seemed a bit shell-shocked from his work at Tom's house and we went around the room introducing ourselves. Everything was very somber. He took his seat, facing the circle of family. He began reviewing the findings in very precise and forensic terms, starting with the time he walked into the house.

"We first encountered a male approximately six foot lying on his stomach at the foot of the stairs with gunshot wounds on his back, neck, and head. He was Hispanic, approximately fifty years old, we identified the body as Tom Pacheco..."

It was jolting to hear this clinical account, and I felt myself disassociate, each sentence was like a dagger in my heart. Many of us sobbed and had tears running down our cheeks.

When the detective started talking about walking into the girls' bedroom and finding each in their beds with gunshot wounds to the head, the crying intensified with his sterile, cold way of describing the scene.

"We found a woman approximately fifty years old in the master bedroom laying on her back in the bed, with a gunshot wound in her forehead. She was identified as Amy, Tom's wife. Across her body was the body of Malachi, who had been shot once in the head. We found out from text messages they were the first victims," he reported. We learned that the texts were between Ezekiel and his *girlfriend*.

The detective talked about all the things they found in the house, on Ezekiel, and in the vehicle related to the crime. He went over the arsenal of seven weapons found and all the ammunition.

"Two AR-15 rifles, a 22, two shotguns, a pistol, and 15,000 rounds of ammunition," he said.

I was in shock; I had no idea that Tom kept seven weapons and wondered why? The detective moved on to what they had found on Ezekiel's iPod—an exchange of texts with a young girl that included a photo he sent to her after he had shot and killed his mother and brother. Leo's face hardened in horror as he listened, having to clear his throat to ask a question.

"Do you know who the girl is? Is she in custody?" he asked.

"She was questioned and released," the detective responded.

The detective passed around screenshots of the texts between Ezekiel and his girlfriend so everyone could read them. It was like show and tell, only much more gruesome and painful than I could ever have imagined. Ezekiel and his girlfriend had texted the day before the murders and during the killings. We read texts where she, a twelve-year-old, was egging him on with sexual overtures.

Ezekiel texted "I feel insane," and asked for pictures of her breasts after killing Amy and Malachi and sending his girlfriend the picture of them dead.

The girl responded with a photo of her chest, "Get it over with, I'll see you soon."

After the killings, Ezekiel met up with her at Calvary and spent the day like any other teenager.

When the detective left, we fell apart. We could hardly speak a word or make sense of it.

I thought to myself, "Why was this detective so graphic and detailed in his report to a grieving family?" It occurred to me that they were beginning to build a case against Ezekiel, and they wanted to convict him and send him to prison. It would go more smoothly if the family had a similar mindset. Perhaps shocking us with the details of the murders was a way for law enforcement to turn the family against him. Their idea of justice might have been death if New Mexico had the death penalty. It seemed crazy to me that the U.S. Supreme Court had only relatively recently outlawed the death penalty for children in 2005.

The next morning, I received a phone call from the State's victims advocate, and she introduced herself and her role. "The Victim's Advocate Office is committed to offering resources and support to victims of crime and their families. We work proactively to ensure that your rights are upheld throughout the criminal legal process."

I was confused at first, not recognizing myself as a victim. "We love our nephew, we don't know what happened," I said and felt myself starting to cry again.

I never heard from them again.

CHAPTER 6

GUARDIANSHIP

The next day, Tuesday, Mark was the first one to go to the property. His task was to find family files and bring them to Leo's house. Jenny coached him on where to look. He went to the property alone and was able to bring back various files and papers he had found upstairs. He didn't share much of what it was like to go into the house, except to say that things were very disorderly.

After sorting through the papers in the laundry room/office next to the living room at Leo's house he came into the living room. "I didn't find a will," he announced. "I created a log of accounts, insurance, and anything that seemed like we should follow up on," he continued. "I found the name and information on the home insurance and made a call. They're going to call me back." He then said, "I also found a substantial life-insurance policy on both Tom and Amy and a lesser policy on the children," seeming surprised by that fact.

Mark set about contacting the agents for the insurance and verifying that the life insurance policies were still active. He spoke with the home insurance company about the correct way to bring in cleaners for biohazards and found someone to come in the next day.

Meanwhile, we learned that the coroner had custody of the bodies and were examining them in detail, and that they would transfer them to a funeral home shortly. Carla and Jenny took charge of deciding things like the funeral home, the services, and the interaction with the community who knew Tom and the family. Our family spent part of the day developing the obituary to put in the newspaper. Carla and Jenny secured a commitment from Calvary to conduct the service on Friday. It was amazing how hard we all had to work to stay ahead of the requests and decisions that had to be made.

We selected the urns that most represented each family member, starting with Tom and ending with Grace. The immediate family worked together every day of that week at Leo's house, dividing up the tasks and making decisions as a family. We grieved amid decisions and discussions that were difficult. It was a relief to have each other.

The defense attorney, Jack Douglas, assigned to Ezekiel's case by the Law Offices for the Public Defender for the State of New Mexico came to Leo's house to talk to the family on Wednesday evening. He was a thin and wiry older man, with gray hair and a gray trimmed beard. He wore glasses and had a very intense expression with eyes that squinted a good amount of the time.

Jack had been representing defendants in these tough cases for a long time and he was one of the best in the business. He introduced his co-counselor Fay, a middle-aged female attorney. In that conversation we learned how Ezekiel's case would move forward and that Jack knew the prosecuting attorney.

"She's inoffensive but strict," explained Jack. "If there is to be any plea or any deals the DA will have to sign it." He mentioned that he had been to see both the DA and Ezekiel before our visit.

"Ezekiel makes no bones about what he did," Jack said. "He seemed disassociated and subdued, and he broke down a couple of times. I think he's afraid."

Jack had given Ezekiel the road map of what would happen next.

"We have to document his whole life and we're going to need records that are private, which might be difficult to get," Jack continued. "And we also need the details of Ezekiel's questioning the night he was arrested."

We probed Jack on what Ezekiel's options were.

"He'll be charged as an adult with five counts of first-degree murder," he explained. "If we can get those down to second degree, that would allow us to petition for him to be tried as a child. He will be charged at an arraignment, and we will make a motion so that he won't have to appear before the court. We want to keep him out of the public eye for as long as we can."

We were grateful for any reprieve from more public scrutiny. Already the headlines were painting Ezekiel as a psychopathic killer. The trolling was downright cruel. It turned out the sheriff took Ezekiel's confession, which was more like an interrogation, and without discretion held a press conference recounting what Ezekiel said, including the part where after extensive questioning he said he considered going to the Walmart near his house after what he had done and shooting up the place— something he likely learned from the video game *Call of Duty*, which we learned that he played regularly. This was the "confession" of a fifteen-year-old who hadn't slept for two days, was out of his mind, and had no legal representative or family member present. We considered this an egregious violation of his rights and of the family.

If they tried Ezekiel as a child, he would get an *Amenability Hearing*. *Amenable to Treatment* was a term that we would learn every detail of in the months and years to come. It meant that he was salvageable and would potentially spend little to no time in adult prison.

Jack emphasized that the State had to "prove a negative," that he wasn't *amenable to treatment*. Being an engineer, I knew in my bones that proving a negative was a challenging thing, it gave me a glimmer of hope for Ezekiel and the family.

Jack said, "If he is tried as a juvenile and is found amenable, he could get out at age twenty-one, but the judge has a lot of discretion in that case. If we're unsuccessful with getting him tried as a juvenile, we will pursue a case of insanity, though that is a long shot." Jack recounted how often those cases are not successful.

"We are likely going to have to go after Tom, Ezekiel's father, because nothing happens just based on Ezekiel being a flawed human being," he said and paused to take in our reactions.

"There is the possibility in all this of using *Restorative Justice*," and he gave us a name of a leader in the Restorative Justice movement in Albuquerque.

Restorative Justice is a response to a crime where meetings between the victim and the offender, and sometimes with representatives of the wider community, are held to create a consensus for what the offender can do to repair the harm from the offense.

"He would meet with circles of people, all the stakeholders in this case," Jack explained.

I had heard of restorative justice before when we lived in Washington, DC. One of our friends used it in his mediation practice for complex cases, in the churches, and in other work.

He then walked us through what would come next; first a Grand Jury would indict Ezekiel, and then an arraignment and assignment of a judge would follow.

"They will assign a judge in two weeks," he explained. "We get to strike the judge once; the State gets one opportunity, as well."

Next would come the discovery process. "I want Ezekiel to appear in street clothes in court, I don't want him in a jumpsuit looking like a criminal, he's a child," he commented.

"It's not likely that we will get a change of venue. There's no place to go, except maybe Santa Fe or Taos." Since there was so much media attention about Ezekiel, the potential for another venue would allow for jurors who might be more neutral. Santa Fe and Taos are in northern New Mexico, which is more liberal, especially when it's about children's rights, than the southern half of New Mexico.

Jack said Ezekiel would stay in the county detention facility for juveniles (aka, juvie) until he was eighteen.

Then he launched into a stern warning. "Don't talk with him about the case. Let him know he shouldn't talk to the counselor or the other kids about it either. I'm not sure he can keep his mouth shut."

He warned us, "The victim's advocate works for the DA and the county detention facility is run by the State. They keep their ears open and record conversations and make copies of all written correspondence. If you get a call from anyone, tell them to talk to Jack Douglas."

Ezekiel would have a team of professionals working with him. We learned that one of the mental health professionals would administer several standard tests, but she wouldn't testify. A forensic psychiatrist would conduct a psychological evaluation and spend time with Ezekiel and would testify in court as an expert witness.

We ended the visit with Jack saying, "You will have to determine who will be Ezekiel's guardian."

This immediately got my mind racing; Leo was in the process of looking for a position in the Washington, DC area. John was looking for employment out of state after his retirement from the Air Force. Carla was going back to California. Jenny and her husband were about to move to Arizona. It dawned on me that I was the best choice, and I felt somehow called in that moment to do it. There was an emotional connection I had with Ezekiel, maybe because he reminded me of his father when he was younger.

The next day, Thursday, was the second visit with Ezekiel, where we met the Juvenile Probation Officer (JPO) assigned to Ezekiel. She explained to Jenny, Carla, and me all the information Ezekiel gave concerning his status as a juvenile detainee; where he lived before his crime, how each of us were related to him, his weight and height, answers he gave to alcohol, drug abuse, suicide, and previous trouble with the law.

We learned that he would sneak a bit of alcohol at family gatherings, that he was able to occasionally smoke marijuana at Calvary with the other boys, and that he had hidden a smoking habit from his parents. Ezekiel later shared that he would gather cigarette butts that weren't completely spent and smoke them.

They didn't find any information about previous trouble with the law, which we already knew because Tom kept a very close eye on his children and they spent most of their time at Calvary or at home. What startled me most was that he reported that he had tried to commit suicide a couple of times by taking pills he found around the house, but the most they did was to make him very drowsy and sick.

The JPO asked, "Who is going to be Ezekiel's guardian?" Carla, Jenny, and I huddled together, and I told them I was willing to do it. They both considered all the options I had already weighed.

Carla said, "OK, but we want to be able to visit Ezekiel anytime we want to."

The JPO chimed in about the visitation rules and that they could be listed as *regular visitors*, which meant they could visit once a week, like I could, and everyone else could visit on *special visits*.

The JPO asked me if I had any ID or birth certificate for Ezekiel.

I told her that we were still sorting through my brother's house and that we would look for those things.

The three of us then were able to visit briefly with Ezekiel that day. Before our visit, I told Carla and Jenny that his personality had changed in a strange way and that he was on suicide watch. He was very guarded, first looking closely at our faces for any signs of judgment or condemnation, especially from his older sister Carla.

"Hi Ezekiel, it's good to see you," Carla said when she saw him.

"Hi," he said almost inaudibly, and he sat down with his hands cuffed and on his lap in his jumpsuit.

"I've been praying for you," she said looking at him.

He glanced at her and looked away, "I'm alright."

We were careful not to talk about the elephant in the room or ask the question *why?* I knew Ezekiel couldn't answer that.

By the end of January 2013, I met with an attorney to become Ezekiel's guardian with the recommendation of Jack to use Pegasus Legal Services for Children, a nonprofit legal group dedicated to helping children with legal matters for minimal cost or free in some cases. We used their services since Ezekiel was now an orphan. The court granted me guardianship.

CHAPTER 7

FLOODED WITH MEMORIES

The cleaners went to Tom's house on Wednesday, and they contacted the sheriff's office about items they found, including a note pad with a child's drawing of a person with a gun pointed at another person. The sheriff's office took most of the items associated with the crime, including bullets from the walls. They went back to the house on Wednesday and took more photos, secured the note pad, a gun sight, a revolver, more ammunition, and a couple of other things. Jack told us that the detectives took over 1,400 pictures and videos.

When the house was ready for us to enter, Mark again took the initiative to scour the house for papers. Meanwhile, the defense team wanted to get in and look around as well, and he arranged to meet them there over the course of the following week. The sheriff's detectives removed all of the weapons and almost all of the ammunition from the home and seized Tom's minivan that Ezekiel had driven to the church after he killed the family, but Mark found even more ammunition.

Again, Mark methodically searched the entire house for paperwork concerning the estate, for example bills, insurance, a will, loans, and credit cards. In that process he took photographs, and by about his second or third time there, he cleaned the kitchen out of habit. Mark couldn't stand the smell of food sitting out all that time. It was clear that Amy made a meal for Tom that sat on the stove and that they hadn't cleaned the kitchen or stove in a while. Mark also noticed that there was scant food in the refrigerator and that the food in the cupboards were mostly expired cans that came from the food bank.

Mark never found a will after searching and organizing all the papers he found, but he came across a letter in Tom's personal items that I had written him years before when I was worried about him after he left the military and moved to California. I was in graduate school in Tucson when I wrote it. With a new baby and school, I hadn't seen him in a while. The fact that he kept the letter so close touched me and I read it, sobbing.

Sept 9, 1984
Dear Tom,

It's been almost a year since I last talked to you, but you're always on my mind and in my prayers. It seems it's been a rough year for you, and it's been a busy one for me.

My daughter's almost a year old and she's about walking, she's got four teeth and lots of curls. She's a real joy, always being a comedian. Don't know when we'll be able to see your son and the new baby girl, but I hope it's before too long.

I hear you've got a steady job, that's good in these hard times, though it's getting better. I hope you're taking care of yourself and going to mass every once in a while.

I think about things from time to time and I wish that somehow, I could alter the past such that I could reach out to you more and somehow make a difference. You know I love you, and I really do try to put myself in your place and understand what you're feeling. It's been hard for you; out of the four of us, it's been hardest on you, and in my mind it's a wonder you've kept your wits about you and done as well as you've done. I know I've not always done the best I could to help you, in fact I may have caused you some hurt through the years, and for that I ask your forgiveness, as I know my imperfections are great. I do love you, through and with all, I do love you. I am reminded of you when I read this book called "Secret of Staying in Love" by John Powell. There's this part, my favorite part, that I wish to say to you.

"But I want you to know that I do know what you need, even when I cannot give it to you. My own limitations and weakness will impede my performance, but I know that my greatest contribution to your life will be to help you love yourself, to accept your own limitations more peacefully in the perspective of your whole person, which is uniquely valuable. To give you all that you need would require a wholeness in me that I do not have. I cannot always come through for you as you need me to. I am living at the outer rim of my own ideals, hanging on only with great effort. But I can promise you this much, I will try, I will try always to reflect to you your unique and unrepeatable value and worth. I will try to be a mirror to your beauty and goodness. I will try to read your heart, not your lips. I will always try to understand you rather than judge you. I will never demand that you meet my expectations as the price of admission to my heart.

So do not ask me why I love you. Such a question could invite only the response of conditional love. I do not love you because you look a certain way or do certain things or practice certain virtues. Only ask me this, "Do you love me?" That I can answer: "Yes, oh yes.""

I know it's a little mushy, but it's the way I feel, and it makes me cry when I read it because I know it seems to you that I do place conditions on you, but that's just my weakness, it doesn't mean I love you less if those conditions are not met.

Anyway, I picked up this card at the San Xavier mission and I hope it will bring you some strength. Know that God loves you and is watching out for you or you wouldn't have come through everything as good as you have. I will continue to pray that God give you strength of mind and a soft heart. I will always think of you as gentle and compassionate of heart for I know through all the shells and walls there's a heart that cares about all and loves as Christ loved to his death.

Please forgive me for my boldness but, I think of you so much and I just want you to know I care no matter what. You are welcomed here or wherever I am always and for as long as you need to stay or want to stay. May God's peace fill your days, and his love warm your heart.

I Love You My Brother,
Gina

My mind flooded with memories of my brother and all the struggles he had and how he was a target of Mom's abuse. There was a time about a year after the divorce when Mom had a man over and they were sleeping in the only bedroom in our four-room house. The four of us kids woke up in the living room and began playing and bantering with each other as usual, and our play moved into the kitchen which was next to the bedroom. Mom came out of the room angry that we were making so much noise. She grabbed a pan that was sitting on the kitchen table and threw it toward us. It was going to hit Tom's head, and he ducked, and the pan went through the glass in the kitchen window. Mom's rage escalated quickly; she lunged at Tom and because she pushed him into the broken glass, he was bleeding. Mom beat him on the head a few times. "Clean this mess up, you're going to pay to fix the window," she yelled. He was eight at the time.

Remembering our time in Florida, I cried harder thinking about when Amalia punished him for wetting the bed. Amalia berated Tom hysterically in Spanish in the front yard. Mortified, I obeyed as she commanded me to get a pitcher. Once the neighborhood kids gathered, she stripped Tom down naked, and then insisted that the kids pee in the pitcher. She poured it over Tom's head.

A couple of years later, Tom went to Long Beach with Vincent and Amalia at Mom's request. He ran away a couple of times because of how cruel and crazy Amalia treated him. That is when he first learned about gangs. Tom told me a friend died in his arms after a drive-by shooting. He was only fourteen. He never recovered from what he experienced with Amalia and hated her until the day he died.

My heart ached so much for Tom.

After a false start with one funeral home that someone at Calvary recommended, Carla decided to go with a more reputable and well-known funeral home. In deciding the services and burial arrangements, Carla and Jenny got commitments by the funeral home and Calvary that they would cover much of the costs associated with taking care of the family remains and the services. It was an astonishingly generous offer.

Carla told us where the family's burial site was, and it was such a blessing because it was the same cemetery where they buried Mom, Grandma Lucero and her brother, Grandma and Grandpa Pacheco, and other family members. The gravestone was in the shape of a lectern set in a garden area. They would place all five of the family's ashes together in the pedestal. There was an outpouring of generosity and help from so many, and many donations to the *Pacheco Family Memorial Fund*. My colleagues from all over the world contributed, many contributed who knew Leo as a public figure, all the community who knew Tom through his ministry, and many countless others.

After the coroner had completed the necessary examinations and transferred the remains to the funeral home, they asked for someone to go and identify the bodies. None of the immediate family could bear to be the one. John and Jenny's husband, both family by marriage, volunteered. When they returned, they told us that the undertaker had put our diseased family in fresh clothing and hid wounds with hats, including a baseball hat on Malachi. "They looked very peaceful," they reported.

The coroner's office released their report, but none of us were ready to hear more forensic details of how and when they died. It was all too much, and there were other matters like organizing the memorial service and arranging for all the women in the family to go to buy black dresses together.

In anticipation of the memorial, we greeted family members from out of town, most from California or Denver, including my father and his wife and their family, Amy's brothers and sister with their families, and my paternal aunts and uncles. Each time we greeted a new family member who had arrived, and they cried, we cried too. Family and friends brought food to Leo's house and it was doled out freely. Each of us survived that time on what they brought.

CHAPTER EIGHT

A GRAND MEMORIAL

The memorial service was so much more than I had imagined, a grand event. The immediate family met at the mortuary, and we boarded five large limousines. Once we boarded the limos, a fire engine, many firefighters, and law enforcement escorted the procession. We first went to one of the Fire Departments where many members of the Fire Department Chaplains stood outside as we drove by slowly and they saluted the remains and the family. Tom was a Fire Department Chaplain and highly respected by that community. On our way there, the city shut down the interstate highway as well as the streets that lead to the Fire Department. As we left to get on another interstate, they shut it down for our travels as well as the final major road that led to Calvary.

When we arrived, there was a fifty-foot American flag held by up by two fire trucks with their ladders fully extended. They drove us to the front of the church where they were assembling the procession that would enter the church first.

The procession of urns, each brought in by a Fire Department

Chaplain, went in first followed by Tom's children, then Tom's siblings, then Amy's siblings, and we sat in reserved seats in the front of the church. Mark and my son walked in with me, and we sat next to Mark's eldest daughter, my daughters, and grandsons. Clinging to both Mark and my son, my grandsons caught my eye but I was too distraught to respond.

There were so many extended family members who filed in endlessly and they all wanted to sit near the front, which stalled the service until they accommodated all of them. The church filled and filled. The news later reported that there were over two thousand people who attended; the church was at capacity.

Calvary was an exceptionally large Evangelical Church that emphasized professional-quality music of praise. Tom was close to a cousin who also attended Calvary. He was a mentor for her and encouraged her when she decided to go to nursing school. She was up front and sang *I Know My Redeemer Lives* beautifully. She also sang at my wedding which Tom presided over, and I was touched by her presence.

Five large banners hung at the front of the church, behind the alter, and each had a larger-than-life photograph of our deceased family members. A headshot of Tom smiling with his mouth shut, bright eyes, and a thick horseshoe mustache. A portrait of Amy with haunting eyes, her lips pursed shut with dark plum lipstick, and her long dark hair in loose curls cascading around her face and shoulders. Malachi laying on the floor with a joyful smile, chewing on a straw, buzzed hair, one arm behind his head, legs crossed wearing jeans, a wolf T-shirt, and a camouflage jacket. A portrait of Miriam taken with a Christmas tree behind her, smiling with her beautiful full lips, mouth closed, wearing pigtails on the front of her shoulder-length brown hair, a red sweatshirt, holding a Curious George stuffed animal. A full body photo of Grace, the two-year-old, looking up with a serious look on her face and big eyes; she was wearing the black and red Christmas dress we gave her and a flower in her short hair on one side.

The chaplains placed the remains on pedestals, starting with Tom in a large silver cube urn with a cross on it; then Amy's urn, a burgundy Asian style vase; Malachi's like his dad's only smaller and gold. Miriam's paid homage to her girly nature, it was white with purple flowers like a large Victorian sugar bowl, and finally Grace's which was a white angel offering flowers. The sorrow was overwhelming. After the remains were in place, the service began.

The pastor began with a blessing, welcoming everyone and expressing condolences to the family for the great loss and tragedy. He gave an introduction talk and a prayer followed by "God's people say." Then a recording of the first pastor in California who took Tom and the family under his wing played and he gave the main sermon on "I am the resurrection and the life."

Then it was time for family members to get up and speak, and we were to do this in groups. First up was Tom's siblings, and Janice, Leo, our youngest half-brother, and I got up. Speaking first, I read from a eulogy I carefully prepared by reflecting on Tom in meditation then writing a love letter to him in my journal. This was my eulogy for my brother Tom:

> I want to tell you all about our brother Tom.
> About his big and tender heart, which was his gift.
> His smile, that many times came from a joke he would crack himself up with or an inside joke he shared with Amy. Although Leo could get him going pretty good.
> About how beautiful it was to watch the joy in his eyes as he interacted with his baby girls Miriam and Grace.

Some say he looked intimidating, and I know he could be, but I never once in my life feared my brother. I knew his heart since we were children together, playmates, sparring partners, confidants.

He was a pastor, he was a friend, he was a brother and father not only to his blood relations, but to so many.

When I contemplate his life, I see that his heart of gold was forged in pain and struggle.

His journey was a hero's journey, he overcame so much.

In the early part of his life his heart, which could be so easily broken, was a burden. It is not cool to cry in the barrio.

When his love for Jesus, his hero, broke his heart wide-open he was able to bring his gift to the people.

Fearlessly he went where many would not go, recovering hearts, transforming lives, restoring families. He had a warrior's confidence and a heart leaking with love.

Being there for his family was a blessing for him, he loved to participate as officiate, as best man, as brother, cousin, uncle, son...family was a priority for him...and his family was big and went beyond blood.

There is no way to sum up the life of this beautiful man, I can only share glimpses. His love for wrestling, the way he danced to funky music, the way he spun me when we danced rancheras, his love of New Mexican food, his lumbering walk, the way he ended every visit and conversation with an "I love you" and "God bless you," his fervent prayer ending with "God's people say."

What is true is that he was present. When he was in the room, he often didn't say much, but you felt his presence, you felt his love...what is true is that we loved Tom and his family deeply...what is true is that he will be missed...what is true is that our hearts are broken.

There is no easy explanation for this tragic loss, but perhaps we can, by his example, use our broken hearts to heal the world and treasure the many people in our lives.

Janice went next, speaking from her heart about her experiences with each of our deceased family members. Leo thanked everyone and cracked a joke, then he spoke very articulately, expressing the support for Ezekiel that we all felt, saying,

You know my brother wasn't perfect, he never pretended he was, as a young man he had a lot of troubles, and he found God and he found faith, and he decided that he was going to spend the rest of his days trying to help people. I know as much as we are all mourning, I know in my heart that what he would have wanted is that we show that same compassion and kindness and forgiveness to Ezekiel. I know that if he were here, he would have wanted all of us, all of us, no matter how angry or sad we are, to not make this tragedy include a sixth life, that is over, that is ended, that is disposable. So today is a celebration of his life, the broken vessel that he was, so imperfect, but as we see here and of all the stories we've heard, an incredible, powerful messenger for compassion and redemption and peace. I hope that we will show his son, his troubled son, the same compassion, that you will join me in making sure that he gets the treatment, the fair treatment that he deserves, and that Tom would want for him. Because justice for Tom and his family would be to stand by his son and to find out why this happened and to make sure he gets the fairest treatment possible. We love you Tom...we love all of you.

Then Amy's four siblings got up to speak, none of which I had ever met before this tragedy. They never traveled to visit Amy in New Mexico as far as I knew. The eldest expressed his love and remembered that he and his sister had it tough growing up, but they found compassion and strength in each other. When her only sister talked, she mentioned Ezekiel saying, "We're all here with you." She talked about how Amy took care of her and her two youngest brothers, acting like a mother for them. Amy's three youngest siblings were from another father and were much younger. They lived with Tom and Amy for a while when they lived in California. Tom had them distributing material from his church and Amy's younger siblings found their way to the church because of Tom and Amy.

Then all five of Tom's children from California and Jenny went to the front. It was the first time I had seen Tom's eldest son since he was a baby, and the first time I met his eldest daughter. I hadn't seen his daughter, who was born four months after Carla, since she was little, and now, she was married with three children. She came with her mother, and it was the first time I met her. Tom couldn't see these three children initially because of lack of child-support; in fact he only saw his eldest son once as an adult and he was trying to see his eldest daughter as an adult before he died. It was a bittersweet reunion of Tom's surviving children, minus Ezekiel.

Jenny spoke first reflecting on the unique qualities of each of her family members, including Ezekiel.

Then Carla spoke saying, *"I'm sure many of you are wondering as brothers and sisters of Ezekiel where we stand… We stand alongside our brother and we will support him because we know, we really know, that is exactly what our dad and Amy and all our siblings would want us to do. We stand confident that God will take this tragedy and use it for something good."*

A slideshow followed commemorating each family member in turn as music played. The first slide was Tom as a one-year-old baby. It was moving and you could hear the crying throughout the church. The pastor came up again and read testimonials to Tom by other people and gave a calling for people to turn their lives to Jesus. He ended with a prayer.

Carla and Jenny then got up and sang songs of praise and hope dedicated to their family. There were more songs of praise. Finally, the Fire Department Chaplains came in again and got each of the urns, and two members of the military led them down the aisle, followed by family.

Our extended Albuquerque family hosted a reception that evening at a Knights of Columbus Hall close to our house. Family sat in groups at separate tables in their family unit, occasionally requiring two tables.

At the burial the next day there were mariachis playing. The immediate family arrived and there were a few chairs, primarily for the women, and a canopy set up closest to the burial site. The extended family encircled the immediate family and then out from there, including close family friends. There were about a hundred people.

Tom's older children were part of the ceremony, and when it came time to put the remains in the pedestal, they were unable to fit all the urns. It was an awkward moment. Luckily, the ashes were in bags, and Carla and Jenny combined ashes in selected urns and placed them. It wasn't until I visited the grave months later in the springtime that I fully appreciated the beauty of the location with the flowers in the garden blooming.

CHAPTER 9

THE MEDIA FEEDING FRENZY

During this time, the media was covering every turn of events related to our family and the investigation of the crime. It felt invasive and cruel. Media covered every salacious detail of the deaths. In one segment, a local television news channel featured a minivan similar to Tom's that they drove to the Walmart near Tom's house, sensationalizing the comment Ezekiel made at his interrogation. The coverage made me so angry, and it only amplified the stress and sadness. It made it harder to deal with all that I had going on in my life.

Leo was getting multiple invitations for news stories and appearances on talk shows. He took charge of drafting the statements to the press. He was a master at it because of his public servant career and media training. He also was leading the charge to change the narrative about Ezekiel to a child with mental health issues. This was a statement released soon after the deaths occurred.

Pacheco Family Statement:

Our family is heartbroken over this senseless tragedy. We have not been able to comprehend what led to this incredibly sad situation. However, we are deeply concerned about the portrayal in some media of Ezekiel as a monster.

It is clear to those of us who know and love him that something went terribly wrong. Whether it was a mental breakdown or some deeper undiagnosed psychological issue, we can't be sure yet. What we do know is that none of us, even in our wildest nightmares, could have imagined that he could do something like this.

There is so much more to the Ezekiel we know than what the media is portraying. We know him as a bright, curious, and incredibly talented young man. He was a brother, nephew, grandson, and cousin.

From the time he was a young boy, his father Tom supported his love for music. Thanks to his interest, practice, and natural ability, Ezekiel has become a very accomplished musician. He plays guitar, drums, and bass. For years he has played at youth and other church services at Calvary and elsewhere.

The idea that he was a loner also has been manufactured by the media and those who simply did not know him. He had many friends at Calvary, where he spent most of his free time playing basketball or music. Like his father, who was a champion wrestler and coach, Ezekiel also competed in wrestling tournaments throughout the state and country.

His parents were always involved at Calvary, and Ezekiel shared their commitment to community service. He accompanied his father on missions to Mexico, where they helped local faith communities. He helped with Calvary's youth ministry and played his guitar or drums whenever someone needed him, including his aunt's wedding. At home, he helped care for his younger siblings and the many animals the family kept.

Like his great grandfather, grandfather, father, and several aunts, uncles, and cousins who are either veterans or on active duty, he wanted to serve his country. Because of this long family tradition of military service, he wanted to enlist when he was old enough. He dreamed of attending NMMI and talked of studying engineering or history. The pictures of him being circulated in his dad's old fatigues were part of his interest in someday being a soldier.

To be clear, our family has differing views on gun rights and gun control. What we do agree on is that those who wish to score political points should not use a confused, misguided, fifteen-year-old boy to make their case.

We ask those in the media, and those who would use the media to make their political case, to not use Ezekiel as a pawn for ratings or to score political points. He is a troubled young man who made a terrible decision that will haunt him and his family forever.

Five lives have been senselessly and needlessly ended. Ruining one more without trying to get to the bottom of what really happened and more importantly—why—would be equally tragic.

After the first few days of coverage portraying Ezekiel as a monster, Leo decided to accept an appearance on *The Dr. Drew Show* and went on the defensive about the media reports from the sheriff's office. On the morning of the memorial service, both he and Jack were in the paper with words condemning the actions of the sheriff with a headline "Attorneys: Bad Rap for Ezekiel."

We started meeting regularly with the defense team, and as a family we asked to meet with the DA's office. We delivered to her a signed letter expressing our wishes that they treat Ezekiel as a juvenile. Tom's daughters, Leo, Janice, and I signed the letter.

January 29, 2013
Dear District Attorney,

We represent the surviving family members of Tom, Amy, Grace, Miriam, and Malachi Pacheco. We understand that we have a right to confer with you about the recent deaths of our family members. This letter is to let you know how to contact us and to request a personal meeting with you before you present the case against Ezekiel to the grand jury.

Tom and Amy Pacheco dedicated their lives to reaching out to people who were considered by some to be unredeemable. Our entire family is united in our belief that justice for our family and for Tom and his family will not be served by locking up Ezekiel in an adult prison.

We feel strongly that Tom and his family would have wanted Ezekiel to take responsibility for his acts as a child within the juvenile system. Pursuing adult sanctions against Ezekiel would be unjust and contrary to the victims' wishes.

Ezekiel had no criminal record, no record of violence against others, and no previous threats of violence against others. He is not a hardened criminal that deserves prosecution to the "fullest extent of the law." He is also only fifteen years old.

We don't know what caused Ezekiel's brain to malfunction the way it did. We believe, however, that with proper mental health evaluation, treatment, and support, Ezekiel can be rehabilitated and rejoin society.

We hope that you will meet with us in person this week so that we can relate to you our feelings and concerns in greater detail. Thank you.

Carla, Julie, Jenny, Janice, Leo, and our spouses met with the DA. We sat around a set of conference tables in a U shape. Each of us told her that we wanted them to treat Ezekiel fairly in the juvenile system, not as an adult.

Jenny said through tears, "I have already lost five family members; I don't want to lose my brother as well." Most of us were crying because we all felt the same way. The DA seemed to listen, and she commented on how the media attention was backfiring on the case and said she contacted the sheriff's department.

That week, Leo arranged a conversation with an AP reporter at his house, where all the family would again speak out on behalf of Ezekiel, which resulted in an article titled "PACHECOS: Give Him a Second Chance," with a subheading "Family Concerns over BCSOs

Handling of Slaying Case." It featured a photograph of Tom's family taken at Jenny's wedding, a photograph of Tom and Amy, and a photo of Ezekiel and me when he was about five. They did an extensive bio on each of the deceased family members and reported how we wanted redemption for Ezekiel as we shared memories of him, and how we believed he deserved a second chance after proper treatment.

The Grand Jury Indictment came on February 4, 2013, five Open Counts of Murder and three Counts of Intentional Abuse of a Child Under 12 Resulting in Death with a Firearm. It went on in detail, throwing as many charges at Ezekiel as possible that would end up being duplicate charges for the same act. Again, we issued a statement from the family.

Pacheco Family Statement on Grand Jury Decision

Tom and Amy Pacheco dedicated their lives to reaching out to people who were considered by some to be unredeemable. Our entire family is united in our belief that justice for our family and for Tom and his family will not be served by trying Ezekiel as an adult or locking him up in an adult prison.

We feel strongly that Tom and his family would have wanted Ezekiel to take responsibility for his acts as a child within the juvenile system. Pursuing adult sanctions against Ezekiel would be unjust and contrary to the victims' wishes.

Ezekiel had no criminal record, no record of violence against others, and no previous threats of violence against others. He is only fifteen years old and solid science on brain development demonstrates that as a juvenile he did not possess an adult capacity for decision-making or consequences.

Moreover, the irresponsible way in which his confession was taken, with no adult in the room, no attorney, and no opportunity to speak to adult family members has deeply damaged his right to a fair and impartial trial. The confession was promptly released to the media and has made him the subject of a public trial and conviction before he has had a chance to even be evaluated by psychiatric professionals for his state of mind or ability to be tried at all.

We don't know what caused Ezekiel's brain to malfunction the way it did. We believe, however, that with proper mental health evaluation, intensive treatment and ongoing support, Ezekiel can be rehabilitated and rejoin society and our family.

About a month after the family died, Leo scheduled Janice, himself, and I to appear on *New Mexico In Focus* on the local Public Broadcasting Station to talk about what happened and about mental illness. A panel of experts discussing mental health issues preceded our appearance. We sat at a round table and a moderator named Matt asked questions.

Matt: "Leo, you say this wasn't a gun issue. Why?"

Leo: "Obviously, guns were part of this tragedy, of course. What we've been trying to come to terms with is that none of us saw this coming or knew what was happening with our nephew's mental health status. What we could have been, should have been, looking for, what should any family be aware of…central to this conversation is what was happening in this little kid's life."

In family discussions and in interactions with the media, Leo had been trying to keep the family together by avoiding the gun issue. He held strong beliefs about gun laws, but there were family members on both sides of the issue.

The conversation continued.

Matt: "A human reaction is to look back on it, asking could I see something?"

Regina: "We didn't see anything unusual as a family...we honestly keep scratching our heads. ...There is nothing that we saw in Ezekiel that would indicate the severity of what happened."

Leo talked about how the people at Calvary didn't see anything alarming in Ezekiel either, and he spent significant time there.

Leo: "As a society we all scratch our heads. ...Are we doing enough to screen for this, are we doing enough to destigmatize this?"

Matt: "The President has talked about bringing some kind of parity with mental health. ...Are we afraid to take a closer look at this?"

Regina: "We're OK with kidney failure, heart conditions...people are really reluctant to think of the brain as an organ that could potentially have issues. Somehow that throws our society off, and that concerns me. ...Getting back to screening, I don't think parents are taught what to look for."

Leo: "We hope that something good will come of this...we hope that there will be a greater awareness that mental health issues are real and exist in every family. We as a society need to give it parity with other health issues. ...This is an illness...we hope that our nephew will be able recover from it, we hope he will be given the opportunity to recover from it and the access to care to recover from it. Right now, all of those thigs are in question. Is there even access to care? Is our justice system so biased toward punitive measures? Even for a fifteen-year-old kid whose family overwhelmingly say that this is not the kid that we knew? ...I hold out hope that some good will come of this."

We talked about the conflict between Ezekiel getting true treatment and the legal pending case, and I shared my hope that he might get into a treatment center.

Leo: "We understand that public safety is important. ...However, I think the bias in our system very much, even for adolescents, even for kids, is on the punishment, is on the accountability, even for someone whose brain wasn't developed, and certainly had some serious mental health issues going on. ...So we're just hoping we will learn from this."

Our family was now immersed in the juvenile justice system and a media feeding frenzy. We were weathering it as a united front. Without realizing it, we were caught in a dualistic system; the family for now united to defend Ezekiel's rights as a child, while the sheriff and the prosecution were gearing up to put him away for life in an adult prison.

In the conversation with Jack, another disturbing reality was forming. To defend Ezekiel, Jack had to "go after" Tom. To free the child, he had to reveal the father.

PART TWO
REACTING TO THE INCONCEIVABLE

CHAPTER 10

THE CHALLENGING AFTERMATH

It was an act of courage to return to work the Monday after the memorial service and simply face my colleagues and try to stay composed and focus on work. Talking with anyone about what happened to our family reignited the feelings of fragility and shame about everything. One of the first things I did was apply for our Employee Assistance Program (EAP) which paid for a set number of therapy sessions. Knowing I needed help, just as I did when I had lost Mom suddenly years ago, I looked also for a place of retreat. The stakes were much higher now dealing with Ezekiel, the legal case, Tom's estate, all the family dynamics, and a leadership position at work on top of everything else. After finding a retreat center for grief and loss, I applied for and received two weeks of Medical Leave from work and began preparing myself and my family for my absence.

Every week I visited Ezekiel. He was assigned to one of five units appropriate for his age, and while his unit had a designated visiting time for the entire unit, we didn't go during the designated time for his unit. We had an earlier slot on Fridays, when there was at most two other visits going on, because they wanted Ezekiel protected from scrutiny or comments by others. Jack told us not to talk about his case because there were listening devices and many people watching and listening to the interaction. My initial weekly visits with Ezekiel were troubling, many of which Jenny or Carla or both would attend.

Ezekiel had created an alternate reality for himself; a reality that somehow was congruent in his mind with what he had done. He imagined himself to be a big-time gang member, and fragments of his story resembled what we had heard from his dad's stories about his time in gangs or his time in the military. We met his counselor. She had a quiet and calm disposition and spoke softly and slowly, making eye contact. Her hair was gray and wavy, a bit longer than shoulder length, and she wore jeans with a T-shirt and a large belt buckle. Concerned by Ezekiel's behavior, I asked her how I should handle his alternate reality.

"Don't challenge him on it," she said. "His personality is still split, and he is coming to grips with all that happened."

She told us that they had put him on antipsychotic medication. A psychiatrist at the county detention facility evaluated Ezekiel and would continue to see him once a month. They tried different medications on him, and I learned to recognize when medications made him worse, not better.

We began meeting with Ezekiel's defense team at a building located near the courthouse and sheriff's building near downtown Albuquerque. We got to know the team. It included Jack the lead counsel, Fay his co-counsel, a social worker, and an investigator.

We learned what the defense team planned to do and more about the expert, a forensic psychiatrist they planned to bring in to spend two days with Ezekiel. They were also going to interview many family members, neighbors, and church attendees and look for records associated with Ezekiel and his family.

Later, Mark and I worked with the defense team to search Tom's house for the kids' schoolwork, any medical files, and anything else that would be helpful. We found a few violent video games, scant records of schoolwork done by the children, almost no medical records except a visit to a chiropractor, and a few childish sketches depicting scenes of violence with a gun in the hands of a stick figure.

Since we didn't find a will, Carla and Jenny moved forward with becoming the personal representatives for Tom and Amy's estate. They met with a probate attorney recommended to the family. After their initial discussion, they asked me to meet with them and the probate attorney. Mark joined me for the meeting, and the attorney explained that since I was Ezekiel's guardian, I would have to sign the paperwork on his behalf that officially made Carla and Jenny personal representatives. In that discussion, Carla committed to divide the life insurance up seven ways for the benefit of all Tom's surviving children, including Ezekiel.

Carla promised her father that if anything should happen to him, she would take this responsibility. After the discussion, I committed to signing the paperwork, confident that Carla would follow through in good faith and include Ezekiel in the split of the money. There would likely be unanticipated expenses with Ezekiel. We didn't know what the long-term situation would be for Ezekiel, and if he spent time in prison, he would need something to start his life with after leaving.

Believing that Carla understood this, I followed through and signed the necessary paperwork. The insurance money for Tom and Amy was in Carla's name, so none of the other surviving children had rights to the money legally. It was the promise she made to her father that compelled her to split it with Ezekiel as well as Tom's other surviving children. The paperwork I signed gave them rights to decide on the estates of Tom and Amy, which were separate estates. Only Jenny and Ezekiel had claim to Amy's estate. My expectation was that they would continue to treat Ezekiel like any of Tom's other children.

Tom had two properties, the large property with their home and multiple buildings and a previous residence that Tom rented out. On the main property, he rented out an apartment and a loft, and there were tenants in both when the deaths occurred. The tenants were a part of the investigation and were interviewed by the defense team. Carla and Jenny gave all of the tenants notice. It was clear after looking through all Tom's papers that the house they lived in was underwater. Tom used that house to borrow against to pay back child support for his children in California and to stay afloat, but after the housing market went bust in 2008, the property almost went into foreclosure, but for a deal with the bank.

Tom and I had a discussion about the potential foreclosure. He was upset and defiant saying, "Let them try to take my property." He was able to make a deal with the bank and he kept the house. It was clear after his death that the property would be foreclosed on based on what he owed and the number of repairs that it needed before they could sell it, not to mention the fact of what happened on the property. They would sell the other property because it had more equity.

Sometime early in sifting through the house, we decided to move everything downstairs. It was in that time I first saw bullet holes in the wall. Carla and Jenny initially would come by to look through things and decide what they wanted done and look for mementos. Jenny eventually stopped coming because it was too painful. Carla gave several personal items to family members, and she allowed me to have a polo shirt with the Fire Department Chaplin patch on it.

Mark visited the place for months to help clean it out while I was at work. Many times, Janice joined him. She volunteered to be responsible for clearing out the house. There was the main house, the garage which had an extended storage area, the two-bedroom apartment, a barn with the apartment loft that was full to the gills and had some leaks in the roof. There were many bikes, mostly kids' bikes, outside and a professional wrestling mat they found in the barn. Mark found charitable organizations that wanted them and picked them up from the house.

We brought in a full-sized dumpster to the property and filled it two times. Janice and Carla orchestrated a yard sale in the vacant lot next to the house closer to the road and sold what they could. In clearing things out, we discovered a blood-soaked blanket, and it brought back the horror associated with all that had happened. Mark immediately put it in a plastic bag to discard separately.

Mark also collected items that his sisters didn't want that we thought might eventually be interesting, either to the defense team or to Ezekiel in the future. It finally dawned on us that they were going to foreclose on the property. We did enough of a job to remove anything of sentimental or monetary value, as well as all the items that could be useful to the investigation or by the defense team.

In those early months after the deaths, the relationships in the family started to fray because of the tension. It was in this time that Carla made a comment about the life insurance.

"I'm working on how to disburse the life insurance money," she explained.

I asked how she planned to handle Ezekiel's portion, and she looked at me and said, "Well, Ezekiel will probably get life and my siblings aren't sure they want him to get anything."

Jenny gave her a nervous look and nodded along. They clearly were about to break the promise they made to me in the probate attorney's office.

Puzzled, I pleaded, "Carla, we are working so that he won't get life," and reminded them of the things I said in the probate attorney's office. They both gave me blank stares in response.

She then brushed me off saying, "Well, we don't know what's going to happen." Then said, "I got to go, God bless you." And they turned to get in her car.

This was crushing. I started to feel I couldn't trust Carla. I also felt that I had let Ezekiel down…maybe I should have gotten the agreement in writing.

CHAPTER 11

A NECESSARY RETREAT

R ight after the deaths of my family, I needed to fall apart and be put back together so that I could be strong, especially for Ezekiel. That's when I requested two weeks of Medical Leave beginning at the end of February 2013 through early March 2013. After searching for places in New Mexico, California, Arizona, and Colorado, I decided on a place in Taos, New Mexico, called Golden Willow Retreat: A Sanctuary for Grief and Loss.

The man who started the retreat center, Ted, had gone through three successive episodes of loved ones dying. First his brother died in a boat accident, then his wife to cancer, and finally he lost his two children in an automobile accident. After his own difficult journey of recovery and learning about grief, he came back to New Mexico and started Golden Willow. The program involved time with a therapist, teachings about grief and loss, ceremony, massage, Reiki, yoga, and meditation. After talking to Ted, I completed the intake forms and we created a schedule of activities for the nine days I would be there. Even though I was worried about being gone and not being able to visit Ezekiel, only a month after becoming his guardian, I knew it was important for my wellness.

After meeting Ted in Taos, he led me to the retreat house. The first afternoon and evening was spent settling in, eating dinner, getting a tour of the place, a review of my schedule, and the pattern and expectations for the time I would be there. He was an energetic man. He was also a busy therapist, and his main job was at his therapy office in town. His wife had a southern accent and played hostess as part of my arrival. They both attended a seminary together in North Carolina where they met, which was part of his healing journey.

They both managed the retreat center and lived in the house, but in a separate wing from the place where visitors came. Between the two wings was a large room that was my living space. There I would receive my therapy sessions, teachings, massage, and Reiki. We planned to start the next day.

I had a session with my therapist the next morning. His name was Jim and he was also a trained shaman in the Apache tradition. I selected him as part of the intake process, and I was looking forward to the time I would spend with him. Jim was a mild-mannered white man and looked like an older hippie. He sported shoulder -length, mostly gray hair, wore sandals, had a kind, neutral face, and an infectious laugh. After the first session, in which he mostly asked questions, we went over the schedule and he gave me some writing assignments. Jim would also be the one conducting the drumming journey, which I had never experienced before, and a sweat lodge ceremony. I had attended several sweats before with a Lakota leader and I loved the experience that acknowledged the divine, all our relations, and the circle of life. What was explained to me was that it was their version of a church service. The sweat would be on the last evening of my stay.

Ted came that evening for my first teaching. While I was familiar with Elizabeth Kubler-Ross's work on grief, what he taught me went further. Kubler-Ross focused her work on the person who was dying, not for those who stayed behind. Ted's model had two more steps, a liminal or unknown time, and relocation or new normal.

He also described how trauma worked with the metaphor of a boat with a good-sized mast. Each time we experienced trauma the mast was hit, and another layer of trauma would be layered in the boat, but more than that, it would rattle all the other layers of trauma and we must go back in time to deal with old trauma, especially if it was unresolved. It is a model that would help me from that time forward and I was grateful.

One of my big assignments was to write letters expressing emotion to everyone who I was angry with or had strong emotion toward. It was a cathartic and exhausting process. On the last day there would be a ceremony, where I could invite Mark to come. I would burn the letters in an open fire outside the chapel where the final ceremony would take place.

The chapel was a standalone adobe structure on the property a little ways from the main building. Ted built the chapel himself with several teens he worked with on grief, abandonment, and substance abuse issues. It was a small building that had an eclectic display of statues from many religious traditions, and it also had a place for pictures of the loved ones of previous clients. Selecting a photo of Tom's family, I included it as part of that display and would visit the place regularly to meditate and pray.

The first time I got a massage, the woman came to the retreat house and set up her massage table in my living space. It was just what I needed and I cried in the process, having held so much emotion. At one point I asked for another massage, and she wasn't available to provide the massage, so they took me to another massage therapist in town, who was a medical intuitive and healer. We spent a good amount of time talking about what happened and my life. After the massage, she said something that I never forgot, "You have been prepared your whole life for this." It sent chills over my body, and I wept.

Daily I worked with a yoga teacher who also came to the retreat center. We would go to the chapel for the yoga sessions. When I did yoga, the teacher had me do some heart-opening poses and I immediately began crying. The time with her was very healing, but she backed off a bit from the heart poses. Months later when I would go to yoga, I was able to eventually manage the heart-opening poses. It was a gradual progression toward healing.

One of the first experiences new to me was Reiki. Ted's wife performed the Reiki in my living space. Reiki is a different sort of *massage* that involves energy work. I first became familiar with Reiki when Mark told me about his experience with it during the last days of his deceased wife's life. They explained it as touchless massage, which Mark first scoffed at, but later began to believe in after it became the only way to calm his wife toward the end as she was entering a coma.

I followed Ted's wife's guidance, and I had a vision as she worked on me. What came first was the picture of Tom's family and the murders in the house. Anger for Ezekiel came; asking him why, how could he, what was he thinking? I then saw each of the family members in turn fly up as spirits. Tom was very pronounced, Amy more reluctant, and the children like little birds. I then went to write a letter of love to Tom apologizing for not visiting him more or inviting him over more. I thanked him for being there and told him that I loved him and will always love him. I asked him to be a special guardian in my life and help me (us) to strengthen our family. Toward the end of the Reiki treatment, I felt deep love for the family and Ezekiel. It overwhelmed me and permeated my heart.

For the drumming journey, I went to Jim's house nearby. It was a sprawling adobe structure on a large property with a cliff face behind in the distance. Later, I would return there for the Sweat Lodge, for which he used the tent and fire pit in the back of the property. He would also conduct Vision Quests on that property from time to time. When I entered his home, which he built largely by himself, I was nervous, not knowing what to expect. From the entrance area I went into the main living space with a kitchen that was open to the living area.

The living area had many couches and chairs and was decorated mostly with Native artifacts. The large windows opened to the cliff face, and it was a peaceful place made more so by the quiet, gentle man who lived there. After pleasantries, like getting something to drink, we settled in and he explained a bit about the drumming journey. "Find a spot on the floor or one of the couches to lay down. You will be there for a bit, so you need to be comfortable." Jim would be drumming and would guide me through the process while he drummed. I settled in on the floor parallel to one of the couches with my head toward Jim, using pillows as necessary to make myself comfortable.

As Jim began drumming, I felt my body sink into the floor and allowed myself to relax. I listened to Jim's words, "Seek your power animal. Let your imagination drift…"

Soon the drums put me into a meditative state. At first, I saw what looked like buffalo, then a parade of a bunch of other animals that looked like they were in a talking circle including an owl, coyote, wolf, and eagle. Then raven came and flew around as if he wanted me to follow him. He joined other ravens then asked me to fly with him. "I can't," I replied.

"Lift your feet," he said flying ahead, so I did, like a plane lifting landing gear. I took off flying over the river, the cottonwoods below outlined the Rio Grande.

We went to Tom's house, coming down on the roof of the house. "I'm not sure I want to be here," I told raven. He said I had to see and that it was important. I flew with him through the extra apartment, the garage, the barn, the extra rooms behind the garage and barn. Then he led me inside as we went in the familiar kitchen entrance. We went around the countertop island, and I shuddered like something was under there. Raven started pecking at the end of the island but I didn't want to get too close. Part of me wanted to check under the cabinets, but I didn't like the energy in my body.

I coaxed raven away and he went up to the ceiling and we went into Miriam and Grace's room. I told raven, "I want to honor the girls."

"Draw a circle," was his reply.

I drew a circle, but was interrupted by a three-headed serpent that was rattling away, talking and talking their heads off in the corner of the room. I'm not sure what they were saying, but they made me uncomfortable, and I told raven I wanted to go to Malachi and Amy. I was in the hall looking in the direction of Amy's room and I saw Malachi's face. I danced or jumped toward the bedroom with the sound of the drum.

On my way there I saw Grace as if she were an angel, translucent. As I got closer to the bedroom, Malachi went away. I looked into the room…on the far wall I saw Amy's body drop to the floor then go up. Again, I asked, "How can I honor them?"

I particularly wanted to honor Malachi because he saw Ezekiel, who he idealized, kill him. I looked up and saw Amy holding Malachi like a Madonna figure in a Pieta pose, and she said, "He's OK, I'm comforting him."

I asked her, "How can I honor you?"

She replied, "A red rose."

"Do you want more than one?" I asked.

"One is enough," she replied.

"What about Malachi?" I asked with no real reply. The only thing that came to mind was a drumstick, because Malachi eagerly learned to play drums from his big brother Ezekiel. I laid the rose down with the drumstick across it and bowed my head to leave. I looked around the room trying to think of what else I could do. The walls were sparkling white.

Looking at raven I asked, "Are you my power animal?"

He shook his head "no." Then he disappeared, and a black panther appeared. I asked the same question. She gave me a growl in the affirmative.

I said, "What about my brother? I want to honor him." We went downstairs and I asked, "How can I honor him?"

She said, "Give him your heart," so I put a red heart that came from panther in the place where Tom died. The heart looked very red against panther's black fur.

It was time to leave, and panther led me out to the river and started running, asking me to follow. "I can't keep up," I panted, so she put me on her back. We ran and ran along the river north toward my house, to a sandy area by the river where I walked to often. She took me off her back and started licking me, my feet, and my heart like I was her cub. Her tongue was very dark pink, and it stood out against her black fur. The vision ended there.

When Jim drummed fast signifying the end of the journey, I went backward through the vision as instructed. I experienced the same shudder in my body at that island countertop area. It was a repulsion, like it was evil, and it lingered.

After the drumming journey, I brought myself more consciously to the room. Reviewing with Jim what I saw, he offered some possible explanations but for the most part allowed me to sit with the experience. He was pleased that I allowed myself to enter the experience. Later in the week at one of our meetings, he showed me a Mayan calendar with the page turned to my birth date and it had the jaguar as my power animal. After that experience I accepted and delighted in the black panther as my power animal and looked through a couple of animal totem books and read all I could about black panthers. I also looked up raven, an animal who visited me on a regular basis, and the dove, who visited regularly during my time at the retreat center.

This retreat helped me in those first few months maintain the various roles I was playing at work, with our children, supporting Ezekiel, dealing with the legal case, and the challenges that were emerging with the family.

About a month after I returned from Golden Willow, I carefully prepared Descanso's for my family. Descansar is Spanish for *rest*, and a Descanso is a marker you place where someone died suddenly or unexpectedly to put their soul to rest. Driving down the roads in New Mexico and other places, when you see crosses or some other marker along the road usually with flowers, it is likely a Descanso. For the girls I prepared a Descanso that was a pair of fabric lilies and at the stem I created an *ojo de dios* (eye of God) with a stick crossing the stem and yarn strung in the cross. For Malachi, a drumstick, and for Amy, a deep red rose made of satin. Mark, a Curandera (healer) friend, our cousin the painter, and I went to Tom's house where the deaths occurred to lay down the Descansos.

We smudged the house with sage, particularly where the island was, and performed a ceremony as I lay the Descansos down. In the girls' room, the place of their death, I drew a circle, not entirely closed as advised by the Curandera. In the circle I put my offering of lilies and prayed for the girls, though I already knew they were with God. Next, I went to Tom and Amy's room, where Amy and

Malachi died. Drawing a heart with a peace sign, I placed the rose across the heart and the drumstick across the rose adding some wire with more hearts. We chanted and rattled for a while before leaving to place Tom's Descanso.

With reverence we walked down the stairs, and at the base of the step the floorboards were missing, something the special cleaning crew did to remove all the blood-stained items. They had also removed the carpets in the bedrooms where the others died. After preparing a special heart made with two pieces of red felt fabric, I filled it with mementos and a letter to Tom, along with a copy of the special letter I wrote him over thirty years earlier that we found in the house after their deaths near his personal items. I sewed the two pieces together with pearl thread and used pearl buttons to put a cross on the top and a button with the Virgen de Guadalupe. Tom had a large tattoo of the Virgin on his back, which was his bane once he became an Evangelical Christian. I talked to him for a while and asked for guidance with Ezekiel. We all said prayers and good-byes. This was the letter I wrote for the Descanso and put in the red heart I prepared for him.

April 6, 2013
My Beloved Brother,

It's been almost three months since your passing, longer since I saw you last. I love you deeply and my heart breaks when I think of your childhood, the last year of your life, and your death. I know there were many sweet moments in your life as you dedicated yourself to God and to working with prisoners. The lives you affected; I know there will be/ are exultations to God on your behalf. I know you are in the arms of God at peace and at a place where you understand so much more. I'm sorry that I could not be more present in your life. I'm not sure what I might have done to somehow mitigate this tragic event. Lord knows I would have, had I had the wisdom and the wherewithal to know.

Tom, I forgive you for raising your children and inflicting your wounds and dysfunction on them. I forgive you for keeping weapons unsecured and for teaching your son to use them. I commit to taking care of Ezekiel to the best of my ability. I ask your help in that endeavor. I fear for your son. He needs you to be his guardian angel. I also fear for Jenny's sweet heart. Please send down the angels to make a path, an easy path to her healing. May she wait for children until she has healed.

Know that I love you, that I have always loved you deeply. My heart knew your heart since the day you were born, and I hope to meet with you again in eternity. I trust that you will be an angel helper to me and to the family while we remain in the flesh. Thank you for your love.

I love you always and forever,
Your sister Regina

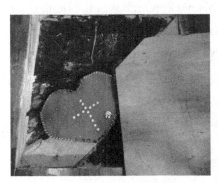

CHAPTER 12

EZEKIEL'S MENTAL HEALTH TREATMENT

In my role as Ezekiel's guardian, I started learning all the players at the county detention facility, all the rules for visitations, and all the rules and recommendations people needed to follow when writing letters to him.

Within a few months, Ezekiel got *super-honors* privileges because he was cooperative, followed the rules, and didn't get into any altercations at the county detention facility. As a result, he was able to have a *special visit* that included family members who were not on the list of regular visitors. In March, I initiated Ezekiel's first special visit with Leo, Janice, Carla, Jenny, and her husband.

I was communicating regularly with two managers at the county detention facility, mostly by e-mail but also on the phone and in person when possible. I asked for procedures and found they were nonexistent or outdated, which the director seemed a bit chagrined about. They managed Ezekiel very carefully due to the notoriety of his case. They scrutinized all mail carefully and scheduled our visits in the late afternoon to minimize Ezekiel's exposure to other people who might stare or make remarks about him.

I couldn't speak to the medical staff or get information about Ezekiel's condition until June. There were laws that dictated that Ezekiel was in control of his medical records because he was older than fourteen years old, and he would have to sign releases to allow anyone access to those records or for me to speak to the medical staff. It was hard to understand the rules, and I talked to Ezekiel on multiple occasions with his counselor present and he agreed to sign a release but did not.

Ezekiel was still very erratic mentally. He continued a fantasy of himself as a gangster saying things like, "Yeah, I got paid $15,000 for a hit."

"Really. What did you do with the money?" I asked.

"I got some food and other things," he said.

"It's hard to spend that much money on food," I said.

He shrugged and said, "I gave some of it away and hid the rest."

It was so ridiculous, but I did not confront him directly. I just asked questions revealing the logic of his story. He claimed that he snuck out at night when his parents were asleep and would meet his gang in the acequia near the house.

I also learned as I visited him that he had auditory and visual hallucinations since about age ten or eleven. There was a particular character we named *Sarge* who would berate and cajole him to do things, calling him a grunt, and he acted like the stereotypical boot camp sergeant.

Sarge was the voice talking to him the night that he committed the murders. Sarge told him that he was a pussy if he didn't complete the *mission*. Ezekiel said it was as if there was a real person standing there that night yelling at him and calling him names every time he hesitated.

Sarge visited him regularly, along with other voices. During the first three months, the psychiatrist was switching out the type of antipsychotic and depression medication and the amount. One of them made him very reactive and uninhibited, and he began to blur what went on around him and what was going on in his inner reality by reacting to others as a big-time gangster.

I treaded lightly during those times, trying hard to understand the effects of the medication. It wasn't until April, three months later, that they put him on medication that seemed to work. At this point, I still hadn't been able to get any medical records or talk to the psychiatrist who was seeing him once a month and made the guiding diagnosis. I was becoming increasingly concerned about his level of care and the fact that I couldn't get the truth on Ezekiel's condition.

I started reading as much as I could about antipsychotic medications and on *parricide*, cases where children kill family members. We began discussing within the family and with Ezekiel's defense team the possibility of hiring an outside therapist who we would pay for and who could visit with him on a regular basis. After looking up my legal options for release of information, I finally contacted the director of the county detention facility to get a release. It took weeks of wrangling.

It was in early April when the defense team brought in a psychologist to evaluate Ezekiel and look at his medical records to help us understand his level of care. She would help us figure out if there was a gap in the level of care that he needed. The goal was for the family to understand the diagnosis or hypothesis of Ezekiel's condition and determine a path that would provide him the care that he required.

Meanwhile, the defense team was trying to decide if he was competent to stand trial and whether there should be a Competency Hearing. It wasn't until the end of April that I finally got the records of Ezekiel's medication and was able to talk to his psychiatrist. This was the second psychiatrist assigned to Ezekiel, and there was a shortage of this type of professional staff available to go around.

The psychiatrist reported that he was suffering from PTSD related to early childhood trauma, that he was still experiencing nightmares, and that he had trauma-related psychosis and thought disorder. They didn't consider him bipolar or believe that he had schizophrenia per se. Instead, he had a bizarre self-perception and a hard time distinguishing reality. The resolution was medication, therapy, and time. We immediately started looking for a therapist to come in and begin working with Ezekiel.

We learned through conversations with Ezekiel that his mother stopped homeschooling when he was in third grade. She told him he was too stupid and lazy to continue homeschool. This led me on another path of understanding the homeschooling laws in New Mexico. It turns out that in New Mexico and other states including California, all you do is declare that you are homeschooling your child and that's all.

You are supposed to have at least a high school diploma, which Tom did, but Amy did not and there is no follow-up. There is no requirement for evaluating the child or supplying any proof that the child is learning and making progress academically.

As I tried to find out what the county detention facility offered for education, I enlisted Lily, Leo's wife, who worked for the Albuquerque Public Schools. The principal reported to her that they were going to do more formal testing on Ezekiel in August. For now, they placed him in ninth grade, and he was doing OK, except for writing. He was reluctant to attend school and instead wanted to stay in the unit. He was struggling with social settings more than academics.

The educational staff was steering him toward getting a GED. I got myself listed as the guardian and later received an e-mail with information on GED scores from a practice test that Ezekiel took. He didn't meet the average score needed to pass, and only scored the average in one of the five subject areas. His worst scores were in math and reading, highest in social studies. Ezekiel loved history and I'm sure that buoyed his Social Studies score.

Jack told us that he secured the services of a forensic psychiatrist, Dr. Newman from South Dakota. Gathering expert witnesses was one of the first things the defense team did. Dr. Newman sounded like a good fit. Besides working with adolescents for many years, especially difficult cases like Ezekiel's, he had a master's in divinity from Harvard. In late April, Jack sent an e-mail with a date that Dr. Newman would be coming into town. He would spend two days with Ezekiel at a private professional office. He would also talk to us and visit Tom's house with the defense team and the psychologist who did the evaluation of Ezekiel in early April. They scheduled the visit for the middle of May 2013.

The team arranged for Dr. Newman's visit, and the transports for Ezekiel from the county detention facility to a private office. The defense team got the judge to issue a sealed order for transport. Thankfully, the DA, the public, and the press knew nothing about it. Indeed, no one at the county detention facility knew aside from those necessary to arrange and conduct the transports.

Jack told us Dr. Newman was a calm, analytical, and patient man. We met him at Tom's house and found he was a gentle man in his fifties with light brown hair who wore western clothing. He asked questions based on what he already knew about the family and Ezekiel from information the defense team sent him and from spending the day with Ezekiel.

The defense team relied upon Dr. Newman to provide reports as to whether Ezekiel was competent, whether he was insane at the time of the murders, and whether on the night of his arrest he had the capacity to wave Miranda Rights. After his visit, where he spent the better part of two days with Ezekiel, he was genuinely surprised by how disconnected Ezekiel was from reality, about the hallucinations, and by the way Tom was training him to be a soldier. He diagnosed him with trauma-induced schizoaffective disorder with severe depression, remarking that he felt like they could prove insanity at the time of the crime.

CHAPTER 13

UNDER THE BUS

After everything I was learning about Ezekiel's home life with Tom, I decided it would be a good idea to visit my father and his wife to understand his relationship with *his* father. I also wanted to check in and see how he was dealing with the whole situation. We planned a trip the weekend before my father's seventy-ninth birthday, which was May 30, 2013.

I didn't get to spend too much time with them when they were in Albuquerque for the memorial service for Tom and the family, so I thought it would be a good time to see him, especially given his poor health. My father is an alcoholic; in his later years he had to curtail his drinking because he was suffering from alcohol-induced Parkinson's disease, and he had a massive heart attack.

We stayed at my younger half-brother's house. My half-brother took over a contracting business my father owned and seemed to be doing well for himself. His wife was a nurse and they had two little boys.

Our conversation revolved around two subjects over the course of the three days we were there: my father's history and what was happening in the case. I wanted to know more about my father's childhood, his relationship with his father, and the work he did as a young man. Over the course of that visit I learned that my father had no relationship with his father because he was gone much of the time, and when he was home our father avoided him.

He said, "The only time I spoke to my dad was after he would he hit me upside the head and then ask me what the hell I was doing in his way."

Grandpa Pacheco, like our father, was a womanizer, and stole Grandma Pacheco away from a suitor in Naco, Arizona. She was twenty and he was thirteen years older. He then took her all over southern Arizona, New Mexico, and Texas looking for work, finally landing in the mid-eastern side of New Mexico homesteading in the llano.

The conversation became animated when we talked about Ezekiel. I told them about the number of firearms they found in the house and about how Tom taught him how to use them. Ezekiel regularly referred to his father as "the General" starting from about eleven years old. Ezekiel reported that Tom would drill him like a drill sergeant, putting him through the routines he had learned in basic training. Drawing on his experience from the military and as a gang leader, he taught Ezekiel how to disassemble and reassemble firearms, clean them, what each firearm could do, and which firearm to use when.

Ezekiel also said his father would take him on runs where he had to wear combat boots and a heavy backpack. He would even wake Ezekiel early in the morning and have him patrol the property, sometimes having him perch on the roof armed and get a line of sight to the neighbor using the gunsight. Tom was in a battle with his neighbors, who reported to the attorneys during deposition that they were surprised that something hadn't happened sooner.

My half-brother chimed in at one point saying, "So, Tom did not change much since he was in California." He and my father went on to describe one of the incidents where Tom got in a fight with his girlfriend and held her at gunpoint waiting for the cops to show up. My father had to talk him down so that the situation didn't end with the police killing him.

The conversation changed in tone when my stepmother mentioned that Ezekiel's defense team had contacted them.

I said, "Yeah, they are in the discovery phase of the case, and they are talking to everyone including neighbors, the boarders at Tom's house, people at the church, and any family who participated in their lives."

She sneered, "They were asking about your father and whether he supported you when you were younger." I sensed her sensitivity about how they conducted themselves with regards to us when we were young. I wanted things to remain pleasant, so I changed subjects.

The Sunday evening before we left, Carla joined us for dinner. She had returned to California, where she lived and worked, in mid-May, and we arranged to have her visit while we were there. In the conversation that evening, she wanted to catch up with things in Albuquerque and I told her how Ezekiel was doing.

We talked about where things were in terms of her father's estate, the property they lived in, which was in foreclosure, and the struggle to get the renters out of Tom's other house. While we were talking about some of what the defense team was learning, the topic came up about what happened in the house with Ezekiel before he killed the family.

Carla had a plaintive way of talking. It was always as though she was explaining herself. "Oh, you know, Ezekiel was always a bit stubborn, and Amy tried to teach him, but he didn't do the homework and my dad was always working. He loved Jesus and had a heart for the people he served." She spent time in Albuquerque after graduating high school. She lived with Tom and Amy while she attended ministry school when Ezekiel was eight and was aware of Amy's homeschooling activities at that time.

She became very defensive of her father saying, "I hope they aren't planning to throw my dad under the bus."

I took the cue to back off.

Later that week, she called and left a message. "Hey Auntie Gina, it's Carla. I wanted to tell you it was really good to see you when you came out here. I was super-blessed to hang out with you guys." She let me know she was planning a visit in early June and said she would deal with the details of selling the property then.

The defense team asked, on behalf of Dr. Newman, to obtain as many records as possible for Tom and Amy, from birth forward, to determine if there were any histories of learning disabilities or psychological issues. The simplest and easiest way to obtain these records was to have their personal representatives, Carla and Jenny, sign a release. Dr. Newman was trying to establish whether waving the Mirada Rights was something Ezekiel could understand and if there was any history of mental illness. This was a necessary part of the due diligence as he tried to formulate or reconstruct what drove Ezekiel to do what he did and what happened with the police confession.

In an e-mail response to the request from the attorneys, Carla said she would not sign the release, saying that she was sure they were going to use the information to discredit her dad.

"Although they made mistakes both big and small as parents and people," she wrote, "I truly believe they loved their children dearly and tried their best to give their kids a good life, and I cannot be a part of any attempt to destroy their characters or discredit the godly image they left behind."

The term "image" stuck in my head. She didn't want *the image* of who they were damaged. In the e-mail she expressed that she was walking away from the legal case because it was too overwhelming. Leo was deeply concerned about the e-mail, knowing that her position and decision to *walk away* was not good for Ezekiel. She retreated into the black and white world of being *saved* and serving Jesus, and yet she didn't see Jesus in her brother. She wanted repentance from Ezekiel, and he was incapable of that right now.

Mark and I went on vacation to celebrate our fifth wedding anniversary and we spent the second week of our vacation in northern Scotland. The weather was beautiful. The locals said it was unusually sunny. We rented a car and were venturing out from our timeshare to see as much of the green landscape as we could that second week of July. On one of the trips, I received a phone call from Carla. She was angry and insisted she wasn't going to sign any release of records.

"They're just trying to blame it all on my dad," she said. "They want to throw him under the bus to save Ezekiel."

"Carla, if your dad has nothing to hide, that is what they will find. You know your father had a stuttering problem and Amy's family has a history of mental illness. Maybe there's something that can explain what happened," I tried to reason.

"No, anything they find, they will use it against my father." She was unmoved.

After more back and forth, I said, "You know the truth will come out," and that brought the conversation to an end, though we did manage to say, "I love you and God bless you."

The constant calls made our vacation paradise fade like watercolors dripping off a page taking away the vivid scenery and joy.

When I returned from Scotland, we had a conference call with the defense team, Carla, Jenny, Leo, Janice, and myself. The defense team again pleaded for Carla and Jenny to sign releases. The defense team first would pursue the competency angle and determine if Ezekiel was incompetent to stand trial. Then they would address if Ezekiel was insane at the time of the murders. There was a chance that the competency and sanity proceedings would sway the State to negotiate a plea bargain.

If they found Ezekiel competent, the defense team was convinced that the State would try to go for maximum sentencing. A full out trial would be very painful for the whole family, and both sides would pull out all the stops. It was a nightmare scenario I wanted to avoid.

Even under these circumstances, I believed that Tom would have had compassion for his son. Even in the best case scenario, Ezekiel would struggle for the rest of his life. I grieved daily over the situation from many angles, as did most of the family. I loved Tom, but making the situation harder on Ezekiel would not bring him, Amy, and the kids back.

We all had to balance the needs of Ezekiel, Tom's legacy, and the burden on the family. My fear was that "getting our backs up" was only going to cause added pain in an already painful situation.

I sensed that Carla and Jenny were in their grieving process. Jenny didn't want to pay attention to the legal case and Carla was struggling with anger. I couldn't help them go through their process, but I couldn't let that stand in the way of good judgment, and I knew that throwing Ezekiel's life away to retain Tom's *image* in the community was wrong.

Carla and Jenny did not sign the releases and the defense team pursued other avenues to obtain the necessary records. It took until March of 2014 to get a court order to obtain the records. The defense attorneys gave notice to the judge in mid-August 2013 that they intended to pursue a "Not Guilty by Reasons of Insanity" plea.

A day later, I got an e-mail from Jenny. It read:

So I wanted to update you on both my parents' estate. I recently found out that both estates are almost ready to close. ...But there is only one problem. Ezekiel is pretty much the only thing holding us back from closing the estate. Ezekiel still has rights to the estate because he has not been convicted, therefore the estate cannot close. There are only two ways the estate can close. First is we wait and see what will happen to Ezekiel's case, which can take a few years, and if he gets convicted then Ezekiel will lose his rights to the estate. Another way is I would get all my inheritance and I would give some of my inheritance to Ezekiel and I would be in charge of his money. But the way to do this is Ezekiel would need to sign over his rights saying he doesn't want anything to do with the estate legally. But of course I would still give him part of my inheritance. Just this way the estate can close sooner and it would be one thing off our plate. So let me know what you and Ezekiel thinks, and let me know yes or no.

Jenny
2 Timothy 4:17-18

I didn't know how to respond. At that point it became clear to me that they were not going to include Ezekiel in with Tom's other surviving children. I showed the e-mail to Leo and told him I didn't know how to respond. I took a few days to think about it and I crafted a return e-mail and sent it about five days later that repeated the concerns I had for not including Ezekiel as gently as I could.

Dearest Jenny,

Sorry I didn't respond right away, I had to pray and think about your request. I completely understand your desire to get the estates off your plate, especially since Ezekiel's case is likely to drag on for years and he might be found not guilty by reason of insanity. I feel so deeply for you, and I know what happened has caused you inexpressible pain and grief. My heart and prayers are always with you.

Ezekiel has a long hard road ahead of him. He will need ongoing psychiatric help, medication, and probably additional legal help. All of this will be expensive for the next several years. He will need a substantial amount of money to pay for all the things so he can be functional at all.

I know you love your brother very much and that you want to do your best by him given the circumstances. I also know that there is no telling what the future holds for any of us. I also know you are planning on having children. When the time comes for his release, which could be anywhere from five to thirty years from now, you understandably may not be in a position to offer him a home and financially provide for his needs. Your priority will be your husband and your children.

It would be best if we created a trust account to take care of these expenses. The way I figure it is that his half of your mom's estate is more than $30,000 and his portion of the life insurance money is a little over $70,000. While this money seems like a lot, Ezekiel will need a lot of help now and after he gets out of whatever institution he ends up being sent to.

Having said all the above, I would be happy to sign a waiver on both your dad's and mom's estates once I get legal notification that a trust is in place for Ezekiel in the amount of $100,000 (it will have to come out of the insurance money initially). The stipulation on the trust can be something like:

"To be administered by _____ (maybe by your attorney or someone that doesn't charge as much) this trust is for the welfare of Ezekiel Pacheco to be used now or in the future for mental health care, medical care, legal expenses, or upon release from prison an amount no greater than $500 a month for housing or educational needs. Upon Ezekiel's death, if trust funds remain, they will go to Jenny Pacheco. The trust funds should remain in an interest-bearing account invested conservatively."

I hope you agree that this is the fairest and most compassionate way to handle this difficult situation.

Let me know how you want to proceed. You can discuss it with Carla and your attorney and let me know. Leo might have good references for people who can handle trusts as well.

Love, Auntie Regina.

I sent a copy of the e-mail to Leo, and he said to let him know how she responded, but I never heard back.

CHAPTER 14

DR. HEALY IS A GODSEND

Before we left on our anniversary trip to Scotland, a news station approached Leo about doing a story on Ezekiel. Leo referred the reporter to me since I was his guardian. Still very wary of the media, I had a discussion with the reporter. She said she would supply the questions ahead of time and I agreed to the interview, which would take place in my home.

I tried to get across the fact that Ezekiel suffered from mental illness and that he was only beginning to stabilize with medication. I shared that I visited him weekly and that was a cycle for me every week of being reminded of the tragedy and trying to do what I can to help him. She asked how Ezekiel was doing and I told her he was a super-honors student and that he follows all the rules, doesn't get into trouble, and does what is asked of him. The interview closed with me showing her a picture of Ezekiel as a child.

She showed me the transcript of the story she planned to air before it aired, and I was comfortable overall. Leo agreed that it went well, and I was relieved. I hoped to help others see Ezekiel as a child who needed help, not a monster.

We struggled for weeks to get a special visit that included Leo and Janice, finally having to sit down in a meeting to hash it out with the counselor, managers, and director at the county detention facility with Leo, Janice, Jenny, Jenny's husband, Carla, and myself in July. Some connected by phone. The super-honors visit with Janice and Leo followed in early August finally after several months of trying to arrange the visit.

The visit was a bit stilted, and I took the initiative at one point and asked Ezekiel, "Do you have anything you want to say to Uncle Leo and Auntie Janice?"

He apologized saying, "I'm sorry for what I did," but added, "It wasn't all my fault…things were terrible…and I couldn't take it anymore."

My stomach sank and I realized I should have kept my mouth shut and not pushed him, especially because they hadn't seen him since before the murders and the whole situation was tense. His response made everyone uncomfortable.

I quickly jumped to another topic. "Can you tell them a bit about how you spend your days?"

"I watch TV on the weekends…I can see the TV from my cell," he replied. "During the week I go to school…we play basketball," he continued.

I continued to set up monthly special visits from then on, including the holiday visits for anyone, usually Leo and Janice, or whoever was available. Jenny took part when she was in town. By June 2013, she had moved to Arizona.

While trying to set up a special visit in October, Carla sent an e-mail saying, "After a session with my counselor and time to reflect, I need to take some time away from seeing Ezekiel to work on myself."

She never visited him again.

After pursuing multiple leads on therapists for Ezekiel, in late July Leo found one who was perfect. Dr. Healy was an older, very experienced psychologist who worked on cases like Ezekiel's regularly, often providing expert testimony at trials. Besides having a practice, he taught at the university and the psychologist who did Ezekiel's evaluation had been one of his students.

We met with him and found him funny and direct, and we were so excited that he was interested in the case, clearly a godsend. Leo told Carla that we found a therapist, and she agreed to the terms of his visits and expressed hope that we could start getting some insight into what may have gone wrong. She committed to paying the therapist from the money we had in the family fund or the insurance money. We initiated the visits with Dr. Healy, checking in with the DA, Jack, getting permissions, and making contact between him and the county detention facility staff. Dr. Healy started working with Ezekiel by late August.

In late September, two months after finding Dr. Healy, Carla informed us in an e-mail that she was only going to pay for four visits total and that she preferred a *Christian* counselor who believes in the Bible.

Leo and I were beside ourselves, and Leo responded by e-mail saying, "We spent an enormous amount of time and effort to find a therapist with the experience, availability, and willingness to see Ezekiel. It took us several months and many tries to find someone who could see Ezekiel. Dr. Healy is literally the best in the state. He has deep experience working with seriously disturbed kids and came highly recommended."

I was discovering in my visits with Ezekiel that the hyper-Christian environment that he grew up in had damaged him. He would talk about how he was sure God hated him and he was going to hell.

Ezekiel developed a relationship with Dr. Healy; he was a grand-father figure for him. Leo and I both felt that taking him away at this point was a terrible idea. It turns out that the unique Christianity that Tom, Carla, and the family took part in believed that psychology and psychotherapy were cult practices.

In fact, Ezekiel never voiced to his parents his visual and auditory hallucinations because he was sure that they would think he was possessed. The notion that he might have brain issues would not have occurred to Tom and Amy. Since he was homeschooled and had no regular contact with other adults, no one knew what other indications of brain illness might have been present. It became extremely difficult to know how to talk to Carla about therapy for Ezekiel.

Leo, Janice, and I met with Dr. Healy the first week in October after he visited Ezekiel four times to see how it was going and to get insight into what he was discovering. He received the Rorschach psychological evaluation that the psychologist conducted on behalf of the defense team. He used Ezekiel's dreams as a way into his psyche. Dr. Healy said unequivocally that he was not a psychopath. In his dreams, Ezekiel experienced feelings of regret, remorse, compassion, empathy, and fear.

Dr. Healy said, "Psychopaths do not experience emotions of regret, shame, or fear about doing something wrong, not even in dreams."

He said that dreams are an unfiltered way to access the true nature of humans. The insight from the Rorschach evaluation was most valuable to me in understanding how he was encouraged into action by his girlfriend on the night of the murders.

Dr. Healy explained, "We can't understand that situation based on our experience of the world. …Ezekiel had no one he bonded with beyond this young woman."

In my conversations with Ezekiel, it was clear that he wasn't able to bond with his mother and I never saw anything between them that indicated that he was bonded to her. He loved and looked up to his father when he was younger, but over time, starting at about age eleven, the bond grew to be one based on fear.

"The need to bond with another human was so intense in him, and the promise of physical connection with this young woman, that his psyche would have convinced him to do anything to consummate a human bond," Dr. Healy explained.

It made me cry to hear this; just the sense of abject loneliness that he must have endured for such a long time. My guess was that he felt it more after Jenny left the house twenty months prior to the murders. The relationship between Jenny and Ezekiel seemed difficult. Jenny had to be a mother figure for Ezekiel and Tom and Amy had set up a survivalist environment in the family where there was a scarcity of food and they walked on eggshells, cueing in on Tom's mood and dictates.

During this time, I was struggling, still dealing with the paradox of my role with Ezekiel. I had such compassion for him, but I was not sure I could forgive him.

When he spoke in more detail about the events the night of the murders, those details were hard to take. Driving home from visits I would often cry. At one point, he told me of how he waited with the AR-15 until he saw his father's van approach then went into the downstairs bathroom. He knew his father would walk past him from the kitchen entrance to get to the stairs and go to his bedroom. After Tom passed him, he came out of the bathroom and shot toward him multiple times in the dark, hitting him in the back and neck. Ezekiel then turned on the lights and went over to where his father had fallen to check whether he was dead. Tom reached out for Ezekiel's boots and startled him. Ezekiel reacted by shooting him in the head, and at that moment they locked eyes.

This story gave me nightmares for months. It was also one of the events that gave Ezekiel nightmares and that he cried about late in the night.

I went back to Taos in September 2013 for a Sweat Lodge conducted by Jim. I also attended a coaching conference held in Santa Fe, a yoga retreat, and joined a writing group. All were ways to keep me sane and functional. In late October 2013, I had a very vivid encounter with my brother Tom. It happened as I was trying to fall asleep. For me it was real, and I was awake, but I would explain it to people as a dream or that I was in a dream state. I wrote about it during a weekend writing retreat.

My brother Tom visited me on Tuesday.
I heard and felt the presence of someone in the house;
  a somewhat common feeling for me.
I was afraid at first, but then I went into the living room.
It was my brother. His presence was unmistakable.
I could feel the largeness of his body, and he was sitting and leaning
  with his elbows resting on his legs that were spread apart and his
  hands together near his mouth.
It is a familiar posture.
I think he knew I was frightened, he looked very casually in my direction,
  but did not move or say anything.
I ran back to my room. I was frightened at first.
I knew my brother wouldn't harm me, but still he was visiting from
  the other side.
I finally calmed myself and asked, "What do you want, why are you
  here?"
He came to my room. I could feel him cross the room and he came to
  my bed.
He leaned in close to my cheek, as tender as a parent kissing a child
  goodnight.

He said to me in his quiet voice, "I'm sorry for all this, I'm really sorry."

Then he said, "I love you Gina."

I said, "I love you," and tears came.

His presence lingered and I fell asleep.

CHAPTER 15

ONE YEAR PASSED

Ezekiel remained a super-honors inmate. He developed a rapport with his unit leader and continued talking with his counselor once a week. He was experiencing a significant amount of emotion and grieving as he came into greater awareness of what he had done and the repercussions of his act.

He was still considered a suicide risk, so he wasn't allowed to go outside. He was in school again after a summer break and now only had to have one person escort him around. He started a dance class that included rumba and salsa, which made him happy. It also made me happy that he was experiencing some joy.

Toward the end of the Fall semester, the county detention facility invited me to an open house that the school hosted. The staff led me to an area behind the normal visiting area, where there were displays of the students' work. Ezekiel was there, as were a few other students and a couple of other parents. There was a table with lemonade and cookies. Going from table to table, the teacher pointed out Ezekiel's work.

When I looked at the work, I was shocked at the rudimentary nature of it. It looked like work done by a third or fourth grader. Trying not to betray my dismay, I smiled and asked Ezekiel about the work and gave him any praise that I could find. His writing was barely legible, and the sentences had numerous misspellings and were incomplete. The artwork looked like something most children would have done in second grade. Ezekiel was sixteen years old by this time, and I couldn't believe what I was seeing. It made me incredibly sad, and I knew we needed to get him more help.

We started pushing the defense team a little harder to find out if the adolescent treatment center was a possibility for Ezekiel. They had other clients who had made the move, and the resources and programs there both for mental health and education far exceeded what was available to him at the county detention facility.

On December 8, 2013, Tom's birthday, Leo arranged a small memorial at a chapel. It was a chapel that was in the north valley behind a house belonging to a friend of his, a local artisan. He had built the chapel himself in honor of his mother after her death. It featured beautiful Christian *bultos* (statues of saints), *retablos* (a local form of art with saints painted on wooden boards), and punched tin art local to New Mexico. The benches were solid wood with no backs, and the one-room chapel was all adobe with stucco walls with *nichos* or nooks carved into the walls and artwork placed inside them. It also had a beautiful main altar at the front.

Leo brought his guitar and played for Lily, Mark, and me. He played and we all sang songs we knew from growing up in the Catholic church. Leo still played guitar for mass at the church we had attended growing up. We also sang *American Pie* by Don McLean because it was one of Tom's favorite songs. Together we exchanged memories of Tom and expressed our love for him. I shared the *dream* I had about him. We ended by singing him *Happy Birthday* in English and Spanish.

For Christmas that year, Janice organized a celebration for the family. It snowed that week, and everything looked beautiful. It was a bittersweet celebration, being the first Christmas gathering without Tom and his family. The food was plentiful. Only Leo's son opened gifts, and we skipped the normal adult gift exchange. It felt extremely hard to do it all without Tom, Amy, and the children. After the holidays, Janice and John were moving to Georgia for his new job, and their house was on the market. The special honors visit the first week in January would be the last visit Janice would take part in for a while.

Leo took the lead on planning a one-year memorial service for Tom, Amy, and the kids. He was able to secure use of the university chapel. With input from the family, he prepared an invitation and sent it to about fifty of our family members. We were trying to keep it manageable, and we were planning a reception after the memorial. The media approached us, asking for interviews for a story on the anniversary of our family tragedy. We declined and instead issued a statement from the family.

It has been a difficult year for our family as we mourn the tragic loss of our loved ones. We miss all of them very much. Our family thanks the community for their outpouring of support. We continue to support Ezekiel as he addresses his mental health challenges. We are hopeful that he will be treated fairly by the judicial system and that the wishes of his family will be honored.

Many family members attended the memorial service, and I arrived early at the chapel about the same time as Carla. It was good to see her, and we laughed as we looked for a way into the chapel. Five of Tom's surviving children were at the service, including Ezekiel's eldest half-brother and half-sister, Carla, Julie, and Jenny. A few aunts attended, including a paternal aunt who was closest to us and always reached out to us after our father left.

We planned to have a blend of Evangelical Christian and Catholic traditions for the service. A Deacon friend of Leo's, who was Tom's best friend growing up, participated in the service. He still lived in the Barelas, the neighborhood where we grew up. He served at Sacred Heart where we had attended church when we were growing up. The pastor who hosted the service the previous year at Calvary, also a good friend of Tom's, was there on behalf of Tom's time at Calvary.

The cousin who attended Calvary and sang at the first memorial a year prior sang two songs accompanied by guitars played by Leo, Carla, and others. She opened the ceremony and they played a slideshow that Lily carefully prepared for the service. The Deacon read the scripture that the family requested from Romans 8 and gave a very moving remembrance of Tom and their lives together growing up. He then invited family and friends up to share. Most of what was said was about Tom and the family and their contributions to the Calvary community, family events and gatherings, and how he made himself available to help anyone who asked.

Leo mused about growing up with Tom, choked back tears talking about how hard family celebrations were without Tom, Amy, and the kids, and again made a statement about supporting Ezekiel. My daughter also shared her faith journey through the past year. I was proud of her when she got up and shared.

I got up and shared by carefully prepared remarks.

Good afternoon family and friends. This year has been one of the hardest, if not the hardest, in my life. I don't know what I would have done without Mark, the most beautiful man I know. I imagine this year has been one the hardest for many of you as well, and certainly it has been the hardest overall for us as a family. Some of you may know that in March last year I went to Taos to a grief retreat center called Golden Willow for nine days. It was very helpful. I experienced tremendous healing and visions related to what happened. Many of you know the stages of grief that are taught based on Elizabeth Kubler Ross's work with the dying: the stages are denial, anger, bargaining, depression, and acceptance. At Golden Willow they talk about two other stages for those of us who remain on this side of death: the unknown and relocation. The unknown stage is the stage of experiencing grace, forgiveness, and connection; what some native tribes call the seventh direction. The relocation stage is when we experience transformation and a call to service based on the loss. It is where we are able to internalize that Tom, Amy, Malachi, Miriam, and Grace are not really gone at all. When native tribes in New Mexico talk about "all my relations" there is an inherent awareness that we are all in God. Or as I believe, in Him we live and move and have our being.

Perhaps many of us are in the unknown stage, which is where I am. It is a liminal space; a threshold between what we were as a family and where we will be in the future. Families, like systems, find a new normal after a loss, especially this magnitude of loss. We get to choose what that future will be.

Right after losing Tom and the family, I experienced the inrush of the sacred in the wake of the vacuum created by the loss that held me; a sense of holiness and nakedness of soul, stripped of my understanding. As time goes on and I choose to operate out of the Source, the storms of sadness, insecurity, fear, darkness, guilt, and neediness still come, but they move on, and I have confidence that I can get to the other side. I trust God's process and I welcome transformation. I know the chisel of the Master is at work in my life.

This chapter in the story of our family is hard to hold, but it is our story. Our story is centuries old in this part of the world. How can we move from this heaviness to delight in the abundance and richness of all our relations? Tom, Amy, Malachi, Miriam, and Grace and their legacy is ours to remember and bless. Ezekiel is still with us, he needs us, and he is ours to love. One of the things that Jesus said the most is to not be

afraid and to love. That is what this family is about. We are strong, cou-
rageous, and fierce in our love for each other even when we don't get
along, even if we don't agree with each other, or see each other all the
time. Especially in hard times when there is unimaginable tragedy. Our
reaction is to love. Can we hold the story and not get lost in the story?
What can we create that will transform this tragedy?

The ceremony was beautiful, touching, and extremely emotional for all of us. The reception was a celebration, a sort of reunion, especially for the cousins. The hall we had reserved used to be a school in an older part of Albuquerque, with wood floors and thick walls painted white and a high wooden celling, the kind that echoed when you walked in heels if it was empty. We brought in New Mexican food from a local favorite restaurant, including trays of red and green enchiladas. Tom's children were enjoying the time together and we took many pictures capturing four generations of family. We missed Mom and Tom terribly. People lingered and enjoyed the family connection that we had in that moment.

CHAPTER 16

THE TREATMENT CENTER

The defense team sent Ezekiel's application to the adolescent treatment center the week before the one-year anniversary of our family's deaths. Dr. Healy and the psychologist on the defense team provided their assessment of Ezekiel. I was thankful for the decision to include Dr. Healy as part of his treatment. The defense team was still in the discovery phase of the case, contacting and interviewing as many people as possible, including many at Calvary.

In addition to visiting Ezekiel weekly, we would have special visits that included Leo. Ezekiel had the distinction of being the longest-serving inmate at the county detention facility and had the most super-honor days. Jenny talked to him weekly. The counselor would use her personal cell phone to call Jenny and allow them to talk. He longed for the connection he had with Jenny.

In February 2014, Jenny crafted an e-mail informing the counselor that she was going to stop the weekly phone calls. She ended the e-mail with, "Please let him know that I do love him, and that I hope that he stays focused on school and that he really tries to work on himself."

She then sent an e-mail to the family informing us of her decision explaining that over the course of her recent phone conversations with him, he was encouraging her to "get pregnant" in a way that made Jenny uncomfortable. The last straw was right after the one year memorial, when he told her that she needed to get over the deaths, which made her angry and she felt that he wasn't showing remorse for what he had done and that talking to him was too disruptive to her life.

She said in the e-mail, "So now I'm going to take some time to heal and not talk to him for a while." She also said that when she was ready to talk with him again, she would write to him. She informed us that she had changed her phone number and gave a different mailing address, which was a P.O. box. She never resumed visits or phone conversations with Ezekiel again. It was sad that their connection ended, but I respected Jenny's decision and it was clear that Ezekiel's healing was difficult and detrimental to Jenny's healing.

As Ezekiel's seventeenth birthday approached, I sent out an e-mail to all his siblings, his aunts, and uncles inviting them to send letters or cards. After checking with the county detention facility, I gave explicit instructions to the family on what they could send. Based on that e-mail, his only maternal aunt, Amy's sister, asked that I set up a special visit for her early in April, which we were able to conduct. It had been over a year since she had seen him. They chatted away; he was so happy to see her and to hear firsthand that all of the family on his mother's side were supporting him and loved him.

I got word from the social worker on the defense team that the treatment center was going to interview Ezekiel, and I was thrilled. He seemed agitated for a couple of weeks and started talking about things not being worth it. It made his counselor nervous, so they increased his medicine. The counseling provided by the county detention facility was intended only to mollify him so that he would not be a risk to himself or others, but it was not intended to help him heal. He was in limbo at the county detention facility and I prayed he would get into the treatment center. He really couldn't address the emotions he was dealing with at the county detention facility.

He did well in the interview, and they later talked to Dr. Healy and me. In mid-April we got word that the treatment center had accepted him and that the insurance would pay, but they still had to talk with the judge and DA to arrange transport. As the defense team was addressing getting a transport legally, I received a call from the lead psychologist of the treatment center saying that they had decided not to accept him.

Panicked, I called Dr. Healy and he called the psychologist at the treatment center. They had a lengthy conversation and he addressed her concerns. I called and e-mailed everyone I could think of, including the head of the treatment center, the Deputy Secretary for Department of Health, and others who might be able to exert influence in this situation. We resolved the issues with the help of Dr. Healy, and Jack ordered the transport.

After they accepted Ezekiel, Dr. Healy called and said, "I'm delighted that he's in a much more humane and humanizing place." He discussed his role as a supporter, with Ezekiel's therapist at the treatment center in the lead. Once Ezekiel moved to the treatment center, Dr. Healy stopped seeing him, which was sad, but I understood the need to have one person lead his treatment and Dr. Healy had a busy practice.

At 7:00 p.m. the night before Ezekiel's transfer, I received a call from his new therapist, and she asked that we bring street clothes and comfort items like a pillow and blankets. Mark and I went to Target that evening and bought him some clothes. I was so happy for him. They transported Ezekiel on Wednesday. On Friday I attended my first monthly team treatment meeting (TTM) and enthusiastically met his treatment team.

In mid-April 2014, Leo contacted Carla about the fact that she had not paid Dr. Healy. She wrote an e-mail reminding us that she didn't approve of Dr. Healy and had asked for a Christian counselor, saying in the e-mail, "I believe firmly in the power of God, and I believe only God has the power to save my brother and truly heal him from every ailment, including mental ailments."

Leo and I didn't know how to respond. We both had deep faith that was the bedrock of our lives, but we also believed that mental health and trauma needed experts and treatment. It was becoming clear to us that Tom never truly healed as Carla said she wanted Ezekiel to do in her e-mail, using "the Bible and God's Holy Spirit to change people from the inside out and make them into new creations." We knew Carla didn't see it that way.

In early September 2014, I received a phone message from Dr. Healy saying that he talked to Carla, and she didn't intend to pay beyond the first four visits and hadn't authorized beyond those visits. We talked on the phone after I called her. Trying to keep my cool, I explained that he would not be seeing Ezekiel anymore but that we needed to pay him for the time he did spend with him.

In our conversation, we got into a discussion where she expressed her anger and hurt toward Ezekiel saying, "You don't know what it's like. I won't have a dad to walk me down the aisle…he won't meet my kids." Her perspective had fundamentally changed in the year since she last saw her brother.

I felt great compassion for her, and I expressed that to her. I knew what it was like to have an absent father and a mother who died too young.

She said, "I want justice. My God is a God of justice!"

At this point I wondered to myself what justice might look like, and who would impose that justice. Responding, I said, "Well, my God is a God of mercy and love."

We were able to agree on one thing: we both wanted something good to come out of the tragedy and the devastation it had caused in our lives. After talking with Leo, we came to an agreement to use the remainder of the *Pacheco's Family Fund*, which was where we asked everyone to send donations after our family died. Leo arranged with Carla to gain access to those funds.

Since the deaths of the family and all that I was discovering about Tom's household, as well as the conversations and interactions with Carla, I was questioning, "What is faith? What is love? What is forgiveness?" A poem began bubbling inside of me and it felt like a manifesto on my faith:

MY FAITH

My faith is beyond any religion, church, or building.
It is beyond any historical text or book.
It is beyond any person who has ever lived.
It is not based on any priest, prophet, or king;
   though I have many teachers.

My faith is not tied to my country, my tribe, or my family;
   though my faith in them comes from the same source.
My faith is not rooted in the company I work for,
   the titles or degrees I hold, or the sum of money I have in the bank.

In God, I live, and breathe, and have my being.

My faith is based on the fact that the divine appears
   every morning with the sunrise and at night with the moon.
It is based on the fact that my heart keeps beating without my will.
It is based on the fact that flowers and weeds tenaciously cling
   to the most precarious places in the cracks of rocks or concrete.

I know in a deep and intimate way That which holds all,
   and That which holds me.
I know that I am not God, but I am not other than God either.

Having said that, there is no-thing I **need** to do, or have, or be.

Fay, the co-counsel on the defense team, left in early 2014 to take another job in the Capital Crimes unit and we were sad to see her go. She seemed excited by the new opportunity. In July 2014, we met Jack's new co-counsel Robert. He was younger and looked very studious. He was quieter and more mild-mannered than Jack. He wore a pair of practical glasses that slid down his nose and spoke directly in an even tone. We learned over time that he genuinely cared about the kids that he represented, and was pained each time they were sent to prison.

I told Ezekiel's siblings, aunts, and uncles about his transfer to the treatment center and I put them all on the lists for phone calls, mail, and visitors. His therapist decided to go slowly with having visitors, starting with those who were visiting previously at the county detention facility. The treatment center was night and day compared with the county detention facility. Ezekiel was excited to be wearing regular clothes. The visiting rooms had couches, chairs, and tables like a small living area. A member of the staff would sit outside the room and there was a window on the door so they could watch things, as necessary.

I was able to bring food and snacks to him, including takeout. I started visiting him three times a week: Saturdays I usually brought New Mexican food and Mark would often join us, Thursdays I visited after work on my own and usually brought snacks or occasionally a burger meal, and Mondays, which became a time for family therapy that included Ezekiel, Leo, his therapist, and myself. Saturday and Thursday visits were an hour. The Monday therapy usually ran ninety minutes. It was a more pleasant and productive way to connect with Ezekiel, and his demeanor brightened tremendously. It was indeed a humane and humanizing place.

The county detention facility never evaluated Ezekiel educationally, which was the first thing they did at the treatment center. They also did a vision and hearing screen and a speech and language screen and I received a report. He passed the screening with a comment that he "exhibited some slight delay in both expressive and receptive language." His educational screen revealed that he was reading at an eighth grade level, his language comprehension was at ninth grade, spelling at second grade, and math at fourth grade. Comments on his motor skills said they were adequate but that "his handwriting and letter/number formation are very poor."

They went on to say in the report, "Ezekiel was very attentive, polite, and put forth great effort in working on the tests." In the summary they wrote, "Ezekiel is a young man of average intellectual ability whose academic achievement profile is somewhat scattered." They made recommendations on which grade levels to start instruction for each subject area. His reading abilities were based on memorizing words, and he had poor letter-sound associations, so they were going to focus on "explicit, systematic, and synthetic phonics instruction." I was so relieved to finally know where he stood academically.

There were no previous educational records, so they had to establish some baseline in the classroom before they recommended any special education services. By the fall semester they determined that he had specific learning disabilities in speech, language, and math and would be put in an Individualized Educational Program (IEP). A comment made in the report was that "he is unable to compute money or make change."

He was now seventeen years old. This was clear neglect on the part of his parents, and I couldn't imagine what he might have done once he was eighteen or even twenty-one if all this had not happened. He might have gotten into the military or maybe a minimum wage job. The whole situation made me sad and a bit angry at Tom and to a degree at myself for not following through on my intuition telling me that things were not right with Tom and his family. I saw clues like the way their children interacted around Tom, scared to say much at family gatherings, but didn't follow up.

Ezekiel loved history and was already much more knowledgeable than me. He had a propensity for memorizing the timeline of history starting with the Visigoths in Spain, to the Roman Empire, to the first and second World War and beyond. I was a math and science aficionado, and while I had a rough sense of historic events, I didn't keep a mental model of the historical timeline. I didn't know which battle happened when and who the major players were in the Roman Empire or the World Wars.

Ezekiel's main teacher loved history as well, and Ezekiel really enjoyed him. He made learning fun and encouraged Ezekiel. He also had a speech and language specialist working with him who was remarkable, upbeat, extremely knowledgeable, and encouraging— another godsend. I was so delighted and relieved that he was in this treatment center. Leo and I would inform other family, like my sister Janice, about Ezekiel's progress when they asked, but most people went on with their lives and rarely asked. Our children were informed and a couple of them visited while he was at the treatment center.

Ezekiel is naturally a good musician. I was able to bring him an old iPod I had, and they helped him download the music he wanted, *heavy metal.* He was also able to eventually get access to a guitar and had it in his room. Music was such a wonderful source of expression, stress relief, and it gave him an outlet for all the emotions he would be dealing with as he began his treatment in earnest. Later in his time at the treatment center they brought in a music teacher; a volunteer student from the university. He praised Ezekiel's abilities, finally asking him to do a solo in a big show about a year after he started at the treatment center.

Ezekiel had received mostly C's and a few F's at the county detention facility, but once he was at the treatment center, he was getting mostly B's, with A's in history. Science was always his lowest grade, and we would have interesting discussions about the subject. He learned growing up that evolution wasn't true and believed that the earth was only four thousand years old, which was determined by the Bible's lineage of people (all the begets) and how long each supposedly lived. He was a *Creationist*. It was a topic of very animated discussion with him as was politics. Tom raised him with beliefs on the far-right end of the political spectrum.

I told Tom several years ago to stop e-mailing propaganda after he sent me extreme anti-Muslim articles that said that Christians had to multiply as much as possible so the Muslims wouldn't take over the world. Tom held very fundamentalist beliefs, and the four of us siblings would occasionally engage in very animated discussions. My brothers were political opposites of each other. We usually avoided politics during family celebrations to avoid ill feelings toward each other. Ezekiel absorbed many of Tom's beliefs, though when challenged he couldn't defend them. When we talked to him about inequities in the system, he would express thoughts that were liberal without realizing. It was an interesting dance we did as he started to explore what he really believed.

In December 2015, they evaluated Ezekiel's academic progress. He was reading at a twelfth-grade level (a difference of four grade levels), his language comprehension was at twelfth grade (a difference of three grades), spelling was at sixth grade (a difference of four grades), and math at fifth grade (a difference of one grade). His progress was astounding in just nineteen months. He was clearly not too stupid or lazy to teach, even if math wasn't his strength.

CHAPTER 17

YEAR-LONG IMMERSION

After starting a new position in late January 2014, I hoped for renewed energy. The previous year had been a slog at work with everything in my personal life going on and my leadership responsibilities coming to a natural end. Retirement was four years away but I was counting the weeks. It was exhausting to compartmentalize work, my children, and what was happening with Ezekiel and the legal case.

I enrolled in a yearlong program conducted by Animas Valley Institute (AVI), an organization dedicated to the inner work of becoming a fully conscious adult or *soul work*. They combined Jungian philosophy, indigenous practices, and nature on their retreats. We would meet four times in 2014, and camp out for about eight to ten days for three of our meetings, and there would be *homework* between those meetings. Everything was taking a toll on me emotionally, and I hoped that this experience would give me a way to work it out.

The first meeting was at the end of February. Our theme "wholeing and self-healing" required us to read a book titled *Wild Mind* by Bill Plotkin, the founder of AVI. Our cohort exchanged e-mail because we each had meal preparation responsibilities and we were coordinating travel so we could carpool when we got there. They held the first meeting at The Valley of Fire State Park outside of Las Vegas. As many trips as I've made over the years to Las Vegas, I had never spent any time there and it was gorgeous. A crop of jagged red rocks silhouetted by a range of blue mountains and the clear blue sky. The first meeting was about the Severance Phase of Adult Development.

I was not doing well when I went to the Valley of Fire in late February 2014, but I had been to several AVI programs starting after the death of Mom in 2002, and I knew what to expect. I was familiar with the model they used for healing trauma through soul work, talking circles, and work we did in nature.

The rules for talking circles created a safe space for sharing: they included 1) speak from the heart, 2) listen from the heart, 3) speak to the heart of the matter (brevity of speech), 4) spontaneity (let yourself be surprised in what you *overhear* yourself saying).

We were camping for six nights and I prepared all the gear they had recommended. I looked forward to my time in nature. Our main guide, Peter, was someone who I did many of the programs with, including a Vision Quest. He was a therapist and had previously been a priest. He was about twenty years older than me and loved the guiding he did in the wilderness. During our time when he was discussing the "whole-ing and healing" he emphasized several times the need to address the addict and escapist in ourselves (our sub-personalities), citing several addictions including alcohol and television.

At one point we had a one-on-one and I talked with Peter about what was happening in my life and my involvement with Ezekiel. He looked at me and very firmly said, "Are you trying to save him, do you think you're his savior? That's not your job."

Peter startled me; he was usually very mild and rarely became what felt to be confrontational. After trying to explain myself, he asked more questions and gave me some exercises in nature to address my relationship with Tom, because we associated the need I had to help Ezekiel with the helplessness I felt as I tried to help Tom in his childhood and young adult years. He said I should bring in my ancestors, invite them to a talking circle, and discuss Ezekiel.

Peter's admonition stuck with me, as did his teaching about the addict and escapist sub-personalities. I made a commitment to refrain from all alcohol and television when I returned until our next meeting in May three months later.

When I got home, I locked the liquor cabinet with the wine, which was mostly what I drank. Mark and I had a habit of finishing a bottle of wine most evenings. We put scarves over our television, and we stuck to not watching television or drinking for the entire three months. I also gave myself limits on the computer and smart phone as I noticed that I was spending too much time on those *screens*.

It did make me confront more of my emotions, and I did many of the practices recommended at our retreat and offered in the books they recommended such as spending regular time in nature, developing a Soul Mandala, paying attention to my dreams, and others.

In March, I contacted Peter because I was struggling with healing from secondary trauma. The memories of Tom's trauma as a child were inundating my thoughts; it was a form of PTSD. I met with Peter by Skype, and he led me through a reflection that I had done in the past with other memories, where you bring to mind the scene that is traumatic and see yourself as a child in the scene. Then you introduce into the scene the adult who is you today and have your adult-self comfort the child and tell her the things she needs to hear and take her from the situation to your present reality.

The scene was from those many years before with Amalia in the front yard where she was punishing Tom by pouring urine over him as he stood naked in front of other children. My adult-self reassured my child-self that there was nothing I could do to stop her, and that I knew how much she loved our brother. I told her that it was OK to be angry with Amalia and to cry. I gathered her in my arms and told her that I would always be with her and picked her up and carried her from the scene. It was very healing. I met with Peter a couple more times and he helped me with the raw emotions I was experiencing due to my current trauma.

We continued our talking circle by e-mail with our cohort, and our guides would chime in when we shared. We developed a bond with the guides and with each other. The second retreat was for seven nights, and we camped on BLM land near the Capital Reef in May, right before I went to visit my father for his eightieth birthday. We would be doing *Shadow Work*, which is work dealing with the parts of the personality, positive or negative, that we are not conscious of, or the unknown side of our psyche. Carl Jung first introduced this work.

I was listening to poetry often and came across the poem *Panther* by Rilke. It resonated with the caged feeling I experienced at work, and I saw the weeks I had until retirement as the bars. After my drumming journey experience with black panther and this poem I took the soul-name *Heart of the Panther*.

A sub-personality called the *destroyer* was visiting me in my dreams as an expert marksman, gangsters, and lost or dismembered children. Although I have a real aversion and disdain for weapons and violence, especially guns, AVI taught us that the scary characters in dreams are there to upset and inform the ego. The ego paints them in the dream as *bad guys* because they signal a change in the ego's control. It felt like my nights had more going on than my days.

One of the more pleasant dreams I had was where I had an object that I was returning to some Native American people. When I got to their place, it was a single-room circular red mud adobe structure. It had a tree growing in it that went through the ceiling, a fireplace, and a bed where elders were resting. I took the object to them, and they melted it with water or some other liquid, and as the red mud streamed down from their hands, they licked it and were so happy. During the entire dream I felt like I belonged to this *red mud clan*. There was a celebration of life, and I left the dream feeling content with a sense of wholeness.

The campsite in Capitol Reef was close to a dry riverbed. It had many trees and a dirt road leading to the place where we camped. One of the things we did the second day into the retreat was a deep imagery meditation. Before the meditation, the guides instructed us on various exercises in nature that we could do afterward. During the meditation I became agitated because I was cold; it was colder than I expected in Capitol Reef. I was resisting the cold as I do other unpleasant aspects of my life.

Cold brings up trauma for me because I grew up with no heat in the bedroom I slept in, and often went to school without a coat in the winter. After the meditation, I became defiant of the cold and went to a place near the dirt road and started digging a hole and put water in the hole with the intent of making mud like the red mud clan. Stripping down to my sports bra and panties, I wallowed in the mud talking to the cold, breathing in my resistance to the cold, and pretending I was with the red mud clan. I stayed there for a long while until the resistance subsided. I could feel it, but I no longer suffered it.

About a month later, Peter contacted me about our retreat and some of the sharing I did during the retreat and on the e-mail talking circle. He was concerned that I disassociated from my body. He asked to set up a meeting, and during that meeting recommended that I find a therapist who did *bodywork*, but I wasn't sure how to find one.

After our discussion, he found a Hakomi-trained therapist in Santa Fe since there were none in Albuquerque. I started therapy with her in July and continued for the next eighteen months. This therapy helped me to stay grounded over that time.

The next retreat would be a Vision Quest, and it would be nine days in the Utah wilderness they called *Beauty Mesa*, which was near Blanding, Utah. They gave us homework to do before the Vision Quest, including to conduct a *Death Lodge* and *Day Walk*. I completed the Death Lodge in my backyard one night, where I pretended I was going into a lodge to die. Setting out various ceremonial items that were meaningful to me, I said my goodbyes then went into a *lodge,* which was a place under a tarp on an air mattress, and waited for the mourners to visit.

Drumming to stay awake as much as possible, I drifted in and out of sleep once I laid in my sleeping bag. My father, mother, ancestors, and others unfamiliar to me visited. The ancestors supported me through the whole night. None of my close family like Mark or our children came, which seemed odd.

During the Day Walk, I fasted for the day as they suggested in preparation of the four-day fast we would be doing during out Vision Quest. In the Sandia Mountains, I had an unusual experience. While I was sitting and journaling, a plant started to shake next to me then suddenly disappeared. An interesting sign for the upcoming retreat.

Beauty Mesa was a wonderful place. We met in Blanding and went up a winding dirt road, and suddenly we were on top of a mesa looking over a canyon with layers of red, pink, and beige rock and sandstone. It had to be over a mile deep. We were going to do a Fire Ceremony on the second day we were there. That was the evening we stopped eating before our Vision Quest the next day, but it was pouring rain. It was a challenge to get the Fire Ceremony going with the rain, but we had a break in the rain and we conducted the ceremony in which we brought things or symbols of things we wanted to burn to rid ourselves of or purify in some way.

The next day we prepared for the Vision Quest, which would last for four days, and we had to carry several gallons of water to our campsite. It was raining, and it took me a while to put my pack together. We did a portal ceremony, and each of us left something dear to us so we would return from the wilderness. Leaving my wedding ring, I went off and found a ledge about half a mile from our main camp, not wanting to go too far. Finding a place for my camp, I immediately put my tarp up and unpacked a few things, including my sleeping bag so I could get warm. Soon there was a break in the clouds and the sun shone and things warmed up. Springing out from under the tarp, I set things out to dry, especially my down sleeping bag, and prepared a proper camp area.

Content on my own, I made my little home. I created a purpose circle where I did ceremony daily, including the prayer in the four directions and the fire ceremony I did the last night. I ritually groomed myself out on the ledge and journaled and drummed in the evenings, overlooking the canyon as I watched sunrises and sunsets. They were spectacular, as the light changed the colors in the layers of rocks and the shadows changed the shapes and faces I saw in the canyon.

Walking a circuit each day, I first visited a grandfather tree that had branches starting especially low to the ground and many more going up the tree in boughs. There was an open space where I did ceremony, including a mandorla which was two circles that intersected and in each you were to act out energies that were opposite to each other, then quietly sit in the almond-shaped mandorla intersection and listen. The mandorla I did was embodying heavy/sad versus light/happy, which helped me to be at peace and have more compassion for the sad part of me.

Going further along the Mesa to a point where there were several trees that had been hit by lightning, I found a magnificent tall tree with twisted scorched bark in brown and black. I named her *Ecstasy*. She was insane for the light and—poof—she embodied it in seconds. I would talk with her, sing to her, and read her poetry. On the way back, I would visit a smaller more groomed tree I called *Louie*. He was French in my mind, and he came from a dream that was about enjoying life.

At night, I would wait for the fullness of the moon, sometimes sleeping a bit with my tarp pulled back so I could watch the sky. When I saw the moon, I would get out of my sleeping bag, put on my *folklorico* royal purple blouse with puffed sleeves and elastic at the waist and a black peasant skirt with satin ribbons of assorted colors horizontally across the skirt. Wearing a red shawl, I danced and sang to the moon, rattling the whole time. That would last at least a half hour.

Hunger wasn't much of a problem for me, only a bit on the first day, but I did get a bit weak over the course of the four days and I had to make a trip back to main camp to get more water. When we returned, we had a talking circle in which we shared our experience and I acted out my tree friends. It was a beautiful respite for me. At the end of our retreat, we went back to where we camped to make sure we removed any signs of our time there and ask for guidance in responding to the phrase "I am the one who." I wrote from my heart, "I am the one who loves deeply and fiercely with the heart of the panther, transcends and includes all that came before, and receives the world open-heartedly with a smile."

The last gathering would be in mid-September, 2014, for six days in a lodge outside of Cortez, Colorado, called Kelly's Place. It would be the first meeting where we slept in beds, and they made the meals. During this meeting we focused on manifesting what we had uncovered on our path to becoming the visionary artisans of cultural transformation. We were to create something that marked our own transformation over the year. Fire was a theme that kept coming to me, the phrase "I am the flame," and when I heard the song *Girl on Fire* by Alicia Keys, it convinced me to work with that theme.

I decided to teach everybody to dance to various Spanish songs: salsa, samba, merengue, rancheras, and others. It was my way of enacting the fire of my culture. Dancing also made me incredibly happy and present in the moment. We had fun and I ended with my own fire dance, complete with several scarves. Saying goodbye at the final retreat was hard, but we stayed connected through our virtual talking circle for years after. The time spent in the immersion allowed me to come home to myself amid all that was tugging at me in the *middle-world*, as the AVI people refer to everyday life on earth.

CHAPTER 18

WHAT REALLY WENT ON IN TOM'S HOUSE

The first mental health assessment at the treatment center reported, "Student has had depressive symptoms including sadness, weight loss, cognitive problems, anxiety, suicidal thoughts, auditory and visual hallucinations, and paranoid thoughts. ...he meets the criteria for major depression disorder with psychotic features and PTSD."

At the treatment center, Ezekiel met multiple times a week with his therapist and they assigned him a psychologist who oversaw his medication. They started adjusting his medication again and I received a phone call from the psychologist when I was at the airport on travel around Thanksgiving 2014. It was the last time they made a major change to his antipsychotic medication.

Up to that time they had him on three drugs: the antipsychotic, depression medication, and something to help him sleep. She wanted him to go from two medications, the antipsychotic and depression, down to one medication, which was both an antipsychotic and used to treat depression. She started that process of transition in December

2014, and would not complete the transition fully until late February 2015.

They took a CAT scan of his brain, and it was normal. He was doing very well in PE, but he still exhibited anxiety in social settings. Ezekiel had a nervous habit of biting his nails, sometimes until he bled, and he popped his knuckles all the time. His therapist started addressing his issues with social skills, trauma, grief work, and getting him to think more broadly. By thinking broadly, she wanted him to address some of the narrow and biased beliefs his father taught him about race, religion, and gender.

Leo and I met every Monday with him for therapy with few exceptions for what turned out to be twenty-two months; about ninety times. It was intensive for all of us. At the county detention facility, we were learning about the relationship between Tom and Ezekiel, but the stories were fragmented and confusing. We couldn't get too deep when I met with him only once a week and Leo saw him once a month. Now that he was at the treatment center and we had quality time with him, especially in therapy, we were learning more.

At times Ezekiel would muse about fun times with his siblings or his friends at Calvary on our informal visits. During the therapy we learned more about what went on in his household with his father. The order of discussing his stories is unclear; many times we would go back to them as we discussed different topics in therapy.

Tom started to be extremely hard on Ezekiel around age eleven. He said his father gave him the rank of *private first class* and he was instructed to refer to his father as *The General*. At that time, there was an incident where Ezekiel wrote a page-long letter the night before he was going to Calvary to attend Co-op, a version of Sunday School.

He had a crush on a young girl with blonde hair and blue eyes, and his parents knew who she was and would remark, "She's ugly." Something they said often when they knew Ezekiel liked someone.

There was a misunderstanding between Ezekiel and this young lady, and he wrote the letter to apologize. The letter had a few cuss words, which he said he learned from his father.

At Co-op, he handed the letter to the young lady under the table. After she got it, she got up and handed the letter to the teacher in front of everyone. The teacher told Ezekiel she was planning to tell his parents. When Amy arrived carrying Malachi, the teacher told her what happened and handed her the letter. As they walked away, Amy told Ezekiel that she was going to tell his father.

When she did, Tom looked at Ezekiel like he was going to beat him and said, "Wait till we get home." This happened in winter, and once they got home it was dark. Tom told Ezekiel to get out of the car and take off his coat. The rest of the family went into the house. Tom led Ezekiel to a basement under the front porch, opened it, and told him to go down there. Ezekiel started crying and protested that he was cold and didn't want to be stuck in the darkness.

His parents would lock him in the closet after horror movies, something Amy enjoyed watching, and his parents would bang on the door and make demon noises. When he would cry or scream to open the door and beg them not to let Satan take him away, they would laugh and let him go up to his room. As a result, Ezekiel hated small, dark spaces.

Once Tom closed the door to the basement, he put his foot on it while Ezekiel was crying and hitting the door, trying to push the door open with all his might, but he couldn't open it. He sat on the basement stairs and wrapped his arms around himself to try to stay warm and he cried. About an hour or so later, he pushed the door to check it and it opened. He eagerly got out of the basement shaking with cold and apprehensively went to the side entry door to the house, which was unlocked.

Ezekiel went in and closed the door behind him. When he turned around Tom came out of a hiding place where he waited for him and trapped Ezekiel because there was a countertop area to his left, the door was behind him, and his dad was approaching from the right. He tried to run and felt a pain on the right side of his face and arm as his dad yelled at him and grabbed his collar and dragged him to the stairs. He let him climb the stairs after he kicked him in the rear end.

Later, while Ezekiel was in his room, Tom walked in and Ezekiel braced himself. Tom yelled, "You're a stupid idiot, your handwriting is horrible, and you can't spell worth a damn!"

His dad ordered him to copy the book of Proverbs, and he gave Ezekiel thirty-one days to finish. It took a month and a half. When Ezekiel was writing at the kitchen table and stopped writing or if he complained about the task, Tom slapped him out of his chair. Tom punished him if he didn't finish a chapter a day. Ezekiel began to loathe the Bible.

Another time, when Ezekiel was twelve years old, his mother and he had a disagreement and he sassed her back. He may have hit her, he wasn't sure. His dad called him into his parents' room, AKA, the COOR, commander of operations room. His father, or the commander, was sitting on his bed looking at him calmly. Ezekiel stood at attention standing between the windows and the foot of the bed. Tom told him to come closer, so he took a small step forward. He knew what might be coming. Tom asked him to come closer again, so he took another small step. Next thing he knew, he's on his back and Tom was on top of him. Tom pinned his arms to his side using his legs and was punching Ezekiel's face. After the fourth or fifth hit, Ezekiel blacked out.

When he woke up in his bed, he remembered what happened and got up and went to the bathroom to look in the mirror. He had a black left eye and a bruised face. Later, Tom called him into the

COOR again. When Ezekiel went in, his dad was getting ready for church. He ordered Ezekiel to be silent about what happened and if anyone asked, he was to say that they were wrestling, and he *accidentally* head-butted him. Ezekiel followed his dad's order when they went to church and people seemed to believe his story; at least no one pressed the issue.

Tom continued beating Ezekiel until the day the family died. Jenny's husband reported visiting with Jenny after they were married and found Tom beating Ezekiel. He tried to pull Tom off of him.

During our therapy we decided that it would be good to have Ezekiel watch the memorial video so he could see the impact that his actions had on others and for closure, because he had also experienced the loss of his family. The first time we tried, he couldn't get past the procession before he became anxious and started crying. We waited another couple of months and tried again. This time he was able to watch the whole thing, silently crying from time to time.

At about a year into his therapy, we went through the newspaper clippings of the deaths and all that followed. He seemed to deal with that a little better. Many of the therapy sessions were hard, and when he would start to make progress something would happen. A disagreement with one of the other students or a remark they made would send him back to his old black and white thinking. He would say something like, "damn redneck," and we had to process his thinking again.

Some of his remarks were alarming because of what Ezekiel had done. A simple "I could kill him" meant a lot more than a casual remark someone would say who was not in Ezekiel's situation. His therapist was teaching him to deal with his strong emotions in other ways, having him practice awareness of his feelings and walking through alternatives he had for how he managed his feelings.

We supported him and we all encouraged any form of mindfulness and breathing in the moment when his emotions went from two to ten. Emotional regulation as he was dealing with his trauma was something we spent a good amount of time on during his therapy. We also worked with getting him to accept responsibility for what he had done and the devastation it caused others, which was hard for him. He did so slowly over time. I experienced him going from blaming others, primarily his mother and father, to acceptance and depression, to self-loathing in a cycle as he came to terms with the *nuclear bomb* he had set off in the family.

CHAPTER 19

A CHILD SOLDIER

Thanksgiving through January was hard for Ezekiel. His father's birthday was in December, and the holidays carried many memories. January, when the deaths occurred, was the hardest. We watched him closely. A few months into his stay at the treatment center he had a visual hallucination that scared him. He saw a small handprint outline on his bed and swore it couldn't have been his or any of the staff. It spooked him, and he was sure that maybe Malachi came to visit him or some demon had come to claim him. It took time before those types of events didn't happen. Ezekiel would talk about times when *Sarge* was talking to him and bullying him to "take action." He became better about recognizing this voice and realizing it wasn't real, and eventually learned to ignore him or talk to him and ask him to leave him alone.

Ezekiel had achieved the rank of sergeant before he killed his family. When I asked him to tell me the story about when he started patrolling his parents' property, he told me this story.

At age thirteen, I had been a grunt for about two years and had already obtained the rank of corporal. I was watching TV with my siblings and our dog started barking. I didn't really pay attention to him. I figured it was some little animal that managed to scare her. I didn't see anything strange through the dining room window, but it being nighttime, I could've been wrong. I heard my parents' door open and my father commander calling for me. I ran up the stairs and into my parents' room. My father handed me a 12-guage shotgun while he was talking. He seemed wound-up and in a fury. I guess someone was in our territory, maybe behind the wooden fence, which is why I couldn't see anything from the dining room window. I guess he saw something I didn't from his upstairs bedroom. This was the reason for the dog barking.

Well, it was time to move out and maybe blast someone unlucky enough to be on the Pacheco's land. When we got to the porch, my father gave me a rundown of how we were going to move on these "ungodly trespassers."

Looking back it seems odd that he was sure who it was, and the exact location of the breach, considering that it was almost ten o'clock at night and there was no light in that sector of our territory. Even from my parents' room on the second floor, you can't see anything but darkness and the barn.

My father was point man and led me outside the gate, to the other side of the property, to the sector where he saw something. From where the broken car was to that sector of wire was known as our "western front." The "southern front" was next to it, like an L shape.

I raised my shotgun at the ready as we were walking this stretch of western frontline. It was dark and there was little noise; mostly our boots and the dog on the other side of the fence. We got to the wire where it separated our territory from our neighbors' (no-man's-land).

No one was there, and there didn't seem to me that anybody was. However, my father took out his flashlight turned it on and got down to examine the wire fence. While he was doing that, I stood behind him with the gun at the ready, scanning from left to right, right to left.

Then he called my name, I looked, he said, "See that there, those bastards clipped wire." Then he touched the wire and said, "It's still warm, too." He had me touch the clipped wire to confirm it. He said, "Let's go back and fix this damn fence."

We walked back the same way we walked in. He went into the garage to grab some tools. I stood outside the door with the shotgun in a cross-carry position and guarded the garage entrance. We walked over again and he began to fix the wire. He had me hold the flashlight on that spot. I had my other hand on the grip of the shotgun resting on my shoulder. He fixed it and we went back. He had me give him the shotgun and wait in the library.

He came down maybe ten minutes later carrying a .22 long-rifle; he handed it to me with the instructions to take guard duty. "No one is permitted to enter this property unless I say so. When a person who's unauthorized enters, the light is green, one shot one kill. Am I clear?"

I told him, "Yes sir."

He told me, "Every night you will be here, do perimeter checks every fifteen mikes, this shift lasts from 20:00 hours or when I say, to 06:30, or when I say. You will be put on active whenever necessary. You are never to abandon your post or shirk your duty. Failure to do this will result in punishment. Do you understand your direct orders?"

"I understand, sir," I replied.

My first night I got caught a couple of times and "smoked out" for going inside. After that I made sure my father was asleep before doing other things at night. Over time I got an AR-15 as a standard weapon for this assignment. Not much went on during this two-year period of guard duty from then until when I was arrested.

In the therapy process we discussed empathy extensively. One of the stories made Ezekiel tear up and wipe tears from the corner of his eyes. He recounted the whippings that his mother would give his younger sister Miriam since about age four when she would wet her pants. Amy would strip her from the waist down and lash her with a thin leather belt on her backside and legs until she had welts. All the time Miriam would cry and try to escape her mother's grasp.

Another story that related to empathy and his confusion around religion happened when he was about age fourteen. Ezekiel said, "It gave me a lesson that life didn't matter much to my father." Here's the way he told the story.

There was a dog in the back area between the guest house and the barn along the western front. The entire family was ready for church and just waiting to leave.

My mother called me into the kitchen. I walked over, and she said, "There's a dog and young puppy in the back area and you need to remove them."

She gave me a plastic bat, like that would do anything. I took the bat and proceeded with her order. When I got to the front, I slowed my walk, but didn't see anything. Then a dog came out from behind the wall; it was big, with big muscles, about half my size at the time. The pup was small and very cute. I continued to walk towards it, slowly, so not to give it a reason to snap.

The dog kept moving forward, then backward, like not sure whether to come or go. I stopped where the water valves were and reached out my left hand. The dog smelled my hand and seemed OK. I began to pet the dogs, then tried to shoo them, but that didn't work. I nudged the dog and it came forward, so that didn't work. I put my hand on the dog's head, trying to think of a way to move it without hitting it.

I tapped the dog's head with the bat, and the dog went wild. Barking, moving a lot, it looked like it was going to spring. I swung hard and hit it in the side of the head, and it went back to normal.

Finally, I was able to get both dogs to follow me, little by little, if I didn't move the bat too quickly. I got them to the gate and slid myself through it to keep my dog from interacting with those two dogs. I didn't need my mother blaming me for our dog fighting other dogs. I walked up the steps and those dogs were just sitting at the gate, waiting for me, I guess.

I went into the house and told my mother, "I can't get the dogs out," but walked out of the kitchen before she could get a hurtful comment out.

I told my father that there were dogs at the gate that Mom wanted gone, but I had failed to do so.

My father just nodded and grabbed the BB gun and went outside. I followed my father. He was able to push the dogs back to the mailbox, further from the house.

The siblings and my mother were loaded up in the van. I was maybe 8-9 feet away from my father and the dogs. He shot the big dog, and the dog went wild like it did earlier.

My father yelled, "Get the shotgun, get the shotgun!"

I ran back into the house and up the stairs. I grabbed the shotgun, checked that it was loaded and took the safety off. I ran back outside and gave him the shotgun and he gave me the BB gun.

Seeing my siblings watching this through the back side window, and knowing what was going to happen, I put my back against the window and with my arms crossed. I leaned back to block their view. I didn't want them to see this.

*Meanwhile, my father was pushing the dog off with the barrel of the gun, then a loud **boom!** The big dog fell over with a yelp and there was a pool of blood within a few seconds. I waited for my father to say something.*

Finally, he turned toward me and like a soldier he said, "No life in his eyes." He told me, while handing me the shotgun, "Secure this, we're going to be late for church service."

I got into the van, put the shotgun and BB gun in between the seats, and put my foot on them to secure them with my arm across the seats to prevent my siblings from touching the guns out of curiosity.

We went to church, did our normal, "God is good. Life is great," and all the rest of the bullshit. When we got home it was nighttime. We could see the dog still laying there. My mother and siblings went inside, and my father and I went to the garage to collect a shovel and a hoe.

We got to the dog and it was still alive, with a bigger pool of blood with chunks in it. I guess it was guts. My father took the hoe and put it under the dog's collar and dragged it a few feet. Then he took the shovel and started to scoop the gravel with the blood and turned it over to hide it, which it did. My father put the hoe under the dog's collar again and dragged it from our yard to the front of the street and left it there. It was gone when we went for a run the next day.

The more we heard from Ezekiel and the defense team about what they learned in the discovery process from others, I began to put together some of the signs I ignored when Tom was alive. The fact that at big events like weddings, the children would all stay seated at the table where Tom and Amy were when all the other children were running around playing with other children and dancing. When we would talk to the kids and ask them a question, they would freeze and look at their father and often not respond. During my time in Washington, DC, I asked Tom if I could fly Ezekiel out for a visit for his birthday to tour around, since I knew he loved history so much. Tom made an excuse about a wrestling tournament he was thinking about going to with him. I learned later that none of his children were able to spend the night with friends or family.

The only time Tom would let them spend the night elsewhere was when there were preteen retreats conducted by the church. Many of the behaviors that Tom exhibited, like paranoia and his tendency to spiral out of control, were similar to what we experienced with Mom. Even though there were times when all we had for dinner was a can of corn to split between four of us, we rarely got food stamps. Mom didn't want anybody "in her business." During many of our therapy sessions, Leo and I heard Mom in the stories about what Tom would say to Ezekiel.

The notable difference was that Mom never kept guns. Had she kept guns, I wonder if one of my brothers would have done something stupid with them. On one visit when Ezekiel was grieving and angry with himself, I told him I would not abandon him no matter what and that if he did something to harm himself or others it would break my heart, but that I would still love him. It occurred to me later that he could very well kill me if he felt betrayed or hurt by me in the future. I said to myself, "Lord, I have no idea what I'm doing or what may come of this tragic situation, all I know to do is to love and if that results in death, then so be it." That possibility would not deter me from my commitment to walk this very difficult journey with Ezekiel; a promise I made to his father after his death and to God.

INHERITANCE

The bittersweet lineage
  slant of the eyes, width of the hips,
  treasure in tenacity, pride, fortitude.

To think of my paternal grandmother alone on the llano for months
  with many little ones,
Or my great grandmother Lupita embittered by the harsh land and
  her harsher husband.
To recognize the ways my brother was just like my mother,
  and how his son like his father, the scapegoat, the crybaby.

Fruit of the tangled vine; conquerors and the conquered.
People who belong to the land claimed by many.

Dare I claim my name after the sacrifice?
What do I claim with that name?

Does this mean that indeed my mother was the black sheep
  and my brother as well?
Does this confirm that my siblings and I were the rats that my
  maternal grandmother chased out of her house?
Was my brother's redemption from LA gang leader to Pastor
  that even I hailed, a farce, a facade?

My sister left the scene and wants to distance her children
  from the controversy, they escaped!

My brother wants to keep things as quiet as possible, he and his son
   have to live in this town after all.

The offender's siblings have scattered and have proclaimed my
   brother, their father, a saint, "El Santo."

The rest of the family, including my father, has dismissed him as a
   bad seed.

I cannot dismiss a child, especially one with my brother's eyes.

He has inherited my love and I continue to hope for redemption.

I see the intellect, the pride, and the tenacity that is our inheritance
   in him.

Yet there remains trepidation in him claiming that inheritance,

   and fear that I cannot love adequately.

CHAPTER 20

THE PLEA AGREEMENT

Ezekiel's judge started canceling court dates in April, and by August 2014, the judge stepped down due to a medical condition (Alzheimer's), and we didn't have a judge. The original prosecutor who Jack was working with ran for a judgeship in Sandoval County and won. They were now working with new prosecuting attorneys and had to bring them up to speed and start the process of collaborating with them. In November, Jack and the prosecutor's office made an agreement on a new judge. Judge Baca was from the children's court, which is what we hoped for after discussing options. The fact that they agreed on a judge was a good sign.

Dr. Newman came back for another visit with Ezekiel in August 2014. He delayed issuing his draft report until the end of January 2015, because the releases for records took so long. After the releases were available, it took a few months for the schools, employment places, military, and medical institutions to supply records on Tom and Amy. The defense team decided to get a brain scan done on Ezekiel at the Mind Research Institute, a well-regarded research institute at the University of New Mexico. Dr. Newman would incorporate those results in the report. The results of his MRI and brain scan showed significant signs of head trauma and developmental abnormalities in his brain. They estimated that his brain development was at least two years behind normal.

The defense team was trying to negotiate a plea with the prosecution team. By August 2015, the plea agreement was a real possibility. Ezekiel was doing well in school and his medications seemed to be working. He was the leader in his lodge and the staff all said he was being cooperative and working hard. Many of the staff members at the treatment center bonded with Ezekiel. He gravitated toward those who had military experience, including an older woman who bought Ezekiel pizza on occasion and a man who Ezekiel looked up to as a big brother. Ezekiel was now eighteen and we were grateful they allowed him to stay at the treatment center for so long. Remaining there after age eighteen was unusual. We expected that he would be there until his case was decided.

The defense team said that after meeting with Judge Baca there was a trial tentatively scheduled for early 2016, unless the prosecution agreed to a plea that was acceptable to the defense team. A plea agreement could categorize Ezekiel as a youthful offender, subject to juvenile sanctions and not a serious youthful offender, subject to adult sanctions. The defense team was getting ready for a trial, as was the prosecution, while at the same time they filed a motion for an Amenability Hearing without a plea.

Ezekiel's defense team, in particular Robert, worked out a plea that was the maximum plea that would still allow him to be categorized as a youthful offender and as such entitled to an Amenability Hearing. Coming to a plea agreement would be a pivotal point in an almost three-year journey; a light at the end of the tunnel. Leo and I, and we believed the entire family, wanted to avoid a long, drawn-out, adversarial trial where our family laundry would be on display for the world to see and a parade of witnesses would be on the stand. The potential for any of 1,400 photos and videos taken the night of the crime, particularly those of the children, passed around to a jury, or worse, displayed in court, was horrifying.

At this point, Ezekiel was on the path to being tried as an adult based on his charges. The Amenability Hearing is an opportunity to show that the juvenile is "amenable to treatment" in the available facilities. Amenable to treatment means they can or are responding to treatment and are salvageable. There are eight criteria weighed in the Amenability Hearing: four related to the crime and four related to the child.

Leo and I met with the prosecution attorneys about the plea, expressing our fear of conducting a court trial and providing them background on Tom and our family of origin. Trying Ezekiel as an adult would be highly contentious and very public. We figured if we told them more about the difficulty of how Tom was raised and the result of that, they might see that there were circumstances that contributed to what happened.

We gave the prosecution the names and contact information that we had for family including Carla, Jenny, and Janice. Leo talked with all three about the plea, letting them know that it would involve an Amenability Hearing and not a court trial. He told them that the sentence could be anywhere from releasing him at age twenty-one, which we all thought was unlikely, to adult prison until he was 105 years old.

According to Leo, they seemed on board with not going through the long court trial and instead going with the plea. The plea would also release the estates for them, because Ezekiel would lose his inheritance if he were legally guilty of murdering his parents. It would allow Jenny and Carla to finish parsing out the inheritance and close the legal records for the estates of Tom and Amy.

The defense team sent a letter to the DA outlining a schedule for pretrial interviews and a plea offer on September 2, 2015. In a meeting with Judge Baca a month later, they agreed to a plea of two counts of second-degree murder and three counts of child abuse resulting in death. Judge Baca was pleased that the two legal teams came to an agreement and scheduled the Amenability Hearing for the week of January 11, 2016. The defense team wanted to keep the actual plea that was agreed to quiet, *without notice*. The only notice was when the Plea Hearing was scheduled. If the details of the plea were known before the Plea Hearing, the media would come out in force.

We were extremely relieved, but I was irrationally nervous that someone would come out of the woodwork and sabotage the plea. We all wanted to avoid the media attention as much as possible. Jack drafted a statement for the press with our input. He planned to release it right before the Plea Hearing.

Ezekiel made his first public appearance at 9:00 a.m. on October 16, 2015, less than two weeks after they reached the plea agreement and thirty-three months since his crime. Judge Baca insisted that they not film his face because he was a minor, so the world saw him on camera from the neck down. He also insisted on having only one camera that would share the film with others. We prepared carefully for his first appearance, buying him new clothes and shoes, thankful that he would appear in street clothes. It was a short hearing where they ushered him in and when Judge Baca came in, he read the plea and asked Ezekiel if he agreed to the plea and Ezekiel said, "I do."

After the Plea Hearing I drove to Taos to attend a writing retreat. Rattled by the media appearing at the hearing, I was concerned about what was yet to come in January at the Amenability Hearing.

Journal entry: November 1, 2015. I do not know what the week of the hearing in January will do to me. I do know that I will take it as an opportunity to heal, to transform, to let go, to allow, and to fall into the invisible or supernatural...that which is unseen and will hold me.

The media broadcast the story of the plea and film of Ezekiel in the courtroom. They again mixed up the facts like the ages and gender of the children, or the fact that Tom was no longer a pastor. Listening to the retelling of the murders was always jarring. They were also again reporting the Walmart comment that Ezekiel had made during his interrogation, without legal counsel, or family to advise him.

There was so much of the story left untold. Leo focused on not alienating anyone. He was sensitive about a comment made by the defense team regarding the fact that Ezekiel was homeschooled and lacked educational opportunities. Leo would repeat the phrase, "We need to keep it together," which meant that we needed to keep the family and the community (Calvary folks) as united as possible in the aims of getting the best possible outcome for Ezekiel. My focus was on supporting Ezekiel the best I could and I let go of control for what others might do.

Once the media quieted down, not much happened between mid-October and right before the Amenability Hearing. Ezekiel continued therapy and school at the treatment center, and we continued to visit him and tried to calm his fears about the Amenability Hearing. In December I wrote a letter and sent it to all the spiritual groups I was involved with, my writing groups, my coaching cohorts, and anyone else I could think of who knew my story and showed concern. The letter asked for prayers during the time of the Amenability Hearing.

Dearest Friends—,

I am writing to ask for your prayers and good thoughts/energy. I believe in the spiritual fabric through which we are all connected, and I trust that you appreciate and participate in the unseen power that it offers. On January 11-15, 2016, an Amenability Hearing for Ezekiel Pacheco, my nephew, is scheduled. This is the most positive possible closure to a journey that began January 19, 2013, when Ezekiel took the lives of his father (my brother), his mother, and his three siblings. He was fifteen at the time. Specifically, we are praying for the wisdom, courage, and discernment of Judge Baca and for the mercy/immunity from the media. Having Judge Baca is a tremendous blessing. He is the most experienced and well-regarded judge in the Children's Court. We are also blessed to have very caring defense attorneys, Jack and Robert, they are the best possible in NM for these cases and they have gone all out for Ezekiel's defense, including getting the plea which allows Ezekiel to be treated as a youthful offender as opposed to an adult. We ask your prayers for them and the prosecution attorneys. Lastly for healing for Ezekiel and the family, this has been very hard for everyone; we are each dealing with it in our own way. The family alliances are fragile, but we are still united in supporting Ezekiel.

Since the death of his mother and father, I have been Ezekiel's guardian; taking care of his personal needs and meeting with medical professionals, teachers, and his defense team. As a part of that role, I advocated for him to be moved from the county detention facility, where he spent sixteen months, to a treatment center where he has been for nineteen months, since May 2014, shortly after his seventeenth birthday. ...

When he moved to the treatment center he was evaluated educationally and put on an IEP (Individualized Education Program). As part of Ezekiel's defense, he has received several psychological evaluations and brain scans and analysis from The Mind Research Network associated with UNM Brain Research. The brain scans revealed he has lesions on the brain indicative of Traumatic Brain Injury (TBI), that he is neurologically two years younger, and that his prefrontal cortex (the thinking/decision-making brain) is in the two percentile developmentally when compared to normal brains of his age.

In my prayer and discernment through this whole thing, I have asked from the beginning "What is mine to do?" What I have heard in response is to walk the journey with Ezekiel. My brother Leo has played the role of communicator and tries to reach out more to the family when it is necessary, including Ezekiel's older siblings (six of them), Amy's siblings, and our sister, father, and two half-brothers who live out of state. I do what I do not just out of love and compassion for Ezekiel, but because I loved my brother very much and he is my brother's son. Tom and I are only sixteen months apart. Four of us were raised by a single mother working as a secretary; we were very poor. She had many of the tendencies my brother manifested as a parent; she was paranoid for others to know her business, she didn't accept public assistance for that reason, and she was a harsh disciplinarian (to put it nicely). Tom got the brunt of Mom's anger and had many other traumatic things happen to him before he was twenty years old, many of which I witnessed. Many times, when we are in counseling with Ezekiel, we hear the words of my brother or even our mother come out of Ezekiel's mouth. Here are some of the difficult discoveries we have made about Ezekiel and the way he was raised:

- *His father was a harsh disciplinarian, especially with Ezekiel, his eldest son in his household. He believed in the phrase "spare the rod, spoil the child." He knocked Ezekiel out on at least one occasion that has been confirmed. Other such beatings were reported by Ezekiel and are likely to have occurred.*
- *His father was training Ezekiel to be a soldier; not just as a military career but because my brother, Tom, was preparing for the possibility of taking on the U.S. government. Tom had a stockpile of weapons, ammunition, and pamphlets that revealed his association with a radical group called "preppers." The guns were all bought illegally from a source that was being investigated by the ATF. He didn't want the government to know about his weapons. We did not know about his stockpile or that he was training Ezekiel, and to some degree, his younger son.*
- *Ezekiel was homeschooled by his mother, who didn't graduate from high school and had speech problems. She stopped teach-*

ing him when he was in third grade, calling him stupid and willful. New Mexico law does not require progress evidence on children who are enrolled as homeschoolers.

- *Ezekiel and his siblings were not on any regular schedule of sleep and meals. Ezekiel was not fed regularly and normally got one meal a day prepared by his mother when his father came home from work (which varied in time). He weighed 105 pounds when he was put in detention; within six months he weighed 150 pounds.*

- *Ezekiel didn't see doctors or any other treatment specialist; in particular my brother regarded psychology professionals as part of a cult (anti-Christian). Ezekiel has been treated medically at the treatment center for many residual conditions, knee problems, and shoulder injuries that he endured earlier in life. Ezekiel started hearing voices and seeing hallucinations around eleven or twelve years old, but kept it to himself. He rationalized it as an artifact of all the horror movies that he watched with his mother and was frightened by the spirit world. He is convinced that his house was haunted. He did not tell his father about his hallucinations, figuring that his father might think he was possessed.*

- *My brother tightly controlled the family and isolated them. There were many occasions when we volunteered to take the kids at various times for periods of time, but he wouldn't allow that to happen. At family gatherings they sat at the same table and the children were not allowed to wander like the other cousins. His wife didn't drive and she was not allowed to leave the house while her husband was away. Ezekiel said he feared being beaten if he shared anything about what was going on at home.*

- *Finally, my brother was dismissed as a pastor at Calvary Church ten months before his death. As you may know from the media, my brother was a pastor at the largest evangelical church in Albuquerque. He did many good things, particularly for men in prison, while he was a pastor. He started that journey after being "saved" in 1992 while in prison, when he faced fifteen years to life for a drive-by. He was released because they did not find witnesses who would testify. He had been involved in gangs since about 1984, when he left the 82nd Airborne disgruntled. After he was fired from Calvary, we witnessed my brother becoming angrier than ever, much like he was when he was in the gangs in Los Angeles. Ezekiel said that things were unbearable at home after Tom lost his job. No doubt there was financial stress, but Tom also lost his identity and redemption story because of losing his status as a pastor. Tom was never truly healed from his childhood woundings.*

I share all of this so that it might shed light on how something like this could happen, not to excuse what Ezekiel did. It was a tragedy all the way around. I often meditate on the heart of Mary as I hold the grief and tragedy of it all, helpless to know how we might have intervened to make things different. It is a small fractal of the human condition, and it hurts.

I invite you to share with discernment and to ask for prayers from all parts of the world the week of January 11-15, 2016. I believe that something good can come of this and I do not know what the "right" decision should be for Ezekiel. If he is judged amenable to treatment, he will likely be sentenced as a youth and sent to the youth detention center or somewhere similar and could get out at age twenty-one (just over two years from now). If he does not, Judge Baca has a lot of latitude. Ezekiel could get up to 120 years sentence as an adult, but we expect it would be more like twenty years. Laws in New Mexico are very polarized; it would be good to get a middle ground of transitioning him over time and letting him out at twenty-five years old. I do fear, though I try not to, what might happen to him if he is put in a maximum-security prison with older hardened criminals. Ezekiel has no previous incursions with the law and was very isolated. He is a good boy. I know that sounds strange given what he did. It would be unfortunate (very difficult for me) to watch him travel a similar journey as his father.

Thank you in advance for your prayers.

Most gently held in the Divine Milieu,
Regina

After receiving many loving responses, I believed that the prayers buoyed me and others through the Amenability Hearing. We had a low-key Christmas and we celebrated with my son and Mark's son and youngest daughter. She was living in Albuquerque now with her fiancé and our newest grandson, our third grandchild. There were no extended family gatherings with Leo, Janice, and the rest of the family.

PART THREE

WALKING THROUGH HELL IN SLOW MOTION

CHAPTER 21

THE AMENABILITY HEARING

We were hoping that the Amenability Hearing would be low-key, comforted by the fact that it was only a hearing and not a full-scale court trial and that they were holding it in the children's court.

Robert helped me with my testimony the week before the Amenability Hearing by giving me the questions he planned to ask. Because I had the most contact with Ezekiel since the deaths of the family, I would be the only one from the family testifying and I was nervous. There was also the threat that I would not be able to stay in the courtroom during the Amenability Hearing since I was a witness. The defense team also explained to us the eight factors they considered in an Amenability Hearing, including:

1. The seriousness of the alleged offense

2. Whether the alleged offense was committed in an aggressive, violent, premeditated, or willful manner

3. Whether a firearm was used to commit the alleged offense

4. Whether the alleged offense was against persons or against property; greater weight being given to offenses against persons, especially if personal injury resulted

5. The maturity of the child as determined by consideration of the child's home, environmental situation, social and emotional health, pattern of living, brain development, trauma history, and disability

6. The record and previous history of the child

7. The prospects for adequate protection of the public and the likelihood of reasonable rehabilitation of the child by the use of procedures, services, and facilities currently available

8. Any other relevant factor, provided that it was stated on the record

The first four factors weighed against Ezekiel, but the defense team explained that the judge doesn't necessarily consider all the factors equally. They planned to argue based on the last four factors given all that they learned from the witnesses they deposed, therapist, psychologist, psychiatrist, other medical experts, the records they obtained, and the brain scans.

We hadn't heard of any other relatives coming in from out of town for the Amenability Hearing except for Janice and her daughter. For moral support, my daughter was coming on Sunday before the hearing and my best friend came on Wednesday the week of the hearing.

Mark and I returned from a trip to Nashville late on Saturday, January 9, 2016, because we needed Sunday to visit Ezekiel, rest, and prepare for the next week.

That evening Leo told me, "Looks like a letter was written to the judge and the *Albuquerque Journal* from Jenny, Dad, and Dad's stepchildren. They want Ezekiel to go to prison."

It was not something I expected. Jenny was meek and not one to write much, and my father was feeble. After Leo talked with Jack, he concluded that it must have been my father's stepson who was behind this.

I was confused. "What does he have to do with any of this?"

The next morning on the Sunday front page of the *Albuquerque Journal* was an article titled "Teen Who Killed Family in Court This Week."

In the article they wrote: *"The tragedy has split much of his extended family. A local aunt and uncle support a juvenile sentence and treatment for Pacheco, but his grandfather, older sister and other family members are urging the judge to impose an adult prison sentence."*

This was the first time I knew that our family was split. Who were these *other family members?* Surely, they weren't taking about our stepmother's children. We barely knew them. Our father and his wife left when I was eight, and our father rarely came around or supported us after they left. Tom spent time in California as an adult after he left the army and had relationships with our stepmother's children. He would hang out with them and get high. I guess you could loosely call them *family.*

The Amenability Hearing started at 9:00 a.m. on Monday, but we wanted to be there when Ezekiel arrived, and we wanted to sit as close to him as possible. Mark and I had worked hard to get him ready over the previous weeks, buying him dress shirts with sweaters to go over them, nice pants, a belt, and shoes. Leo got him a dress coat since it was winter. Everything looked big on him. He was still skinny even though he had gained half again his original body weight since his incarceration.

We arrived at the Children's Courthouse just before 8:00 a.m., pulling into the back parking area at the same time the Channel 13 News truck was pulling in, and my stomach tightened. The media terrified me, and they seemed so menacing. They wanted the most salacious story they could tell, and they didn't care who told it to them. We walked quickly to the courthouse and made our way through the security screening as efficiently as possible and swiftly made our way to Judge Baca's courtroom. We were in that courtroom less than three months prior for the plea hearing, so it was familiar to us.

Mark, my daughter, and I settled in on the bench right behind where Ezekiel and his defense team would be sitting. It was just after 8:00 a.m. Leo and Lily came about 8:30 and settled in next to us. Janice and my niece sat behind us. Ezekiel's sisters Carla, Julie, and Jenny arrived after Leo. Julie had her five-year-old daughter with her. About three of our cousins came, including the one who sang at Calvary.

Carla was very standoffish and sat near the back of the five-bench courtroom, behind us. I hadn't seen Ezekiel's sisters since Carla's wedding almost a year ago. They all greeted us at the wedding, but something changed. Leo went back to talk to her, and she was very terse, avoided eye contact, didn't smile, and generally seemed hurt or upset with us.

Ezekiel soon arrived and sat between the social worker and his attorneys. The guards from the treatment center escorted him, and we knew them all because we had visited often over the last twenty-two months.

The social worker and I talked. "How's he doing?" I asked.

"Fine. He's very nervous and we tried to remind him not to bite his nails or fidget with his hands," she said. Ezekiel barely had nails at this point, and often one or the other of his fingertips were bleeding.

It was going to take a good bit of focus and self-control not to fidget today.

I pulled out my spiral notebook and planned to take notes, partly because as an engineer for years that's how I absorb information, partly because I wanted a basic record of the testimony, but mostly because it kept me busy. The Amenability Hearing was going to be emotional.

Jack questioned the camera operator to make sure he understood that he was only supposed to film Ezekiel from the neck down. He then went to speak with Judge Baca, and the bailiff announced the rules to the media. There was only one video camera, and they would share the feed, but there were other still cameras. Jack also cleared me to stay during the entire hearing because I was there to support Ezekiel and I wasn't an expert witness. The media piled in on the other side of where we were. They also filled most of the row behind us; it appeared that there were more media folks than there were family.

I attended the Amenability Hearing and took careful notes each day. The full transcript and testimony is publicly available.

Day 1: Robert, the co-counsel for the defense, made his opening statement.

The State will focus on the undisputed facts of the case related to the murders. We will focus on his amenability to treatment and not the crime. Ezekiel was isolated, had no friends outside of the church, his father trained him to use assault weapons, and his stunted brain development and traumatic brain injury (TBI) were due to his father's beatings.

When he was finally able to attend a proper educational facility, he showed the ability to improve despite his brain injury and that he was deprived of medication growing up. He has no history of any criminal or drug behavior. He has shown by his own actions the ability to respond to health treatment, and he is amenable to treatment and is not a threat to the public.

Treat him as a juvenile until age twenty-one and keep him in treatment. Give him a blended sentence. A sentence that would keep him in treatment until age twenty-one, then evaluate him. Based on that evaluation, either release him or sentence him to spend an additional five years in prison.

The prosecution witnesses went first, and they called their medical expert in brain scans, Dr. Fisk, and established his credentials. He testified.

After looking at Ezekiel's MRI scans and seeing these images, you might as well consider it a normal MRI. The diffuse axonal injuries (DAIs) in the brain scans that the defense's brain expert Dr. Bill said was a TBI either wasn't a TBI, or if it were a TBI, falling when Ezekiel was roller skating could have caused what Dr. Bill was seeing.

On cross-examination, the defense established that he couldn't rule out TBI and that he was not an expert in TBIs.

Judge Baca adjourned for lunch, and we had over ninety minutes.

Concerned with making sure Ezekiel would get lunch, he was going to stay in a back room of the court; I told the social worker we would get him lunch. In the meantime, Leo was trying to talk to Carla and Jenny, but the victim's advocate seemed to be guarding them, as if Leo was harassing them.

After lunch, the prosecution called Dr. Hahn, the expert psychologist for the prosecution, and established his identity, affiliations, and credentials. Jack got up and questioned his credentials, noting that his training was mostly with the police and that he had no credentials in child psychology. He also challenged his credentials as a forensic psychology expert and objected to his qualifications as an expert in providing an opinion on amenability.

Judge Baca decided he needed to hear Dr Hahn's testimony based on his relevant experience. Dr. Hahn testified.

I evaluated Ezekiel for sanity and found no evidence of gross thought disorder or breaks with reality. He accurately reported historical facts, so other than mumbling and nervousness, I found him sane. Ezekiel told me what happened; it took ten to fifteen minutes to tell me about that night. He showed no affect. He was goal-directed the night of the event. When he was eating lunch with his girlfriend and her grandmother, he didn't want to answer questions.

Ezekiel said he had the lights off so the neighbor wouldn't notice, then turned them on to see what happened when he shot Tom. He was concerned that if his dad saw him, he would have harmed or killed him. He understood the severity of his crime and said that if he went to Walmart, it would be a way to commit suicide.

Ezekiel had remorse for messing up his life and other people's lives but was emotionally hollow. He talked about treatment he was receiving for the abuse from his mother and father and hearing voices. He told me about that night when the voices talked to him. When I asked Ezekiel if he could ignore the voices, he said yes, if he fought hard enough.

Ezekiel was not well educated, his home was violent, chaotic, and neglectful. His only relationships were at church. Deviant behavior reported includes that he had a few fights, stole little things, kicked a dog at church, and shot a bird.

When I asked him why he did what he did, Ezekiel responded that his dad got older and meaner and that things got worse over the years. He also said that he was interested in guns.

I originally thought that Ezekiel had an antisocial personality disorder, but have since broadened it to severe personality disorder. In the DSM-5 (Diagnostic and Statistical Manual of Mental Disorders) it defines severe personality disorder as, "Personality Disorder—Severe; antisocial, narcissistic—fantasy of power, paranoid aspect, deep-seated lack of confidence." Ezekiel's personality disorder is related to his upbringing, and it is difficult to treat. At the treatment center there is the opportunity for suppression of boundaries and rules; the real world won't suppress. Two years was not enough time to treat him; it is a chronic long-term disorder.

On cross-examination, the defense established that he came to Albuquerque one time and spent just over three hours with Ezekiel. He didn't talk to anybody at the youth detention center where they would send Ezekiel (if amenable) or any of his relations, so he wouldn't know if a flat affect was normal in the family. He didn't talk to Ezekiel's therapist who had spent over 160 hours with him, but he talked to other doctors who spent no time with him.

Judge Baca adjourned until 9:30 a.m. the next morning.

Mark had been loud with his reactions expressing his disapproval or disagreement in the courtroom. A few times throughout the day, Leo and Lily would shoot me a look like "he needs to be quiet." At the point when the psychologist said that it wasn't normal for boys to want to hit other boys, Mark blurted out, "Aw, come on."

We got several looks, and I was sure the bailiff would say something to us or throw us out. Leo looked at him and said, "That's not helping."

In my personal preparation for the hearing with the Hakomi therapist, I put an energy barrier of light around myself, protecting me from negative energy and holding me together, and this pierced my barrier.

When we got in the car to leave, I tried to talk to Mark about it and he became defensive, saying, "You and your family have excluded me since the beginning, and I have worked hard to support you all."

I lost it. "This is not about you!" I yelled and pounded my fist on the car door window. "I am barely holding it together."

I honestly didn't have the wherewithal to think about his feelings, which was true about most of my family in that courtroom. We were all struggling and lost in our own hurt. Things were silent between us. At one level, I knew he was right, that in some of the meetings with the defense team or other meetings, he wasn't included, or someone would make a comment about him being there and not being *family*. Mark worked extremely hard after the deaths to help the family, especially dealing with the house. We were silent, both understanding the stress we were under. He was calmer in the courtroom after that.

Carla, Jenny, and others scurried out quickly. Carla and Jenny's behavior confused me, and I had no clue what to do or how to talk to them. Perhaps their grief had turned to anger—Leo had the best chance of reaching them now.

CHAPTER 22

THE PROSECUTION'S WITNESSES

We got there early the next day, and everyone sat in about the same places as the day before. After a brief discussion with the social worker on how Ezekiel was doing and agreeing to get him lunch, I took my seat and meditated until Judge Baca walked in.

Day 2: The prosecution called on a deputy from the sheriff's office. He testified.

I am trained in electronic devices for the purposes of extracting forensic evidence and investigate crimes against children. I assisted with Ezekiel's interview, took notes, and I asked a few questions during the interview. We got Ezekiel's iPod device with text messages and photos and had another staff member produce DVDs and printed the texts and photos. Ezekiel downloaded an app, Text Now, something that other people in his age range use.

On cross-examination, the defense confirmed that there wasn't anything else useful on Ezekiel's iPod and that he saw Jenny in the hallway when they were interviewing Ezekiel after his arrest. Jenny wasn't invited to join them during the interview.

The second witness called by the prosecution was the lead detective who came to our house the Monday after the tragedy. He testified.

I had been investigating crimes involving death for almost two years at the time of the murders. A Sergeant contacted me on Jan. 19, 2013, at 9:00 p.m. When I arrived at the scene the deputies briefed me on what they saw.

I didn't go into the property until after they received a warrant. During the interview at the sheriff's office, I Mirandised Ezekiel and explained each of his rights, and Ezekiel told me he understood. He seemed tired but calm the night of his arrest.

Ezekiel said he found his dad, mother, and siblings dead. I discussed with him who might have killed them, and he responded that someone put a "hit" on them. Eventually Ezekiel told me that he killed his family, and he cried when he talked about his mom.

I briefly interviewed the girlfriend on January 20, 2013, and she didn't understand being Mirandised. She was matter of fact and didn't understand the gravity of the situation, and she didn't have any emotional reaction. She looked like a normal twelve-year-old.

We conducted the interview in an 8 x 10 room with a video recorder in the ceiling. When I Mirandised Ezekiel, I explained that he had a right to have an adult present.

On cross-examination the defense reviewed the time of the interview to be 1:00 a.m. on January 20, 2013, and that Ezekiel told him he hadn't slept in over forty-two hours. The interview was about an hour, and he appeared honest.

The deputy then summarized the text messages Ezekiel and the girlfriend sent to each other the night of the murders.

Ezekiel started with the message sent at 1:00 a.m. on January 19, 2013, "I'm feeling insane." Then texts saying how much they loved each other and sexual conversation. There was a discussion about a plan to kill both sets of parents. The girlfriend said she didn't have the guts.

The girlfriend texted at one point saying, "That's nice, I hope he dies fast," referring to Malachi. Ezekiel sent a photo proving that he had killed his mother and Malachi with an "I love you." Then Ezekiel texted, "I really have gone insane." There was more sexual talk and Ezekiel asked her to send him a photo of her chest; she did, and he said, "Thanks." There were more texts throughout the early morning before Tom got home and they made plans to meet.

Jack rose for a brief redirect. "We are looking at the girlfriend as a suspect. She was taken to a psychiatric hospital because of the homicidal nature of the text messages."

Judge Baca adjourned for lunch and again we went to get food for Ezekiel. There was little conversation between the family.

At 1:00 p.m. they resumed testimony and the prosecution called Jane, the grandmother of the girlfriend. She testified.

I met Ezekiel helping my granddaughter with involvement at Calvary. On January 19, 2013, I spent time with her at Calvary. My granddaughter wanted to be there that morning when the band was playing, and she wanted to meet Ezekiel before, so I dropped her off. My granddaughter would go to Calvary with her school friends.

She wanted to go to church to be with friends and meet boys. She met Ezekiel at the skate park they have at Calvary—he was a boy she liked. He was in the band, and she liked going to listen to the band practice in the morning. I needed to go to work after I dropped her off.

I was texting my granddaughter and arranged to pick her up for lunch.

Ezekiel went with us to Wendy's nearby and I bought them lunch. My granddaughter teased Ezekiel saying, "My grandma will grill you with questions." She said he was going to military school. Ezekiel told me that he moved from California, getting away from the gangs and that the gangs may have followed. His demeanor at lunch was polite with neither a positive nor negative expression.

We then went to my house. I live with my daughter and my grand-daughter. Ezekiel and my granddaughter went to the park for a walk. I remained in text message contact with her. She texted and asked if Ezekiel could spend the night.

When they returned to my house, I asked them why he wanted to spend the night, and Ezekiel said his parents were killed in a car accident. Ezekiel took a nap from about 3:30 to 4:00 p.m. and they were watching TV after the nap.

We went back to the church so they could attend the mid-high service; a service for the youth. Ezekiel and my granddaughter went into the service. I was concerned about what he told me and asked to speak to the youth minister. I recounted what Ezekiel said to the youth minister and he said that it didn't sound right. When the service was over, I met Ezekiel and my granddaughter in the bookstore and we got coffee and cake, until a pastor took Ezekiel. Me and my grand-daughter went home.

I didn't hear anything until the next day, Sunday, January 20, 2013, when they asked me to come to the courthouse with my granddaugh-ter at 1:00 in the morning. I took my granddaughter for the interview and brought her back. After work that day, I learned that someone took my granddaughter back to the courthouse.

The next witness called was a detective on the high-enforcement action team (HEAT) who did field service patrolling. He testified.

There was a dispatch on January 19, 2013, and I responded. I got there at 9:12 p.m. I was the first deputy on the scene and made contact with the Calvary safety officer. I talked with Ezekiel, who was in the front seat of an SUV. He looked me in the eye and shook my hand firmly. He said he came home earlier and found his family dead.

I asked Ezekiel open-ended questions—his demeanor was emotion-less. He told me that he spent the night at a friend's house and that his friend brought him home at 6:00 a.m. the next morning, which was January 19th. That seemed odd to me. Ezekiel went on to say that he found his entire family deceased.

I called for more detectives, who arrived on the scene almost immediately. When they arrived, we got the keys from Ezekiel and made a plan. We approached the house and cleared the residence. Four officers went in, and we stayed together. I held the staircase and we confirmed what Ezekiel said. We found Tom at the stairs, the girls in the first bedroom, no one in the boy's room, and we found Amy and Malachi in the master bedroom.

We were all shocked and we slowed it down and searched again in case there was anyone else, perhaps a child hiding. We took a break after what we discovered.

The next witness called by the prosecution was a deputy first class employed at the sheriff's office for six years. He testified.

I responded to a call to a residence in the south valley on January 19, 2013, because a juvenile relayed a message that his family was killed. A deputy was on the scene when I got there and said it might be real, so we called for more deputies.

I got the keys from Ezekiel and secured him in my vehicle. I first made sure that he didn't have any weapons. Ezekiel was quiet, and he stared at me; it was a long stare. Ezekiel asked if he could lay down in the backseat and I gave him some water.

When I got the keys, Ezekiel pointed out which keys opened the doors. Four to five officers went inside the residence.

The next witness called by the prosecution was a detective for the crime scenes unit of the sheriff's office. He testified.

My supervisor called me to investigate a crime scene and I arrived on the scene at 10:30 p.m. I was the deputy on call responsible for taking photos and collecting evidence. There were deputies outside the residence, and I talked to one of them before going into the residence.

The prosecution stated that they would only show the photos taken by the deputy to Judge Baca. The deputy, prosecution, and defense attorneys approached the bench. They went through each photo with Judge Baca. He reviewed about twenty pictures of the crime scene. I was so grateful and relieved that they didn't show the photos in the courtroom; it was hard enough listening and imagining based on the detective's description.

The detective went on in his testimony.

We didn't move anything. We turned on a light in the boys' room. I did not make contact with Ezekiel. I used a digital camera and uploaded the photos to a database at the sheriff's office. The physical evidence we collected in the house that night included two types of casings, ammunition, two guns, projectiles, and fragments on Grace's hair. There were no casings or fragments for the guns we collected that night. The firearms for the casings and fragments we found were in the vehicle that Ezekiel drove—his dad's van. I also collected Ezekiel's clothes after they took him to the county detention facility.

On cross-examination by the defense, he testified.

The gun chamber lock had a key in the lock and wasn't being used. There were no guns locked. We collected a Smith & Wesson pistol grip and a Remington shotgun with ammunition in the chamber. We found lots of ammunition. The second time we went through the house on January 23rd, we collected more guns, including a revolver with one hundred rounds and a 365 magnum with sixty rounds. On January 24th we were able to get into the vehicle. We found more guns, including an AR-15 that the ATF collected and many more rounds of ammunition.

During redirect, the prosecution clarified that there were two types of casings at the crime scene: a .22 caliber and 223-AR-15. Both casings were downstairs and in the girls' room. The casings matched the guns found in the vehicle.

Judge Baca adjourned for the day. That evening Carla went back to California.

CHAPTER 23

THE CORONER'S REPORT

Day 3: The prosecution called on a forensic pathologist, Dr. Kim from the Coroner's office. Dr. Kim testified.

I supervised all the autopsies and did three of them myself. Two other doctors performed the autopsies on Tom and Miriam. I wrote the final report. We performed all the autopsies on January 21, 2013.

Amy was compatible with her age; she had two wounds to her face done with a rifle at a distance of at least one to two feet. The wounds were to the nose and one to the lip. No exit wounds. Both fatal. The cause of death was homicide—multiple gunshot wounds.

Malachi's body was consistent with his age of nine years and relatively normal weight with normal kid contusions on the body. He had one gunshot wound and one exit wound with a lower caliber firearm. Fired at a distant range. The wound was on the right side and the exit wound was through the left ear. The bullet went through the center of the brain and brain stem. It was a rapid death.

Miriam was consistent with the age of five years. She had minor scrapes and bruises. She had a gunshot wound to the head with a lower caliber firearm. It was on the right side, front to the back of the head fired at a distant range. She probably survived for a brief time because of the inflammatory response; maybe minutes to hours.

On that my heart stopped. Images of her face flooded my mind. I remembered Ezekiel saying something about hearing noises from the girl's room after he shot them and went downstairs. I took a deep breath to stop from crying.

Dr. Kim continued her testimony.

Grace's body was unremarkable and compatible with her age of two years. She had six gunshot wounds, three entry wounds and three exit wounds. The first was on her left forehead near her eye and it traveled on the left side of the brain, exiting through the back of her head. The second entered the right side of the neck, exiting on the left side of the neck where it traversed the path of the first gunshot wound. The third was on her right chest and exited out through the chest. There were two severe gunshot wounds. The manner of death was gunshot wounds.

My eyes welled up with tears and I looked at Leo. He looked like he might cry as well. He had that horrified, steely look on his face that I saw the night the detective visited.

Dr. Kim continued with Tom.

The body had significant injuries and was compatible with age of fifty-one. There were multiple gunshot wounds. Two on the right side of the head with a high caliber that converged right to left and destroyed the brain. The shots were at a distant range. There was significant distortion of his head. There were two wounds to the back with a high caliber gun shot at a distant range. There was a partial exit wound on the left side of his neck with a convergence of shots to the back and chest and a right lateral chest entrance wound.

I took a deep breath and wanted to cry but stopped myself. I closed my eyes and convinced myself that this was the hardest testimony I would hear all week. I took another breath and called on the divine mother as I swallowed hard.

The coroner's report shook me, especially about how many times Ezekiel shot Grace, the baby. The fact that the deputies found AR-15 casings near Miriam's bed also disturbed me. But the coroner said she was shot once. I told the social worker that I wanted to visit Ezekiel that evening because they wouldn't allow me to talk to him while he was in the courthouse. I planned to contact his therapist for a meeting. I needed clarification from him about what happened with Miriam and Grace. It felt urgent to me.

The prosecution then called a nurse from a local hospital who volunteered at Calvary as a worship leader. He testified.

I worked with the middle school group. I led the group and played guitar. The night of the incident, I talked to Ezekiel at mid-service. There was nothing out of the ordinary.

Jane approached me and told me the story of the car crash and the deaths of the family. It didn't sound right. I went to a pastor who worked in the prison ministry and the pastor tried to get ahold of Tom. We went to another pastor's office and brought Ezekiel. He told us that the family was deceased and that it could have been two days. He was not emotional.

The next witness the prosecution called was the Safety Officer at Calvary who retired from the police department. He testified.

I knew Tom for thirteen years as a Pastor and as a Chaplain for the jail. I was not at Calvary the night of January 19, 2013, but I received a call from the pastor. The pastor told me that Ezekiel reported that his family died in a car accident. I met the pastors and Ezekiel at a McDonalds. We all got in my car. I asked Ezekiel what happened, and he said the family died in a car accident.

I decided to go to Tom's house with Ezekiel and we talked in the car. He repeated that the family was in a car accident, but then said their bodies were at the house, remarking, "My dad's past caught up with him." I pulled over and called 911. I then drove to the house and the first deputy arrived within minutes, followed by other officers. They handled the situation from there.

I called Jenny and told her about the situation. Jenny and her husband came to Tom's house hours after they discovered the bodies. We drove downtown to the sheriff's department together.

On cross-examination by the defense, he testified.

Ezekiel was extremely respectful with me; he would shake hands and look me in the eyes. Tom's career at Calvary was chaotic. He was upset and became bitter about being pushed out because they hired a girl as a Chaplain at the jail. When Tom was put on a six-month sabbatical because of issues with Calvary, he was sent to pastor at a satellite in Santa Fe. The family's attendance was on and off after he was no longer a pastor. I never had a problem with the Pacheco children, they never backtalked or disagreed with Tom or Amy. Tom did mention that Amy had a speech disorder.

Judge Baca adjourned for lunch, and I contacted Ezekiel's therapist and we decided that I would visit 6:00 p.m.

After lunch, the first witness the defense called was a neuroradiologist, Dr. Bill. He had an incredible résumé and they admitted him as an expert neuroradiologist with research emphasis in traumatic brain injury (TBI). He testified.

If a scan has any positive findings, I only list plausible causes for the physician. I conducted an extensive Differential Analysis (DA) and a Volumetric Analysis (VA) which is in the report.

Ezekiel had a TBI from blows to the head. I found lesions that were small in nature and 80% of Diffuse Axonal Injury (DAI) scans were non-hemorrhage. In my experience with athletes, scans don't show signs when the patient isn't knocked unconscious. Ezekiel had to have had a blow that rendered him unconscious. From my research, his brain could take years to recover. The brain develops back to front, and the front is the decision-making part. His brain will look more normal when he is twenty-two years old.

The defense then called Ezekiel's speech and language pathologist from the treatment center. He testified.

In the beginning months I worked with him on a reading program. We got along very well. When we tested him almost a year later, he made very significant gains. He went through the whole regiment and worked very hard. Even when he got frustrated with written language, he didn't give up.

On cross-examination he testified.

Ezekiel's cognitive ability isn't an issue. He learned at an appropriate pace. Concept formation is a strength for predicting comprehension. Ezekiel did better than most in effort and his reading skills were generally good.

The next witness the defense called was a mental health supervisor from the treatment center who started working there two weeks prior to Ezekiel arriving. He was the staff member who felt like a big brother to Ezekiel. He testified.

Ezekiel was in lodge A, and I would have contact with him for nine hours a day. At first, he was quiet. For two or three months he missed his family. He would get upset when the other students were unruly, and I would mentor him and teach him coping skills. He learned to cope by playing the guitar, reading history books, and taking space in the courtyard or in his room. He liked hanging around boys who were respectful. Ezekiel would salute me because I had been in the Army. He was a role model for the other kids and carried himself like a leader.

Ezekiel reported stealing food from the church because there was no food at home. His father entrusted him to guard the house and he would police the perimeter with firearms. He told me he respected and feared his dad and that his mother wasn't there in a way that you would expect. He was deeply knowledgeable in history and had an interest in military history and our government. Ezekiel would disengage on his own when needed.

On cross-examination he testified.

I experienced Ezekiel to be better than most kids. His behavior with the other mental health techs was respectful overall. However, a female staff member had to redirect him from a sexual remark he made.

The next witness the defense called was Ezekiel's teacher at the treatment center. He testified.

Ezekiel came in with skills below what was expected. He was particularly interested in history and could talk intelligently about what motivated historic figures and events. His reading comprehension improved tremendously. He is now at 12.5 grade level; an improvement of four grade levels in two years.

Ezekiel is willing to consider ideas that he hadn't thought of before. Other students were not as inquisitive. He has grown over time in that he is more willing to hear opinions and doesn't argue with others.

On cross-examination by the prosecution, he testified.

I enjoyed being in class with Ezekiel. He was one of two or three of the best-behaved kids I have ever taught. He doesn't talk back. He's the most cooperative, most disciplined, and over time he became more sociable. Ezekiel judges himself and others to high standards. He was respectful and followed directions. He would socialize with other boys, but gravitated away from boys that were aggressive, loud, or didn't follow the rules. He is curious about many subjects, but he is a bit stubborn about math and has a personal aversion towards art.

My concerns about Ezekiel include that he looked for a key to power.

He was fascinated with people who had power—searching for his own power through efficacy. The attitudes that I found disconcerting about him were that he talked about Hitler and the Third Reich. He had challenges with race and with black people. He had strong opinions and beliefs and wouldn't change his opinion.

Ezekiel was barely absent, which was exceptionally good in comparison to other students. When he was gone, he usually had a good reason. When he's in class he is not demonstrative of emotion.

Mark and I went to visit Ezekiel that evening. He seemed shaken and numb from the week's testimony. It was hard for him to hear everyone talk about him while he was in the room. When I asked him questions about the fact that he had shot Grace three times, he seemed confused as if he didn't know or didn't remember that he shot her multiple times.

I pressed him, asking, "Could you have just pulled the trigger too hard and multiple shots went off?"

He started to explain how a .22 caliber firearm works, knowing that I didn't know much about guns, when I interrupted him. "Could the bullets somehow ricochet and reenter?" I asked knowing I was out of my depth. Frantic, I wanted to know how he could possibly shoot his two-year-old sister at all, let alone more than once.

He became defensive and tried to answer my questions—there was silence.

I took a breath and realized again that the night when he killed them, he wasn't in his right mind—he had left reality behind.

After a bit of small talk, I asked, "Why did they find AR-15 shells in Miriam's room?"

He looked at the ground and said, "I shot into the room to see how loud it would be. I was afraid the guy staying in the apartment would hear the shots from the AR-15." He shot into the room before his father came home and planned to use the AR-15 on his father because of his size. Learning which weapons to use when was part of the training Tom had given him.

Ezekiel and I had discussed the night of murders and all that happened on multiple occasions. I remembered hearing him talk about shooting the AR-15 into the girls' room before. I said, "I remember you saying that now."

The guy staying in the apartment was deposed by the defense team. He reported many unfavorable things about Tom and the family based on witnessing what went on in the household. I never read his statement and don't know the details. We met him once when we were working at Tom's house, but only discussed his plans for clearing out all his stuff from the property.

Ezekiel and I talked about the fact that his older sisters were there in the courtroom, and he said, "Yeah, I'm trying not to look at them or anyone when I walk in. I have to concentrate on staying calm and not messing with my hands."

"You're doing a good job," I responded.

By the time we left, he seemed a little more himself and I calmed down. "Hang in there," I told him, and we hugged him goodbye.

CHAPTER 24

THE DEFENSE WITNESSES

Day 4: The defense called Ezekiel's therapist at the treatment center. The therapist testified.

Ezekiel and I worked on coping strategies. He had to figure out his own coping strategies through our therapy. He was initially hyper-vigilant. Now he's able to use coping strategies on his own. Ezekiel had anger issues, issues with intolerance and prejudice, grief issues, and grief about the losses. When he watched the memorial services video the first time it was overwhelming; he became incredibly sad. He had trauma issues, physical aggression from his father, and emotional aggression from his mother. He had to self-soothe. We went through events in his childhood a bit at a time using Cognitive Behavioral Therapy (CBT) to change how he thought, which changed how he felt.

He had trust problems. At the county detention facility, he couldn't let his guard down. His parents were very distrustful of most people, including the government. There was lots of paranoia. Ezekiel channeled his father. He has progressed and does very well following the program. He talks about issues, changes his reaction, and is not as judgmental. He's been less anxious and less hyper-vigilant. He is very compliant with therapy and has gotten better over time.

Medication is extremely helpful. Ezekiel had a history of auditory and visual hallucinations and depression. He is treatable. He would normally be stepped down at the treatment center— if not for his crime.

On cross-examination she testified.

Ezekiel sought control over his life. He was very controlled by his father when he wasn't at church. On the positive side, he learned from his father to be gregarious and to help others. He helps other kids at the treatment center. He learned to dislike immaturity—people acting like a kid when they are not kids.

He has self-esteem issues, he isn't good at reading social cues, and naming his emotion is hard. He has had no fights at the treatment center. There were no issues with him stealing and he has not shown deceitfulness. He has a diagnosis of PTSD and major depression with psychotic features.

The prosecution went back to how attracted Ezekiel was to military thinking, guns, and violence. They brought up a reported incident where he stayed up all night finishing the book *The Third Reich*, and at 5:40 in the morning was hyper. The prosecution asked, "How can we feel safe when he stops treatment? He will not stop reading these kinds of books."

The next witness the defense called was the forensic psychiatrist Dr. Newman, who had been working with the defense team since the beginning. The defense reviewed his résumé, which was extensive. He went to Harvard Divinity School, won a *We Believe in Kids* Award, treated upward of 15,000 patients—many adolescents—and spent 20% of his time doing forensic work. They established him as an expert in forensic psychiatry with specialty in adolescent treatment. He testified.

I assessed Ezekiel's past personal history and explored where he lived and his interest in video games and music. His delusions of being a gangster—doing drive-by shootings, hanging out with gangs, and basically glorifying acts of being a gangster, was him faking bad. It was a fantasy that provided Ezekiel context for what he did and to avoid the painful aspects of what he did. People with delusions, if they don't understand what they did, must develop a narrative that can explain what happened.

Ezekiel's mother was distant, antagonistic, and put him down constantly. She said things like, "In the Bible days they would stone you to death." She didn't like him. Tom was a military guy who would allegedly punch, kick, and shove Ezekiel. Tom was struggling to support the family since he lost his job.

Ezekiel said he was compelled to guard the compound. He learned that people outside the compound were dangerous. His mother and father were people who had hard lives. They came together and did their best and make things work. Being born-again gave them a very traditional model. They used messages of conversion but had primitive coping strategies and a very black and white model. They were paranoid and worried about what the outside world would think, and put Ezekiel in a position where he had to develop his own coping strategies.

There was a crescendo of sexual excitement that led to the murders. Ezekiel did not approach dating the way normal fifteen-year-old boys would. There was a level of immaturity and his whole plan was not very well thought out—it wasn't a rational plan. He was homeschooled poorly by his mother, who didn't graduate from high school. He had no other role models. His parents kept him away from any employment opportunities or other experiences. His father taught him to be a soldier, and he wanted to be a soldier; what other model did he have?

He had no medical records at all except for a chiropractic visit and his birth records. He received medical care only after his incarceration. He has no real history of drug or alcohol use. He has no record of illegal activity. He stole food a time or two from church, but no history of rule-breaking, which if he did, would make him difficult to treat.

When the psychiatrist became involved, they found he had a long history of depression, psychotic symptoms, and no treatment. As for malingering, feigning, or exaggerating what happened, Ezekiel didn't mention his hallucinations to me for seven hours during my interview. He only spoke of them in response to a direct question. He didn't blame his actions on the voices. He didn't report the voices to the police. He didn't want people to think he was crazy.

In the text messages he said he was insane, recognizing that the situation was bizarre. The killings and story after were characteristic of those psychotic symptoms.

The crime was violent, aggressive, militaristic, and horrible. Factors include 1) lack of mature thinking skills, 2) very depressed, 3) unable to escape from his family, 4) angry at his parents, 5) sexual excitement, 6) ready access to weapons, 7) command hallucinations that were chronic and persistent, and 8) abuse by his parents.

Ezekiel's mental health status at the time of the killings was depressed, agitated, and he had a poor appetite. His thoughts were disorganized, suicidal, and focused on getting away from his father. He had homicidal thoughts and was focused on being with the girlfriend. He was convinced that if he ran away, his dad would hunt him down and beat him up worse than before. He was paranoid and fearful of his father. He had auditory hallucinations that were insulting for up to three years prior and escalating over the two weeks before the murders. He felt he had no options. The voices would call him stupid and call him a bitch.

When I asked Jenny about violence toward Ezekiel, she confirmed that their dad did hit him with a belt and his fist. Ezekiel couldn't name an adult to whom he was close. Jenny thought her dad did the killings when she first heard about them.

Ezekiel's diagnosis at the time of the incident was schizoaffective disorder, severe depression, and TBI. As to adequate protection of the public the positives are 1) hallucinations are treatable, 2) depression is treatable, 3) Dr. Healy developed a relationship with him, 4) significant progress in school and psychological tests show he is functioning normally now, 5) the adolescent brain is not mature and the frontal lobe won't mature until age twenty-two to twenty-five, and 6) in terms of personality disorders, antisocial behavior in adolescents does not predict antisocial behavior as an adult.

The prediction for adolescents who kill family members is that they are no more likely to kill again than normal adolescents. The analysis of Ezekiel's brain compared to other brains does not indicate that he is likely to be a criminal.

Dr. Hahn's interview technique was aggressive, authoritative, and demanding. He poked at Ezekiel trying to get him to react and had very few open-ended questions. He rushed the interview.

Ezekiel's greatest strength is that he has family who cares about him. His trajectory looks positive. Ezekiel is amenable to treatment.

On cross-examination the prosecution challenged the negative portrayal of the guns in the home, saying, "The guns were for defense. When Ezekiel was trained to use them, they started with a .22 caliber."

When discussing the head injuries, the prosecution pointed out, "Ezekiel said his sister put his head through a mirror, why didn't you mention that and instead focused on his dad hitting him? Isn't it possible that Tom was just disciplining Ezekiel?"

Dr. Newman responded, testifying.

Tom's type of punishment was characteristic of strong male-dominated families. Ezekiel learned aggression as a coping skill instead of other coping skills like reasoning about his actions. He had to figure out his own coping skills. Malachi was fighting for superior authority in the home and pulled a gun on Ezekiel at one point in the months before his death. Ezekiel's issues with power aren't a dominant theme with him anymore.

I would be testifying the next day. I became more concerned about being on the stand after watching the prosecution. I didn't sleep much that week, and in the early morning hours I would rehearse how I might respond to questions while lying in bed. I had prepared by creating a timeline. Reviewing all my records, notes, and e-mails so I had it clear in my mind the sequence of events and interactions after the deaths. Obsessing on the details, I reviewed the timeline repeatedly that week.

People were advising me about how to testify. Mark said, "Look at the judge, don't let her distract you. Answer the question you think should be asked, don't let her lead you." The advice was long, and I tried to take it in.

I met with Robert over lunch to review my testimony. He would ask me a question, let me respond, then he gave me feedback. "Keep it short. …OK definitely keep that." Most of his feedback was to help me clarify my response.

CHAPTER 25

THE COURT-APPOINTED EXPERT WITNESS

Day 5: They called Dr. Newman to continue his cross-examination by the prosecution. Dr. Newman testified.

Hallucinations are a form of psychosis where the receptors in the brain are hypersensitive. The content varies based on the situation. With schizophrenia the voices are derogatory, with depression they are egocentric, and in manic episodes the voices are aggrandizing; for example, "you are special." Ezekiel's voice told him after the murders that "your work is complete and your rise to power has begun." It would be ideal for Ezekiel to remain in treatment until his mid-twenties.

On redirect the defense asked questions and Dr. Newman testified.

The texts showed that the girlfriend was egging him on. The age difference between Ezekiel and the girlfriend makes sense because he is emotionally and cognitively immature. Ezekiel's understanding of girlfriends is immature. His father prohibited involvement with girls.

The next witness called by the defense was me. They went over my place of employment, my degrees, and established my relationship with Tom and Ezekiel as Tom's sister and Ezekiel's aunt, and now his guardian. I testified.

I went to Tom's house about five times a year, usually for the kids' birthdays or church celebrations. I went to Calvary a few times when invited to their prison ministry breakfasts or for Tom's Spanish service. Tom moved into the property where he lived shortly after I moved back to Albuquerque from Las Cruces in 2002, and I helped him move in. The family and kids only engaged in church activities and family functions. The family functions would average two to three times a month, either at my house, Janice's, or Leo's house or a wedding, baptism, or confirmation of one of our cousins, nieces, or nephews. Primarily my mom's family and sometimes friends.

We celebrated Tom's last Thanksgiving and birthday together at my house. Ezekiel wasn't at Tom's birthday. He was practicing at Calvary for music ministry. We then had a family Christmas celebration at Janice's house right before Tom and the family were going to California. On Thanksgiving, Tom was demonstrably angry and bitter. He dedicated himself to the work at Calvary and talked about potentially suing them for wrongful termination. He also had an altercation with somebody at the rescue mission, and when he talked about it there was a lot of bitterness and anger. When he was on his way to California, he talked about carrying a gun.

At Thanksgiving the children seemed very hungry; it was more pronounced than before. Tom and Amy's parenting style was very authoritative, based on the Bible Old Testament. Tom was the man of the house, so he was in control, and Amy followed his direction.

I remembered vividly when Tom disciplined Jenny when she was about four years old at my house in Las Cruces. They had her hair up in a very tight ponytail and she was crying. Tom yanked her hard by her ponytail, telling her to stop crying, and it startled me. Usually, their discipline happened behind closed doors.

Another incident I remember was shortly after I moved back to Albuquerque. Ezekiel was about five years old and Tom and Amy were teasing him ruthlessly while he was crying. I felt so sorry for him, but I didn't say anything. I never saw Ezekiel or any of the other children with any friends.

I tried to see Ezekiel the Sunday after his arrest, but I wasn't allowed to see him. On Monday I visited him, and he seemed strung out or in shock. My goal was simply to connect with him and to make sure he was OK and getting his needs met. It was a supervised visit and there was concern about suicide.

Then on Thursday after Ezekiel's arrest, his Juvenile Probation Officer (JPO), Jenny, Carla, Ezekiel, and I sat down and went through the paperwork. The JPO asked who was going to be the guardian? After a discussion with Carla and Jenny, I said I was willing to do it. We arranged for Carla and Jenny to be regular visitors. Ezekiel talked about persistent audio and visual hallucinations, including a Civil War soldier who would visit him regularly and a woman who passed in front of his bedroom door. He experienced these at his house and sometimes at Calvary.

We've told him that we are not going to abandon him—that we're never going to leave him. I think he takes a lot of comfort in that. I just want him to be healthy, to live a life as normal as possible. He deserves that.

When Robert asked me, "Why have you stood by Ezekiel through all of this?"

Choking back tears in a crackling voice I responded, "Because he's my brother's son…and I love my brother and I love Ezekiel and that's what family does."

On cross-examination I testified.

I had no knowledge of Jenny's ability to write, other than that she texts a lot, and she doesn't like to talk on the phone much. Carla graduated from one of the better high schools in California. Jenny lived with her parents until she married in May 2011. Carla lived in Albuquerque for maybe a year and a half after graduating from high school in California, where she lived with her mother and sisters. Carla attended ministry school in Albuquerque before she went off on a mission with the church in Mexico around 2005, when Ezekiel was around eight years old. She came to Albuquerque very infrequently after that. Her dad visited California once or twice a year and they talked and texted.

It seemed like Ezekiel and Malachi attended wrestling tournaments until about 2010 based on the trophies on the wall at Tom's house. The family went to Calvary often until Tom lost his position, then they would just attend services and Ezekiel practiced and participated in music ministry. My understanding was that Tom was fired and not on sabbatical.

Janice and I bought the iPod as a Christmas gift in 2011 for Ezekiel. I didn't witness him engage less in family gatherings because of the iPod.

Carla and Jenny visited Ezekiel at the county detention facility, but they never visited at the treatment center. At the time that they visited, January 2013 through June 2013, Ezekiel had not stabilized on his medications. He was still hallucinating, had delusional thoughts, and he was depressed.

It was hard to get medical records from the county detention facility. Mark went through the house after the incident very thoroughly and didn't find any records except a chiropractic report. My understanding is that the defense team requested records and didn't get much. My experience is that it's uncommon for someone to take their kids to get shots and then not keep that record.

In the middle of my testimony after we returned from lunch, Carla called the victims advocate and said she wanted to hear my testimony by phone and said she might rebut. She was back in California since she left on Tuesday evening. Judge Baca decided that if the prosecution planned to call her as a witness, then she couldn't hear my testimony.

When I stepped down I was so relieved. Most of the time I talked to the judge, not the prosecuting attorney. I thought I did OK. They called a break and I hugged Mark. Leo said he thought I did good. I worked hard to breathe and take my time because I talk fast when I get nervous. I was glad it was over.

The next witness called was the court-appointed forensic

psychologist, Dr. Berry. He worked for Children Youth and Family Department (CYFD), he had a background in amenability, he had done more than two thousand psychiatric evaluations, and the court ordered him to evaluate Ezekiel. He testified.

Ezekiel was evaluated based on the factors of amenability related to maturity and general functioning. I also did a risk assessment to determine if the public would be safe if he were released. My recommendation is that Ezekiel is amenable to treatment. He is salvageable; however, twenty-one years of age is not enough time. But the chances are small that he will reoffend even at age twenty-one.

I first considered the child's home and determined that it was disturbed as best and bizarre at worst. This was based on the aggregate of all the information I looked at. The father was quite disturbed, the mother was quite disturbed. The father was very controlling, and demonstrated paranoia and an attraction to violence. He was very into guns. He was frightened of the outside world. His family were virtually prisoners. He exhibited control and authoritarian discipline beyond disturbed. Tom beat his son, Jenny said, at least twice a week.

In evaluating the environmental situation, Ezekiel's attachment to his mother was problematic. She hit the kids and was emotionally abusive—never warm. His father showed love but could turn on him. He used guns to patrol, was at war with the neighbors, and thought he might have to go to war with the U.S. government.

Ezekiel did not have normal socialization and did not get enough food. In terms of his mental health, he has PTSD, depression, and auditory hallucinations. He also has low self-esteem and low self-confidence. His maturity with friends and girlfriends appears to have been that of a younger child. His pattern of living includes that he had easy access to guns. His brain development was delayed. I would not characterize him as psychotic. He has demonstrated good response to treatment and is responding to medication. I believe Ezekiel may be able to eventually go off medication.

I disagree with Dr. Hahn's diagnosis of conduct disorders—his diagnosis was wrong. In the police confession, Ezekiel bragged about fighting and invented violent behavior. A depressed and oppressed individual is very helpless and powerless. Ezekiel wanted to emulate a powerful person and build himself up. Dr. Hahn changed his diagnosis to antisocial, narcissistic, and paranoid. He's wrong. He was trying to salvage the work he did. There are criteria for enduring patterns of behavior; it must be across life circumstance. Paranoid people are super controlling. Ezekiel has some paranoia based on living with his father and mother, but paranoid individuals are so hostile they can't cooperate with lawyers. They are angry and bitter, nasty, and difficult to get along with.

Narcissistic people demonstrate grandiosity that extends over a period. They are explosive with others, always building themselves up out of a sense of ego, and believe that they are special.

Anti-social is a pervasive pattern. They disregard others, lack empathy, are exploitative, and criminal behavior is the result.

Dr. Hahn made his conclusions on malingering all wrong. Malingering is purposeful fabrication of symptoms for some favorable outcome. Dr. Hahn's evaluation showed a mild deviation, and he was misreporting. There was no distortion on the scale for adolescents.

I determined in the Risk Assessment that there is adequate treatment available. There is a likelihood of rehabilitation based on all of Ezekiel's progress so far. Tests reveal no cognitive disabilities that would interfere with future therapy. The MRI scans don't indicate long-term effects of the TBI. He has social support and connection with Regina—a good prognostic factor.

Ezekiel hasn't fully come to terms with what he did and the impact on others as well as himself. The paranoia is lingering, including paranoid ideations. He's not violent but still has an attraction to a militaristic view. He is looking at his thought processes and he is doing Cognitive Behavioral Therapy. He needs a structured treatment environment. He can be a productive, contributing member of society and live a healthy and happy life, though he may have lingering depression and self-esteem issues.

In terms of the risk to public safety, it is currently low; at age twenty-one it is statistically low. If he has extended treatment, it will be near zero. In terms of severity of offense, children who kill their family members have a very low risk of killing again based on a few studies. I don't want Ezekiel to go to prison.

"Disturbed at best and bizarre at worst," became the headline in the paper. Many of us were surprised at his candor and directness. The Amenability Hearing would continue on February 10-11, 2016. Exhausted, we left the courtroom quickly.

CHAPTER 26

WE WERE GOBSMACKED

We prepared for Leo's fiftieth birthday party, it was going to be a big event with all the family and many of Leo's friends. It was two weeks after the Amenability Hearing, on January 23rd.

Most of our extended family was there. Several of Leo's friends flew in from other places. Many of the people who knew Leo over the course of his career were there, and all the friends in his men's group were there with their families.

While I circulated around talking to family, many were talking about the Amenability Hearing and my testimony. My *madrina* (godmother) was genuinely concerned, saying, "I'm afraid for you mija, when he's out he might hurt you." I reassured her. We also discussed the fact that I still felt the presence of my brother with me. She insisted that he was gone.

In another discussion with one of my cousins, I asked her if she would support one of her sister's sons if he did something bad. She looked at me with a furrowed brow and said, "Honestly, I don't think so."

I cut short my visiting with family and gravitated to the dance floor.

Less people came to the continuation of the Amenability Hearing in February. Ezekiel's sisters weren't there, nor was Janice. A couple of our cousins came, and there were some people from Calvary.

Day 6: The court called to the stand Dr. Berry, the court-appointed psychologist for cross-examination. He testified.

I recommend five more years of treatment. At age twenty-three Ezekiel would be fully developed. He could be assessed at that time based on his behavior.

Ezekiel's social experience was not normal on average. The prosecution is taking snippets of positive and putting them together. An analogy is when people against the right to die would record a person in a coma for months then create a short video of all the twitches or movement and claim that the person was still actively alive.

Tom gave the impression that he was proud of his son, but Ezekiel internalized that his father was disappointed with him. The beatings were often based on reports from his mother; if there were reports of any misbehavior, there would most certainly be a beating. Things got tough after Jenny left and even worse when Tom lost his job.

Understanding what and why he did what he did won't alone determine if he will kill again. He's willing to talk about his reactions and looks toward the future. His military obsession came from his dad. He felt powerless, so he identified with his dad's power in his past.

I don't agree with Dr. Hahn. I also don't agree with Dr. Newman that Ezekiel was insane at the time of the murder. I don't think falling at the skate park caused the TBI.

Ezekiel has the capacity to get better and return to society.

On redirect the defense questioned him. He testified.

I did not interview Jenny or Carla, but the defense provided a statement for both, and I received one thing from the State with Jenny saying that she was afraid of Ezekiel. There was also the statement Jenny made the night of the incident about thinking it was her father who committed the murders. The State showed a picture of Tom as happy, but the State didn't provide evidence that indicated he was happy. In Tom's work environment he probably was happier because he was contributing. But at home he was different; not unusual.

Tom not only taught Ezekiel to kill, but said it was OK to kill.

The tenant who lived in the apartment made a statement about the family asking for food from him.

Ezekiel has the capacity to go to college. There isn't any reason he wouldn't continue to make progress. Ezekiel made the decision to kill because Ezekiel felt powerless, helpless, and hopeless—severely so. He had a very high level of depression and it still lingers. The only evidence of positive parenting was that Amy never raised her voice. Hopefully, Ezekiel will get better. There aren't any indications that he won't make progress. Everything points to him being able to make changes if he stays on track.

The next witness called by the defense was the youth detention center psychiatrist, Dr. Alexander. The youth detention center is where Ezekiel would be sent if he was found amenable and remained in the juvenile system. He testified.

I met Ezekiel in December 2015 at the treatment center and asked him about his experience at the treatment center. He seemed intact, not psychotic. He didn't appear depressed, but overall hopeful. He had a particularly good relationship with the staff and peers. I reviewed reports submitted by the experts from the defense, the prosecution, and the one submitted by Ezekiel's JPO. My assessment is that he is fully engaged in therapy and has family who is supportive of psychotherapy and trauma work.

At the youth detention center, family therapy is available, but many children don't have viable family. They would delay family therapy about three weeks during his intake, which is when they will place him in his unit.

The intake process at the youth detention center starts with interviews by diagnosticians to review academics, intellect, trauma scales, and personality. They will also evaluate any other collateral from other institutions. They would then talk to available support people. Ezekiel would be interviewed by the staff. Finally, they would make a determination on placement which involves level of maturity, academics, medical needs, and space availability.

My assessment of Ezekiel's needs and whether they can be met at the youth detention center is that in most respects he is like other clients. We've had cases where boys killed multiple family members and we've had success. Statistically, it's rare that these kids will kill again because they are not sophisticated in criminal activity. If Ezekiel were committed to the youth detention center it would be possible to provide a report to the court as he approaches age twenty-one.

On cross-examination by the prosecution he testified.

Ezekiel is like the rest of the population, not in terms of crime, but 95% of their cases are cases of neglect and abuse. It wouldn't be a good idea to keep him at the youth detention center right up to age twenty-one. They try to get kids to a reintegration center. It could be as little as a month, but I prefer three to six months, and family involvement is important. Transition is more important. We can't guarantee a reintegration center or integration coordinator beyond age twenty-one. After release they make efforts to make connections with social services for the kids.

Day 7: The prosecution started with their closing arguments and went through the factors of amenability.

Number one, the seriousness of the crime. He killed his parents and three children in a cold-blooded way. It wasn't a crime of passion, there was no precipitating event. He shot Miriam twice. Woke up his brother before he killed him. He took a photo of his mother and brother's dead bodies. It was not a rampage, he did it coldly, calmly, he was clear-headed. The police made him comfortable, that's why he gave them a confession.

Number two, the offense was committed in a violent aggressive manner. We covered this in number one.

Number three, firearms used. There were two firearms. Tom trusted Ezekiel; if they had been locked, he would have had the key.

Number four, persons or property. This weighed heavily against Ezekiel. It was a violent crime against persons.

Number five, conditions of the child. The facts are in dispute. He had a normal, ordinary home, many amenities, and his basic needs were met.

Number six, trauma history. It's unclear, the State doesn't accept all his childhood being horrible. Other kids are abused. The fact that he doesn't have a history is a double-edged sword. Maybe his history was not reported to officials.

Number seven, prospects of adequate treatment. The doctors don't know why he did what he did. Ezekiel hasn't addressed it. There is no prospect that he will be safe in the community. He is still obsessed with the military, still obsessed with Hitler. Dr. Hahn's diagnosis is mixed personality disorder and he doesn't think they can treat him. Dr. Newman says he was insane at the time of the murder. Dr. Berry says they can't treat him in two years, and he needs reassessment at age twenty-three. Dr. Alexander said he can treat him and make the transition, but it is best if his treatment is under the thumb of the court.

Number eight, any other factor. Ezekiel's teacher at the treatment center found it distasteful that he wanted power. A couple of quotes from the testimony presented were "rise to power" and "power struggle with his brother."

The defense in their opening said they were not concerned with the facts of the crime. You must consider all factors. A blended sentence, although not precluded by law, is illogical. Ezekiel has never shown real emotion. The State is not convinced treatment will work.

The State rests its case.

Jack stood up to make the closing arguments for the defense.

Ezekiel is amenable to treatment and the burden is on the State to prove by clear and convincing evidence he is not. Is he amenable to treatment? Dr. Newman, yes, he is amenable, Dr. Hahn, no, Dr. Berry yes, and Dr. Alexander said he had other people like Ezekiel. There is a significant difference in the amount of time the experts spent on this case. Dr. Newman and Dr. Berry put in the elbow grease. Dr. Hahn, three and half hours. All other professionals agree with Dr. Newman and Dr. Berry.

Why can't we show why he did what he did? Dr. Newman said, "He had a psychotic break, hallucinations, and it's complicated." That is the explanation! Dr. Hahn said, "It was a mixed personality disorder. There are no DSM rules. Conduct disorder based on lame examples like Ezekiel had eleven girlfriends, even though he didn't know what a girlfriend was, and he shot a pigeon. There is no mental illness, just a bad seed." RUBBISH!

He had a restrictive family. Dr. Berry's example of the woman in the coma was apt; the prosecution is doing the same thing addressing a few point examples. They try to normalize the guns; he had an armory under extremely dangerous circumstances. His father depended on Ezekiel to keep the house safe; that's not his responsibility. He used Ezekiel to act out his paranoid delusions.

The people at the treatment center, they have no dog in this fight, they all say he is progressing. Ezekiel showed remorse as reported by his therapist and the mental health supervisor. Everything they have offered him he has taken. Ezekiel's work at the treatment center is the most important evidence. All evidence points in the same direction. Ezekiel is getting better. Ezekiel's type does not have recidivism. His brain will mature.

Ezekiel is amenable to treatment, but the question is, does he deserve a chance? He pleaded guilty. He has taken responsibility. If the court wants a middle ground, find him amenable for two counts and not amenable for three counts and give him a blended sentence.

The defense rests.

When we returned, Judge Baca spent three hours going through his notes in the order of the witnesses and in detail. Then he declared,

"The Court finds as follows, amenable to treatment in available facilities."

We were stunned.

Then he went through his rationale.

- Proving that he is not amenable to treatment is the burden of the State and the standard of proof is clear and convincing evidence
- Standard abuse case was clear and convincing, this tilted the scale
- Case law says in these cases focus on the child not the offenses committed

So, the question is, can Ezekiel be treated adequately so that he can be safe? Based on testimony of Dr. Newman, Dr. Berry, and others who worked closely with him and believe he is amenable, he can be. The only dissenter was Dr. Hahn.

The Court finds that the State did not prove that Ezekiel was not amenable to treatment in available facilities. A Disposition Hearing will be in March.

Judge Baca then banged the gavel.

We were gobsmacked. Robert hugged Ezekiel, as did the social worker. We met with the defense team in a room off the hall across from the courtroom and talked. It was like the dog that caught the tire of a moving vehicle. We were happy on the one hand, though we refrained from showing it in the courtroom, but now we had a big challenge to prepare Ezekiel for a release in just two years!

CHAPTER 27

IMMEDIATE AND PUNISHING REACTION

The media went wild, and there was an immediate call for an appeal. Jenny's friend at Calvary put a *change.org* site up on behalf of Carla and Jenny, the next day after Judge Baca made his decision. I was thankful that Mark and I planned to get away for the Valentine's Day weekend starting the next day. Over the weekend the media interviewed our stepmother. People's reaction and the interview exasperated and discouraged me.

A week later, with Facebook posts that were derogatory about Leo and me from family and the change.org petition circulating, Mark and I decided to write a letter to our children, partly because one of them reposted the change.org petition. This letter reflected our views. It was an extremely trying time, but we continued in the conviction that they should treat Ezekiel as a juvenile. One we held with others since after we learned of the deaths of the family.

February 17, 2016
Dearest Children,

You are all aware that Ezekiel's seven-day Amenability Hearing, the longest in New Mexico history, was finalized last week, with the sentencing portion to come in a few weeks. For those of you who have held us in prayer during this difficult time, we thank you. We were all shocked by the ruling of Judge Baca. The best we were hoping for was what they called a blended sentence, where Ezekiel would be sentenced as a juvenile on two of the charges, and for three of the charges he would get an adult sentence that would reduce to time served and five years probation; ten years total. I think Judge Baca knew that ruling would have been unprecedented and subject to appeal.

The facts presented in the case fully supported that he was amenable, the progress he has made at the treatment center alone made that evident. It is not speculation that he will be amenable to treatment; he is showing it every day. There was nothing the prosecution presented that came close to convincing evidence for ruling that he was not amenable. In New Mexico and many states there are only those two choices: sentence as a juvenile and release at twenty-one or adult prison; nothing in between. We are relieved that he will not go to adult prison.

This case is very complex, as you may imagine, and the three years since this tragedy began has been incredibly painful, challenging, emotional, and revealing. We have supported Ezekiel out of love from the very beginning. Please do not confuse this with defending him or his actions. We have never defended his actions and never will. We will stand up for this child and help him have a voice. Our position has always been that there is a reason there is an adult court system and a juvenile court system, and Ezekiel as a juvenile should be in the juvenile system. We supported his medical care, mental health care, education, and demonstrated to him that there is a family who still loves him when almost everyone has abandoned him.

What has been horribly painful is the hateful, venomous response by others; especially family members. The media and the press have done a great disservice, as they have not reported this case truthfully and have fanned the flames of those seeking not justice, but revenge and retribution. All of those who are outspoken are ignorant to the facts of this case; none attended the seven-day Amenability Hearing (we were there every minute). Some family members wanting revenge have lied to the media; most have only gotten their facts from the inept reporting of the media.

They are now becoming very vocal on social media and regular media calling for an appeal. It's one thing to have an opinion based on misinformation, but to use it to the detriment of a child by putting him in prison for the rest of his life is disgraceful. For example, it is irresponsible to allow Regina's stepmother on camera given that she contributed to leaving Tom and his siblings without a father and in poverty when Tom was six years old. She has very little to do with the family now and her motivation is unclear given how much suffering she's brought to Regina's family.

At change.org there are many incorrect facts on the particulars of what happened, and opinions expressed that are not based in fact, all aimed at eliciting an emotional response. Below are some examples:

- *The description of what happened distorted facts. We were in court for the coroner's report, and there were no AR-15 bullets in any of the first four victims.*
- *There is a chorus of people repeating that Ezekiel is not remorseful. Ezekiel pleaded guilty, several witnesses testified to the fact that he cries about what happened and struggled to watch the video of the memorial service. None of these people has spoken to Ezekiel in over two years, including his sister or half-siblings, until a couple of weeks ago, when Ezekiel initiated a call to Carla. She proceeded to attack him, so he just stopped talking. This repeating of a lie until it sounds like truth is just wrong. Leo and Regina have spent over one hundred hours with Ezekiel in therapy. They believe he is remorseful. He wrote letters of apology to Jenny and Carla. The pain that this kid is living with is punishing.*
- *The claim that the family was swindled. (This claim was made because the family in California was not included throughout,*

especially for the plea deal, and the fact that Carla didn't get to testify). First of all, they had Jack's number, they could have called the DA, and they had Ezekiel's address and phone number. Additionally, enclosed is a letter signed and delivered to the DA when she met with the family, to include Janice, Jenny, and Carla. Also enclosed is a statement to the press given a year later that Janice, Jenny, and Carla helped craft on the first-year anniversary. Since then, Leo has worked very hard to keep them in the loop and called them to get their agreement on the plea. If not for the plea there would have been a three-week or more trial that would have dragged the family through the mud and would have been very adversarial.

Jack, who leads Ezekiel's legal team, did not put many witnesses up on the stand for the hearing that would have confirmed what Ezekiel said, including neighbors and boarders who either lived with Tom or near Tom. He took statements from them and relied on the court-appointed psychologist to have all that information and make his own determination. In many cases, the court-appointed psychologist rules against amenability. In this case, when provided all the evidence and statements (which was extensive), including information from prosecutors, he determined that Ezekiel was amenable. ...

The comments that are out on change.org about Tom's character are all from people who knew Tom in his ministries. Tom did a lot of good things, we acknowledge that; we can hold that he did good things and made bad choices as a parent. He was a different person in public than in the privacy of his home. We saw bits of both, and we were completely unaware of the extent of the difference, particularly the arsenal of weapons and ammunition he had. When he lost his position at Calvary, he began to unravel altogether.

In short, the change.org petition is a reaction and feels more like a lynch mob than anybody interested in the truth. All in the name of Jesus and justice. Enclosed is a link to an article that talks about parricides; much was discussed in the court about the treatability of these cases and recidivism. They exhibit many of the same characteristics, many of which Ezekiel shares, and it turns out they have recidivism statistics of less than 5%. Please do your own research to inform your opinion.

We are not sure what people think our motivation here is other than showing love for this abused and neglected child. This has been hard work for three years primarily for Regina, Leo, Lily, and Mark. Especially so for Regina, as his guardian, who has worked tirelessly to be sure he has received his proper medical and mental health care, his medications, and his education. She fought hard to get him into a full-time treatment center where he has received the care to make the progress he is making.

Both of us respect that each of you may not agree or feel comfortable with the ruling, but we trust that you will show respect and restraint based on our belief that Ezekiel's life should not be discarded. Leo, Lily, Regina, and Mark are all hurting right now; it is not an easy stance to take with the level of attack, venom, and vengeance that some have expressed. It is unfortunate that people are after retribution instead of transformation. We know it comes out of their own woundedness and we are trying to hold them in compassion. If you want to discuss anything with us, we are open. This whole thing is a terrible tragedy, a small fractal of the human condition and there are no easy answers.

Most of all what we ask of you is to keep all of this in your prayers. It is destroying a family, has the potential to ruin a life, and it is causing tremendous strife and emotional stress in the lives of us trying to love. We hope you find the space in your heart to love Ezekiel even though he has done the unspeakable. Our faith and life experiences have shown us that love and forgiveness are the only true ways to go.

Love to all of you

We received a written response from Mark's middle daughter.

Our prayers have accompanied both of you, the family, and those who are part of the case. It is too complex to know the "right" outcome, but I've prayed and hoped that the right thing would happen, and I have confidence that this is part of the unfolding. My heart continues to ache to see the pain all of this is causing. We will continue to pray that God's

will is done through all of this and all of us, and we will continue to sup-
port both of you. Thank you for allowing your hearts to be broken. And
thank you for sharing that love with all of us and Ezekiel.

Over the course of time, we had discussions with our children about the situation. Our sons were neutral about things, not sure what the right answer was.

CHAPTER 28

THE DISPOSITION HEARING

Jack collected all the letters of support which we received and he received from others in anticipation of the Disposition Hearing, which is when the judge would sentence Ezekiel as a youthful offender. He planned to give them directly to Judge Baca. Leo and I coordinated what we would say in our statements and provided each other feedback. I spoke to the fact that trauma is generational and that if pain is not transformed it will inevitably be passed on, referring to what I believed happened with my brother. Leo focused on the fact that the family, including Carla and Jenny, supported Ezekiel being treated as a juvenile. All of them spoke to the DA about their desires for fair treatment in the juvenile system and they agreed with moving ahead with the plea. He also planned to talk about the fact that Tom was able to find redemption thirty years prior as he sat in a jail cell in California after shooting people in a drive-by. Ezekiel should get the same opportunity, which is what Tom and Amy would have wished for if they could speak.

The Saturday before the Disposition Hearing, scheduled for March 2, 2016, Leo and Lily visited Ezekiel. He was not in a good state of mind. He was expressing fear for his future and talked about joining the military again. This really bothered Leo and Lily, and they sent an e-mail to the defense team and me expressing their concern with Ezekiel's attitude and the things he said.

I was with my daughters in El Paso helping to pick out dresses and other wedding preparations for my daughter.

At one point when I was driving in El Paso with five people in my car on the freeway, I started to lose my peripheral vision and began driving very slowly. My daughter in the passenger seat looked at me. I told her, "I think I'm having a panic attack. I'm scared to drive next to the construction barrier with the trucks around me."

She responded, "Get off at the next exit, I'll drive."

I said, "I've lost peripheral vision." And I slowed down to about thirty-five miles an hour on the busy freeway.

"It's OK mom, just get to the next exit." She coached me. At one point I glanced in the rearview mirror realizing I had five people in the car, including my daughter's best friends' daughter. I almost started crying.

I managed to drive until I could get off the freeway and let my daughter drive. I was surprised and embarrassed by what happened. I had never experienced that before, but the ongoing stress of Ezekiel's case was overwhelming.

The social worker with the defense team and I responded to Leo and Lily about their concerns via e-mail. I was dismayed that Ezekiel was regressing, but the social worker, his therapist, and I were sure he was simply scared of the upcoming hearing. He was afraid of his sisters and wondered if someone might try to kill him in the courtroom. He was also scared of leaving the treatment center where he had built a community of support. He would have to gain acceptance in a new place where people would know him only as the boy who killed his family. He had mentioned at a recent visit that he didn't even know how to work the remote control for the new TV in the lodge. Ezekiel was afraid to hope for a better future, because that could be taken from him.

In his fear, he reverted to old ways of thinking to protect himself from harm. The military path felt like a refuge for him because he knew they take care of food and housing and would tell him what to do. Every other route felt nebulous and scary to him. Our hope and belief were that once he moved to the youth detention center and got into a routine, he would continue the growth trajectory we had witnessed up to that point. He was still a *work in progress*. He was still a teenage boy.

We met with him on Monday before the Wednesday Disposition Hearing. We addressed his fears by walking him through what would happen the day of the Disposition Hearing, over the course of the next week, and in the first weeks at the youth detention center. I told him that he had done well so far, there was no reason to think that he wouldn't be OK at the youth detention center. We also reassured him that we would continue to support him at the youth detention center and beyond. He seemed to lighten up and we all felt better.

The Disposition Hearing would start at 1:30 p.m. on March 2, 2016, and end by about 3:00 p.m. We were worried about the backlash within some of the family members and community; especially many in the evangelical community at Calvary. Leo and I would be giving statements on behalf of the defense and Carla, Jenny, the cousin who attended Calvary, and one of the Calvary members would give statements for the prosecution. Each side had twenty minutes. I visited Ezekiel the morning of the Disposition Hearing to see how he was doing and to reassure him. Leo, Lily, Mark, and I met with the defense team at their office at 11:30 a.m. to review things during lunch and talk about any concerns so we could go in as a team.

There was a demonstration planned by some family members, people from Calvary, and a few from the general public at 1:00 p.m. at the courthouse against Ezekiel. The treatment center folks decided to bring Ezekiel through the back gate at the courthouse for everyone's protection. They would transfer him immediately to the youth detention center so he would be going with a different crew to a new location after the hearing, also through the back gate.

At the Disposition Hearing, the defense and prosecution made statements, and we read all of our statements, then the judge formalized sentencing Ezekiel until age twenty-one and signed the transfer to the youth detention center. It was an anticlimactic hearing. It turns out that with the decision that Ezekiel was amenable, his release at age twenty-one was almost automatic. I believe his sisters thought they might be able to change the outcome, but Judge Baca had made his decision in February and the Disposition Hearing was a formality. For us, this was the best outcome given the binary choice available.

After the Disposition Hearing and Ezekiel's transfer to the youth detention center, Leo, Lily, Mark, the defense team, and I met briefly in the side room across from Judge Baca's courtroom. The Disposition Hearing was very tense. The defense team gave us copies of the letters sent before the hearing to Judge Baca for and against Ezekiel. I read the letter we heard about before the Amenability Hearing that Jenny, my father, and his stepchildren signed. I had a good laugh. They said that I was angry at Tom because he went to California to live with my father back in the early '80s. They wrote it in a comical version of legalese, trying to make it look very formal. It was a strange letter.

My sister Janice's letter made me a bit upset. She also took aim at me, saying that I called my brother a monster. This stemmed from misreporting in the news, when I used the phrase, "my brother was demonstrably angry," referring to Tom's demeanor after he lost his job at Calvary. The news reported the story saying that I said, "my brother was monstrously angry." Many in the family and community latched onto that and it became a source of some of the venom I received. I used the word "demonstrably" specifically after the prosecution objected to my testifying to anything Tom told me because it was *hearsay*. I would never call any person or being in creation a *monster*, let alone my brother whom I loved.

In January 2016, I started planning a trip to Washington, DC for a Georgetown Coaching Conference scheduled in March, and I figured the Disposition Hearing would be done by then. I combined a visit with customers at our government oversight organization in Washington, DC at the same time. Later, after a discussion with Mark, we decided to bookend the trip with a visit to Mark's daughter on one end in Cincinnati and Mark's son on the other in Boston. I needed to get out of Albuquerque and put everything out of my mind for a time. By the middle of February, I booked the trip once we knew the date of the Disposition Hearing. The timing was perfect, and after a visit with my therapist on Thursday the day after the hearing, we left on Friday for Cincinnati and returned ten days later.

On April 29, 2016, the DA filed the Notice of Appeal with a statement asking that they put it on the Appellate Court Docket. The defense team assured us that it wasn't likely to go anywhere and that the Appellate Court rarely reversed the decision of an esteemed judge like Judge Baca.

PART FOUR
COMMITMENT IN ACTION

CHAPTER 29

THE YOUTH DETENTION CENTER

E zekiel moved to the youth detention center. A new chapter of learning how another facility ran so we could continue to support Ezekiel. When he first went to the youth detention center, we did not fully understand the hostility he was met with by the inmates and staff there. It was a harsher place where the state sends juveniles once their case is decided, located in Albuquerque.

He was taken to the youth detention center right after the Disposition Hearing on March 2, 2016. I was interviewed as part of his intake process. He didn't get assigned to his *cottage*, Sandia Cottage, until the end of March, and that was when we could start visiting him. They only had weekly three-hour visits, and Mark and I split the time with Leo and Lily. No other family members chose to be involved.

Unlike the treatment center, we couldn't come in the door with anything for Ezekiel. The visits were in the cafeteria and there were about five long rows of red rubber-covered metal tables with benches that were perforated (not solid) and bolted to the floor. When we visited, we were allowed to spend ten dollars in quarters on the vending machines in the cafeteria where they held the visits. We spent the money buying junk food for Ezekiel. We also couldn't sit next to Ezekiel; we sat across from him facing the guard who was overseeing the visit at the front of the room. It was noisy during our visits, which made it challenging to carry on a conversation.

Our first Multidisciplinary Treatment (MDT) team meeting was on March 22, 2016. We were introduced to the team who would be working with Ezekiel and who we would meet with monthly. The team included the Sandia Cottage classification officer, youth care supervisor, therapist, transition coordinator, education coordinator, and Ezekiel's juvenile probation officer. The meetings were chaired by the classification officer, and there was a tempo to the meetings that started with a roundtable, first Ezekiel, then each area, and lastly Leo and me and/or any family who came to the meeting. The classification officer ended with announcements and the risk assessment for Ezekiel made that month and a list of goals that Ezekiel had committed to. We would all sign a paper stating that we heard the report. Occasionally there would be other staff there if they were involved in some way, for example a report from the family therapist.

The therapist and staff were much less receptive to our involvement. Lily and Mark took a more active role now that Ezekiel's release was near. The four of us took part in family counseling together. It was important to us to understand where Ezekiel was psychologically and educationally so we could prepare to support him after his release.

Ezekiel continued his education and had the potential to graduate by the end of the fall 2016 term. Lily and I attended his first IEP on April 28, 2016. She was concerned with what the teachers were reporting on his progress and his hesitancy to ask for help. I expected that the transition in his educational program would be bumpy since it was in the middle of the term and the court proceedings were very disruptive and emotional for him. He was able to enroll in a guitar class as an elective, which was helpful for his stress level.

On April 1, 2016, someone who I had been mentoring for five years or more lost her brothers to gun violence. The national laboratory where I worked hired Deb as an intern when she was an undergraduate and sent her to school for her master's at MIT. She then transitioned back to the national laboratories to work as a mechanical engineer. She is first-generation American, and when her father came to the United States as a teenager, he was instructed by his family to take all necessary steps to bring his parents and siblings to the U.S.

Her father followed up on that promise and brought seven family members, including a brother, to the United States when Deb was in grade school. After Deb's father came to the U.S., he married, had three children, and became an entrepreneur, ultimately starting a successful restaurant business that their community adored. Deb's brothers chose to run the restaurant with their father while she chose to go to the university and study mechanical engineering. Years later, her uncle (father's brother) came into the restaurant, shot and killed her two brothers ages twenty-four and thirty-one, and maimed their father. Her uncle died by suicide in a standoff with the police.

I reached out to Deb, and she told me the whole story and said, "Regina, I knew you would understand more than anyone else could," and we both cried. I attended an outdoor service where they let a bunch of balloons fly from a lookout point on the Albuquerque west mesa. I hugged her and she talked about how she was handling everything. The *Albuquerque Journal* caught a photo of us with me cradling her head in my hands as we talked.

I love Deb so much and I could feel her pain. She took responsibility for the funerals of her siblings. She had moved to work at our national laboratories in California a year prior to the incident, and she planned to remain there after her family tragedy. I was proud of her for not moving back to Albuquerque. It was important that she live her life and heal.

The media continued their sensationalized coverage of Ezekiel's case, including coverage of a demonstration held in New Mexico by our stepmother and her family. It felt like an outrage and brought back memories of the trauma I felt as a child when my parents divorced. I didn't know the people they were calling family when the media covered the demonstration. Our stepmother's family also started a new petition on change.org. It was even more incendiary in the way it went after Ezekiel than the one that Carla and Jenny had on the site.

In late April 2016, soon after Ezekiel was settled in at the youth detention center, he started talking about a woman from the treatment center who was writing to him under an alias. The relationship sounded increasingly like a love relationship, and a dysfunctional one at that. I knew he had many people who cared about him at the treatment center while he was there, including female staff, but they all seemed more like mothers to him. There was one woman who asked if she could send a gift to my address for me to give to Ezekiel because they weren't allowed to give gifts to the clients at the treatment center. It was a T-shirt with his favorite band imprinted on it. I guess that should have been a red flag.

By early May 2016, Leo and Lily became very concerned about the relationship and we agreed to meet and talk about it at our house. When Leo, Lily, Mark, and I met I was not in a good place emotionally. They wanted to talk to the director at the treatment center and tell her about what was happening with this woman who was a staff member there. I felt that the relationship would die out because they couldn't see each other.

"Regina, it's an ethical issue. She's on staff, she's not supposed to be personally involved with the clients. They're children!" Lily emphasized.

I replied, "I know, I just can't deal with it now." It was just over two months since the Disposition Hearing, Deb's event was difficult, and the reporting on our stepmother's demonstration hit me hard. I was also involved in planning a wedding for Mark's youngest daughter in June 2016, and a big wedding for my middle daughter scheduled for October 2016.

I felt very debilitated emotionally and I didn't have the where-withal to deal with Ezekiel's secret relationship, and our meeting didn't end well. I wrote a letter explaining myself to Leo and Lily the next morning before leaving for work. This is an excerpt from that e-mail sent May 6, 2016.

Leo and Lily,

I'm sorry about my demeanor last night. I have not been able to process all the hurt and stuff that came up after the media circus. I have also been in physical pain. Frankly, I have lost myself through this whole process; it has just been too much for too long. I need to work that out, but in the meantime I am doing my best and showing up and being present, especially for my kids and Ezekiel. ...

I think that you being present as a man for Ezekiel is awesome. I respect the work that you have done in your own life and for others. ...I think Mark is right, it is probably a good time to set some forward-look-ing goals with him and help him make steps and hold him accountable to commitments.

I think the biggest thing is that we both have to come from a more centered place. Right now, I am in a state of hurt and pain, you seem to be coming at it from a place of fear at what might happen. As Mark said, and it has been my belief since the beginning, I am not in control, I am working on behalf of God, the universe, the angels, and ancestors. The best I can do is influence, show up, show I care, try to influence his thinking and behavior, help him get the help he needs, love him, pray, etc.

Know in your heart that I love you very, very much, that I am very proud to call you my brother and sister, and that I know your intentions are pure. I know that this is hard for you, as it is for me, and we are bound to make mistakes. I also know that this process would have likely killed me had I gone through it on my own.

Regina

Leo responded the same day and the issue of reporting the secret relationship went by the wayside for the time being. Here is an excerpt of the response from Leo:

Thanks Regina. I appreciate your words very much. Lily and I both felt really bad about how things went last night. I'm sorry I was not able to be more understanding and supportive of where you are. You have borne the brunt of the anger and venom of all of those in the family who can't deal with this. I know that must be really tough.

Mostly we are worried about you. It was clear last night that the anger and pain is really getting you off center. I should have come from a more sympathetic place and not talked about how I am handling it. This is all new territory for all of us and no amount of past therapy, recovery, or wisdom could have prepared us enough. We just have to do the best we can. ...

Going forward, let's both try harder to come from a place of support and respect. I am so incredibly grateful for all you have done for Ezekiel in this difficult process. He is truly blessed to have you.

I love you very much and know that God has a special place for all of us on the other side of all of this hell. Let's try to be kind to each other and to try to forgive or at least have compassion for all of those who are putting out so much hate and judgment.

It was nice to read the serenity prayer in your bathroom last night before we left. It is a prayer that has helped me so much to remember I am not in control and that I can only work on myself and leave the rest to God.

I love you.

About a month later, Leo and Lily invited us over for dinner. They brought up the topic of Ezekiel's secret relationship again. It had not gone away; in fact, it had gotten more alarming. After we last met, we encouraged Ezekiel to distance himself from her. He wrote a letter telling her he needed to back off and then didn't write for a while. She wrote mentioning another client at the treatment center who she was possibly having a relationship with to make Ezekiel jealous. I was still not sure I could deal with what might happen if we talked to the treatment center director. Leo assured me, "We'll ask them to keep it private as an internal investigation."

I agreed and we met with the director on June 9, 2016. I explained that I had thought that this woman was just one of the people who were cheering Ezekiel on, like at least three others at the treatment center who I knew cared for him. She assured us that they would begin an internal investigation and that our reporting would be private. That was a Thursday. By Friday, the police were investigating the matter and they went to the youth detention center and took all the letters in Ezekiel's locker and interviewed Leo. They called me but I was unable to return the call before they had what they needed. By June 15, it was all over the news. The *Albuquerque Journal* headline read, "ABQ treatment center worker arrested for alleged relationship with teen killer."

It turned out that she knew the spots at the treatment center where there was no camera coverage. I knew Ezekiel was constantly supervised, and I knew about all the cameras in the place because the first thing you see when you check in is a guard looking at all the cameras in the facility. What I didn't know was that the employees knew where they could hide from security, and since she was one of the people responsible for his supervision, she was able to engage in a relationship with Ezekiel. A relationship that involved kissing and touching, no undressing or anything close. It revealed my naivety again.

Two days after the media reported the relationship, we started to receive guests for Mark's daughter's wedding. I couldn't even process what happened with the woman at the treatment center and the media coverage. Lily texted me to check in and I did not respond. I blocked everything out and focused on my family. The timing was terrible. Leo and Lily went to the wedding, but I spent most of my time with our grandson and didn't want to talk about what had happened. It took a while before I could have a real conversation with Leo and Lily again. I knew at one level they were right, but it was all too much.

My relationship with Leo and Lily recovered by August 2016, when we went out to dinner to celebrate Lily's and my birthdays. We continued our journey together supporting Ezekiel, and in November 2016, the four of us started family therapy with Ezekiel and a different therapist than the one Ezekiel saw individually at the youth detention center.

Ezekiel had some time off school in the summer 2016, and he seemed to be settling into his new situation. He was engaged in therapy, taking his medication, participating in their exercise program, and going to school and passing his classes. He didn't like the group sessions, where they had discussions and activities.

Overall, there were no significant issues with Ezekiel discussed at the MDT team meetings. He was making the progress they expected. He started to stall on moving to stage 3, which required him to complete several personal tasks, including listing the things that his father had taught him. He generally didn't like talking to people about his father, other than with his therapist. It stirred up grief and he didn't think people needed to know his business. They said Ezekiel needed to work on anger and mood management. His transition coordinator was working with him on life skills and social skills.

By the end of 2016, Ezekiel was engaged in deep therapy, and it did affect his moods. He had a couple of friends. He started talking about wanting to go to Colorado after he got a bachelor's degree in New Mexico once he was released. We strongly encouraged him to work hard on his therapy and life skills. Ezekiel spent a lot of time reading. He read several books, including one on Roman mythology.

In November, with the help of Ezekiel's therapist, Leo sent a saliva sample for Ezekiel to *Ancestry.com*. We did this because he was still working on racism in therapy. It would still come up when he was angry or triggered in some way. The results showed that he was about 50% Southern European from the Iberian Peninsula and Greece, 30% Native American, and that he had a small amount of African blood. He was surprised by the results. We would remind him that he was multiracial when he made any remarks that sounded racist. His therapist used the results to work with him in their sessions.

We had our first formal Transition Planning Meeting with the cabinet secretary for the Children Youth and Family Services Department (CYFD) in November 2016. She was a younger woman, small in frame, and very perky. The cabinet secretary reported directly to the governor of New Mexico. The transition coordinator chaired the meeting and we decided to look at three possible locations in New Mexico where Ezekiel might settle in after his release. She was tasked with creating a report of all the services (i.e., therapy, training, case management) that would be available, as well as housing and employment opportunities.

The transition coordinator made it clear that there were no transitional living places available to Ezekiel, writing in her report after the meeting, "In terms of transitional living, he will likely have to reside in his own apartment in the community after transitioning from your home. Reason being, virtually all adult transitional living programs are geared toward specified populations." In our first meeting we learned that he couldn't go from the youth detention center to any group living situation, either because of his crime or the populations they served. Mark and I were considering taking him into our home for a period of about six months or so. We knew that he would need a support system and guidance when he was first released before he could be on his own.

We figured out how the youth detention center managed the holidays and how to mail packages to him with extra goodies for Christmas. My daughter's wedding in October had been beautiful, and they were away on their honeymoon over the holidays. On top of the tough year we had with Ezekiel, it was an election year, and we were dealing with stress that some of our children were experiencing. We were so glad that 2016 was over as we celebrated New Year's Eve at a nice restaurant with Mark's daughter and her husband.

CHAPTER 30

REFRAMING MY COMMITMENT

At our first MDT meeting on January 3, 2017, we learned that Ezekiel met the requirements to graduate from high school. It was a very confusing meeting, and after follow-up with the staff at the youth detention center, Ezekiel met the requirements with a 2.26 GPA and 25.5 credits; more than required.

Leo sent an e-mail to the classification officer saying: "*As discussed today, we were surprised and dismayed to learn that Ezekiel may already have sufficient credits to graduate. We have been inquiring about his educational status since he arrived at the youth detention center so that he could graduate as soon as possible and start community college.*"

By the end of January they were able to enroll him in three classes at the community college as dual enrollment with the high school, because technically he couldn't graduate until June.

At the January 2017 MDT, we also learned that they had taken him off all his medications, and they were working with him to stabilize his moods. The reports on his behavior were generally positive at the MDT meetings in the spring. By April he had a job working as a porter for the administrative offices ten hours a week. He was also back on antidepressants by April. I became concerned about how they were taking him on and off medication.

In early March, we learned that Ezekiel wasn't doing well in classes. We brought it up with him during family therapy and he said he had to respond to homework and discussions through an online forum and he was worried people would recognize his name. We talked about it and the teacher worked with him on an alternative accommodation and helped him with his responses to the discussion board.

In late March 2017, I had a particularly troubling phone call with Ezekiel. After returning from a writing retreat, he called as I was sitting down to a meal at a restaurant with Mark. He was able to call on certain evenings from Sandia Cottage. The week before, I had a phone conversation with his teacher, and she said he still wasn't doing his work and he would likely fail two of his classes. During my visits with Ezekiel, when I asked him if he was doing his classwork, he said that he was. I decided to confront him on the call.

"I talked to your teacher, and she said you're not doing well. You're still not doing the work and you will likely fail your classes," I said.

He replied, "I'm not interested in college." Which was a surprise to me.

"Ezekiel, it's not about you taking college classes, it's that you haven't been telling me the truth," I responded.

He said, "Well, the teacher shouldn't be giving you information unless I let her."

"Ezekiel, I had to ask my son to leave and get his own place once I knew I couldn't trust him not to throw parties in our absence when I asked him not to," I said.

"Well, that's probably why he doesn't visit you anymore," he retorted.

That made me angry, he had no clue what he was talking about, and I said, "I'm going to have to rethink having you come to live with us if I can't trust you." I hung up saying, "We'll talk later."

I realized after I hung up that I became very loud, and that people in the restaurant were looking in our direction. It took me a while to calm down, and Mark and I discussed again Ezekiel coming to live with us.

Leo took the initiative to set up a meeting with Dr. Healy on April 3, 2017, for the four of us (Leo, Lily, Mark, and me) to talk with him about how best to prepare Ezekiel for his release, scheduled for March 20, 2018. After my phone call with Ezekiel, Mark drafted a letter that he wanted to review with Ezekiel. Both of us were feeling that the family therapy wasn't particularly helpful and that it lacked direction. In the letter, Mark suggested that we work with Ezekiel on objectives that would help him prepare for getting out. He had me review it and we were planning to share it with Leo and Lily.

A few days before our meeting with Dr. Healy, Mark e-mailed the letter to Leo and Lily saying that he thought it would be good to review it with Ezekiel during our therapy sessions. He also thought we could potentially talk with Dr. Healy about it in our meeting.

The letter for Ezekiel was aimed at having him take responsibility for the future and to show us that he was earnest in his preparation and to create trust in our partnership with him. The fallout related to the community college classes and his untruthfulness damaged the trust Mark and I had with him. Leo and Lily thought we were expecting too much from him, and that he might not be college material. Mark and I had no qualms with him not going to college, but he had to be honest with us no matter what. Leo's demands once he was released seemed to be only that he never used a gun again and that he continued going to therapy. We completely agreed that those were non-negotiables, but we also believed that he had to work toward a future where he could sustain himself financially and stay healthy in the larger sense.

At the meeting in Dr. Healy's office, the tension we were experiencing between Leo and Lily and Mark and I came to a head. Mark didn't hear anything from them about the e-mail and letter he wanted to discuss with Ezekiel, and he was hurt by that.

In the meeting, Mark confronted them saying, "You seem to disregard everything I say, and we are the ones who will be dealing with Ezekiel when he gets out if he lives with us."

Mark got up and went for the door in Dr. Healys' office, and Leo said, "I was hoping we could talk about it in this meeting. We weren't trying to ignore your e-mail; we just haven't had time to give it proper consideration."

I was confused by the whole interaction. Somehow, we managed to finish the hour with Dr. Healy giving us advice on preparing Ezekiel that was based on where he was in terms of maturity and what he was facing.

The next day, Mark wrote a letter saying he was going to back away and take a less active role. He gave me permission to so share it with Leo and Lily. He wrote.

Recently I have taken a more active role in participating in the family therapy sessions, MDT sessions, the secretary meetings and the transition team meetings, as well as visiting Ezekiel during your absence. Notably, my latest action was to propose a plan for us to follow over the next eleven months to accelerate Ezekiel's preparation for his transition, to create opportunities for him to demonstrate his desire and ability to adhere to the three most fundamental requirements of him living with us, and have him prepare contingency plans of action should that not be an option for any possible reason. ...

I will continue to support you, as I have done faithfully for five years, and that it must be in the background is clear to me. So it will be im-

portant that I be kept informed of how Ezekiel is demonstrating those requirements we have agreed upon (effort, truth, cooperation).

I was very troubled by what happened in Dr. Healy's office and even more troubled with how Mark was taking everything. The night after the meeting with Dr. Healy was a sort of *dark night of the soul* or reckoning for me. I was at work the morning I received the letter from Mark, and later that morning we were going to have an MDT meeting and a Transition Planning Meeting with the cabinet secretary. It was clear what I needed to do.

The MDT meeting went first, and I took my place on the couch next to Ezekiel as usual, and when it came time for me to talk, I announced, "Mark and I will not be taking Ezekiel into our home when he is released." Ezekiel looked at me a couple of times with a mix of hurt, embarrassment, and defiance and he shrunk into the couch. Explaining my decision as lovingly as possible, I said, "Based on recent interactions with Ezekiel, Leo, and my husband, I think it's best if we come up with a plan where Ezekiel can establish a residence of his own when he is released. We will support him fully in that process."

In the Transition Planning Meeting I made a similar announcement, and nobody skipped a beat. The lead psychologist said, "I understand, it's a big responsibility," and the meeting continued.

Leo and Lily seemed pleased by the news. Leo settled into the large black leather conference chair and began grilling the cabinet secretary about what options the State had for transitioning Ezekiel. The secretary explained, "We can't guarantee anything, we don't have jurisdiction after he turns twenty-one." It was something I had understood since we began these meetings or even before, when Dr. Alexander talked about transitioning Ezekiel at the Amenability Hearing. I'm not sure what Leo expected.

Over the next few Transition Planning Meetings, Ezekiel's transition plan turned to him selecting a city in Colorado and figuring out how we could help him get set up for success. The transition coordinator did a lot of the work to find out about the services in the city and all of the people we needed to contact and things we needed to do in preparation for his release and thereafter. She developed a plan that grew more detailed over time. She even applied for grant funds for him to get started.

Mark and I were willing to get him to the city he was going to live in, help him find a place to live, and spend periods of time in the area in our own rental to help him get started. That became the basis of the plan. Leo and Lily's role in the actual nitty-gritty of getting Ezekiel transitioned remained unclear to me because it was clear they had obligations to their son and their jobs, but they participated in the planning process.

Mark didn't attend our next family therapy session and it became clear to me during the therapy that there was no good reason for me to attend, either. The therapy sessions wandered, and I felt there were too many people in the room to focus on what we needed to focus on to prepare Ezekiel. Leo accused me of wanting to control things and I decided that the therapy shouldn't be about the difference of opinion between Leo and me. His own need to control emerged because of fear and uncertainty about Ezekiel's future, including the possibility of him hurting someone once he got out. It wasn't something we were able to address in this forum.

I wrote a note to the family therapist saying, "I think we should pause on the family therapy with the six of us for now." There were only two sessions of family therapy sessions planned because Leo and Lily were going to spend the summer in Spain.

Mark and I attended Ezekiel's graduation from Foothill High

School held on June 28, 2017. It was held in an auditorium I never knew existed. It was such a special event. They had a speaker who had previously been incarcerated as a youth and now was a successful businessman. Ezekiel was happy and I could tell he was proud of himself, saying to me, "My dad wouldn't believe I made it." I was sad that his graduation couldn't include his parents, siblings, and our extended family. Mark and I were the only ones in the audience for him. Leo and Lily would have been there, but they were out of the country.

It turned out that Ezekiel had managed to pass two of the three community college classes he signed up for the previous semester. Our conversations during our visits with him became more about what other things, besides going to college, he wanted to do. He started entertaining the idea of becoming an electrician or doing something in the trades, which we wholeheartedly supported. He signed up for a CTech (certified technician) class in the trades on high power electricity. He finished that class by September 2017, and enrolled in a construction class.

In raising our six children, we both took our cues from what our children expressed interest in. We always told them that if they got any education or training for the future, we would help support them financially. If they chose not to prepare in some way for their future, then they would need to get jobs and support themselves. We intended to apply the same principles with Ezekiel.

When Leo and Lily returned from Spain, the Transition Planning Meetings resumed and intensified. It was about that time that the cabinet secretary started attending with her legal counsel. It seemed a little strange to us at the time, but we didn't think too much about it because we didn't know any better and Leo, Lily, and I continued to participate as usual. The meetings usually had many participants, and the director of the youth detention center also started attending on a regular basis. Ironically, the proposals made by the director were similar to what Mark proposed in the letter he wrote before our visit to Dr. Healy's office.

Since Ezekiel had arrived at the youth detention center, we talked about the possibility of changing Ezekiel's name to make his transition easier. In October 2017, his transition coordinator brought in someone from Pegasus Legal Services to discuss the process and what that would mean overall for his future. It would mean that people might not immediately recognize his name, or if they did a search on his name new name, all the media reports wouldn't come up immediately. It could help him in securing a lease for an apartment and a job.

During my visits with Ezekiel, they seemed to be changing his medication quite a bit; they would take him off and then put him back on again. It concerned me, and I could tell when he went off his antidepressants. As the holidays approached, he became moodier and more anxious, primarily because the holidays, Tom's birthday, and the incident all fell in the narrow time between Thanksgiving and January 20th. With the time of his release so close, I encouraged him to stay on his medications; he needed to be in his best state of mind to deal with the next few months.

Mark and I were also preparing for changes in our own lives because I was planning to retire the following year, timing it to occur right before Ezekiel was going to be released. Mark and I were also celebrating our tenth wedding anniversary in 2018, and we had always talked about going on a Mediterranean cruise to celebrate. We moved the timing of the cruise up and decided to take the cruise in November 2017, which is when we had become a couple ten years prior.

CHAPTER 31

THE RUG WAS PULLED

In January 2018, as Ezekiel's release date approached, unexpected media coverage about him began airing. The New Mexico Legislature would begin meeting that month and we initially thought the media coverage was associated with their legislative agenda. New Mexico lawmakers had been trying for years to introduce the possibility of a blended sentence for juveniles who committed serious crimes. Ezekiel's case would be an example.

On January 8, 2018, several local TV news stations reported that the security officer at Calvary said that he had concerns about statements Ezekiel made a few years ago while he was at the county detention facility. He claimed that Ezekiel wanted to kill people from the church. He said the information came from a law enforcement contact.

In the same reporting, one news station reported that the state police chief said to go through everything that Ezekiel may have said during his time at CYFD or any other point in his incarceration to make sure people feel as safe as they can when he's released. If there were threats made, which he said they were trying substantiate, there could be criminal charges.

Ezekiel allegedly made threatening remarks about revenge that he would seek after his release, and those remarks prompted the police to open an investigation. They opened the investigation on January 9, 2018. Eleven different agents investigated the alleged threats by conducting interviews with thirteen people over a three-day period. The youth detention center allowed Ezekiel to be questioned again with no representation or adult present. Ezekiel specifically said to the police that he had no interest in hurting his sisters. Both Carla and Jenny were interviewed and said they did not receive threats from Ezekiel. All the people they interviewed said they had never received any threats. The investigation was closed with no findings and declared inactive on January 23, 2018.

Meanwhile, the police investigation was made available to the public and the media ran with it and read pieces that simply stated that a case was open on allegations by a "confidential informant." They read some of the names of the people being interviewed and allegedly were threatened. They enrolled Ezekiel's sister Jenny in the media circus, interviewing her where she made generalized statements like, "I don't want him released, I think he's a threat." At that point she had not visited or talked to her brother in four years.

Even though Leo and I were given the opportunity to comment, neither of us wanted to enter the maelstrom of nonsense. Leo contacted a civil rights attorney to see if we could push back on the media for putting this kind of information out there. It was one station in particular, and their headlines were extremely misleading and damaging to Ezekiel.

We were crushed and confused. We hadn't heard any threats from Ezekiel; it was never mentioned by his therapist or in any of the MDT meetings. He was bitter and sad that his sisters abandoned him, but he planned to stay away from them. After we got a copy of the investigation report, we realized it was a setup intended to get all of Ezekiel's private records held by the youth detention center, including notes taken by the therapist.

Mark contacted a number of civil rights attorneys once we realized that they used this sham investigation to obtain all private records from the youth detention center. This demonstrated for us that Ezekiel's earnest engagement in therapy and getting better was detrimental overall to his well-being. Ultimately, everything he said, even in the privacy of a therapist's office where he was dealing with his own trauma, would be revealed and used against him. The civil rights attorneys either didn't take cases dealing with the CYFD and the incarcerated or they weren't taking new clients.

Early in 2018, we arranged to have the same psychologist who did the Rorschach test in 2013 conduct another test. We were able to get the permissions and the test was conducted and the results sent to Dr. Healy as Ezekiel's release approached. We met with Dr. Healy on March 6, 2018, and we went over the results. There was a lot of detail presented, but big picture, he said, "Ezekiel goes to facts. He is grieving about loved ones. He wants to find a job, take care of children, and find a hobby but he's afraid that will not be possible. He wants to be in a relationship with someone who is loving."

Giving us direction, he told us, "Focus on rituals and schedule, like regular meals, movies, bedtime. Let Ezekiel know what you expect from him. Teach him cooperation and emotions through an I-thou relationship. Sit together and review your day, best part of the day and worst part of the day. Ezekiel is a work in progress, but not dangerous."

We were relieved to hear that, but with the tumult, we weren't sure what might happen.

It was about that time that we found out that the youth detention center brought in Mr. Thomas, a psychiatrist, to evaluate Ezekiel in late 2017. They didn't let us know until after the fact, and only after we heard it referenced in a Transition Planning Meeting. The head of psychiatry at the youth detention center was very coy with us when we tried to find out more about that evaluation, and it explained why he was initially reluctant to allow us to have Ezekiel evaluated.

Since February 2018, we had been planning how we would get Ezekiel out of the state without anybody noticing. We were working with the director at the youth detention center, and they were willing to meet us out of town at an undisclosed location. We bought a cell phone for Ezekiel. I rented an Airbnb. We were ready to go.

Leo, Lily, and I had a discussion about Ezekiel's move. Leo said, "I don't know when I can go see him and how much time I can spend."

Lily said, "You know my parents are getting old, and our son is in school. We probably can't spend too much time away."

I was glad that both Mark and I were retired; my last day in the office was in February 2018. We were willing to do what we could to get Ezekiel transitioned successfully.

On March 5, 2018, the State filed several motions to stop Ezekiel's release based on this sham investigation, the records they got, and the fact that we were in the process of changing his name. We started meeting with an attorney at Pegasus Legal Services in January 2018, and by March 2018, the legal process to change his name was underway and it was promptly reported in the news.

On March 9, 2018, the Appellate Court reversed Judge Baca's decision and said there had to be another Amenability Hearing. Ezekiel was scheduled to be released on March 20, 2018. He was moved to the adult county jail after a hearing with a substitute judge on March 15, 2018. The State made the case that Ezekiel was a flight risk if he was released before the second Amenability Hearing. Robert issued a statement the day before the hearing.

Media Statement from Ezekiel Pacheco's Legal Team

We are deeply disappointed and concerned by recent media coverage of Ezekiel Pacheco's case. This one-sided coverage, based on misleading and extremely prejudicial information from CYFD, the State Police, and others is irresponsible and unnecessarily raises public fear.

Unsubstantiated reports, never confirmed by the state police, and any comments made over the past five years, made during his therapy or aimed at addressing Ezekiel's personal or mental health challenges, should have remained protected and not used against him.

Much of KOAT and other media outlets' recent reports were based on information from over four years ago and hearsay from sources unfamiliar with all the progress Ezekiel has made with five years of treatment. Since he entered the juvenile rehabilitation system, Ezekiel has received hundreds of hours of individual, group, and family therapy. Ezekiel has already proven that he is amenable to treatment. He has earned a high school diploma and taken community college and vocational courses. Ezekiel's latest psychological evaluation confirms substantial progress and readiness for reintegration into society.

Keeping the public informed is important. However, it is irresponsible to use protected information to stoke unnecessary hysteria and public excitement. We hope KOAT and other media outlets provide more balanced coverage moving forward.

The day before the hearing we also had our last Transition Planning Meeting. The transition coordinator proudly presented a two-inch binder of Ezekiel's transition plan into the community he selected in Colorado. It included information on Ezekiel's name change, housing information, financial support, health insurance, behavioral health, employment, education/vocational certifications, life skills Ezekiel had learned to prepare for his reintegration, natural and

community support, transportation, basic needs, and his recreational/
social plan all for the location where he was intending to start his life.

The cabinet secretary was at the hearing with her legal counsel.
She had also issued various statements to the press about needing to
ensure juvenile offenders were ready for release. It started to dawn
on us why her legal counsel was there. It appeared that she was also
likely working behind the scenes to undermine Ezekiel. When we
saw her legal counsel talking to and sitting behind the prosecution
attorneys at the hearing, it was very clear that they were working
with the AG and DA.

The reversal sent me into a tailspin. It felt like an orchestrated
effort to keep Ezekiel incarcerated. We believed that the appeal
wouldn't go anywhere; at most they might ask Judge Baca to recon-
sider his sentencing of Ezekiel.

Ezekiel took the transition to the adult county jail remarkably
well. We were all concerned. His greatest fear was that the rug would
be pulled out from under him and he wouldn't be released. Maybe
because he had that fear, when it happened it didn't surprise him.

Leo, Mark, and I continued to support Ezekiel in his new, even
harsher environment. The county jail was a nightmare for families
trying to participate with their incarcerated loved ones. They had
specific days you could visit for one hour using video monitors. You
could only visit twice a week and it couldn't be on the same day. They
would go into lockdown regularly, which meant that something was
happening with the inmates that caused them to lock them in their
cells and not allow visitation. If you were on your way to visit or
waiting for up to two hours for a visit and they went into lockdown,
you had to leave. Some of the families traveled two to three hours
to visit their loved ones and they wouldn't get to visit. Sometimes
the video stopped working and your visit was truncated or canceled.

They charged for everything the inmates needed and for phone calls. They recorded telephone calls and video visits.

Leo and I decided we would each visit for an hour each week, and Mark would go with me during our visit. We had to wear headphones when we talked to him and would pass them back and forth.

Ezekiel was in a segregation unit and he wasn't able to take any classes. We sent him a number of books; titles like *The Soul of America* by current historian Jon Meacham, *The Doomsday Machine* by Daniel Ellsberg, *Educated* by Tara West, and *Sapiens, a Brief History of Humankind* by Yuval Noah Harari. He enjoys reading, and while history is his favorite subject, he has wide interests. He was able to see a therapist for about six months during his stay in 2018, and that seemed to help him. He also had a job at the county jail for about six months in 2018.

CHAPTER 32

SECOND BITE AT THE APPLE

The second Amenability Hearing was December 3-7, 2018, almost six years after we lost our family. This time I would not be testifying, but Carla and Jenny would be. We were extremely grateful that Judge Baca was assigned, and we put a lot of faith in him. Janice, Julie, Carla, Mark, Leo, Lily, the cousin from Calvary and her daughter, and I were at the hearing.

Day 1: Robert stood up to address the court.

"The prosecution may duplicate what was presented in the first Amenability Hearing. I ask that you review the Court of Appeals opinion. I ask you to protect against double jeopardy."

The prosecution chimed in saying, "The Court of Appeals said *New Hearing;* the first ruling didn't consider the crime."

Judge Baca responded saying, "Evidence can be provided related to Ezekiel's rehabilitation, as well."

The prosecution opened by projecting multiple pictures of each of our deceased family members on a screen and talking about the family.

"They were protective parents and their household was normal. Tom mentored criminals and sometimes housed them. He taught his son to use weapons to protect the family." The prosecution then went through what happened the night of the murders, including the texting with the girlfriend, and said, "Tom was ambushed by his son. Ezekiel told stories of the deaths that didn't make sense. He was lying." The prosecutor then reviewed the plea, what happened during the first Amenability Hearing and the Appeal. Continuing, she said, "We will show he has not had sufficient treatment to protect society." The prosecution then went through the amenability factors and how they weighed against Ezekiel's amenability.

Robert opened for the defense saying, "Before the Court can sentence Ezekiel as an adult, the State has to show that Ezekiel is not amenable to treatment using clear and convincing evidence. At the last Amenability Hearing they did not do that, and he was sent to the youth detention center. There are options available to the Court, like ordering treatment. All experts believe he is salvageable. Ezekiel still needs treatment and socialization skills. I beg you to use your authority to save this child."

The prosecution called one of the detectives who conducted the interview with Ezekiel on the night of the crime. He gave the same testimony as he did the first time, including the fact that Ezekiel changed his story a couple of times. The prosecution played some clips of the interview with Ezekiel. They talked more about Ezekiel's handling of the guns and where they found fingerprints which they confronted him with when his story was inconsistent. Right before Ezekiel confessed, he made the statement, "It's going to be hard to be called a murderer."

They played a tape of Ezekiel's confession and then discussed the girlfriend. The detective read or summarized the texts. He recapped the day Ezekiel spent with his girlfriend and how the detectives became involved.

The prosecution asked about the impact on the detective, and he testified.

It was devastating the night of the event and thereafter. The way the murders were cold and calculated and Ezekiel's demeanor. Other officers pulled away and sought services.

The prosecution then called the lead detective, the same detective who visited us the Monday after our family died. He went over the same basic facts of his involvement. He discussed all the weapons they found in the house, then began to display the guns Ezekiel used and discuss them in detail.

"Guns don't need to be displayed and handled in the courtroom," Judge Baca admonished. The guns were put away.

They then had Judge Baca watch a fifteen-minute video taken at the crime scene by the deputies. The detective reiterated that Ezekiel's demeanor was matter of fact and that he was personable, polite, and courteous.

The entire presentation by the detectives felt over the top. It was painful to listen to all of the details of the deaths again. Anger at the prosecution bubbled in me; I knew they were trying to emphasize the crime because the appeal was based on their assertion that Judge Baca did not consider the first four factors of amenability related to the nature of the crime.

The next witness called was Ezekiel's therapist at the youth detention center. She testified.

Ezekiel would come to me for therapy and sometimes I would go see how he was doing. I had twelve students who I counseled. Ezekiel wasn't nervous, but he was guarded when I started with him. He was kind, polite, and respectful. We discussed his previous treatment. He interacted with the unit supervisor and classification officer regularly.

Ezekiel had a case worker and one or two staff on the unit all the time. The staff was available 24/7.

His maturity was mixed. His interaction with adults was fine, but he was sheltered and didn't know how to behave with peers. He is above average in intelligence. It took a month to launch into deep therapy. We figured out together what he wanted to work on. I read the diagnostic reports and files from previous treatments to provide direction. We worked on trauma and the depression and anger he felt. We also worked on personal and social development and determining his own identity. We had discussions on morals and values, empathy, and accountability. We built a rapport.

He wanted to work on the anger, which came from his frustration with his peers. They were very different from him; most of them were gang members or drug users. He would often come to me or the unit supervisor and classification officer when he was struggling with his peers. I never witnessed him hitting others. Initially, Ezekiel responded best to the staff that were in the military. He had two friends on the unit, but one left in the middle of his commitment. They all lived in very close quarters. Ezekiel was generally more mature and intelligent than his peers, but he was awkward in social situations.

In terms of relationships with females, he said that he started seeing the girlfriend he had when he committed the crime as a favor to another friend. They planned the crime together. He also had the relationship that he hid at the treatment center.

My assessment of the familial relationships is that there was significant dysfunction within the nuclear family, abuse, and militaristic training; his father was the commander. His mother didn't care for him or his siblings and was emotionally abusive. He did have outings with his father. It's difficult to tell what the future holds in terms of normal relationships. He did build trust with the staff. He has family members who support him, but it will be a struggle to find friendship because he is inclined to distrust.

We watched films that had themes of racism to open the avenues of empathy. Empathy is a struggle for kids who have committed violent crimes. Ezekiel stated that he was racist, but his best friends were black. When we went over the report of his ancestry, he handled it well.

He has anger issues, severe at times—his baseline was high. He angers quickly at times, and most of the time he can bring himself down relatively quickly. He de-escalates by reading, playing or listening to music, breathing, or leaving the situation. He never voiced plans for revenge. At times he would express something like, "I want to punch that kid."

The youth detention center is a protected environment. His trauma history interfered with his ability to assess threats and it was initially distorted, but it got better. Initially there were rumors about threats to him. They discussed it with the group before he came. The unit supervisor was on high alert.

In preparation for his release, we discussed situations he might be put in and how to talk to others. He has more things he has to work on, but he's aware of them. His ability to read others is a mixed bag; because of his trauma he has trouble with reading social cues. He was attracted to a female supervisor and made comments about her. She sat down with Ezekiel and told him that it was not acceptable behavior. He had a crush on his math teacher and had a perception that his aunt was coming on to him, but that wasn't reality. If he was acting on perception, he was generally not good at reading cues. He was good about talking with me about it in therapy. The sexual stuff wasn't much of a focus; we focused on anger and understanding trauma. His history impacted the way he viewed himself and the world, and what he did.

Mr. Thomas's evaluation was done by a different department. Ezekiel's family therapist and I were merely interviewed. I can kind of agree, but in the context of therapy he made himself vulnerable. We made significant progress but there's more work to be done.

There was little opportunity for social interaction at church and the youth detention center is not a normal environment. He's been locked up for six years; these were the years to work on life skills. I believe he wouldn't hurt anyone. Is it possible? Yes. Is it probable? I don't know. I would like him to have support, including therapy and life skills learning opportunities. He does need more.

On cross-examination she testified.

I felt he was on a lot of medication when he arrived. Over time we decreased his medication. He first went down to just antidepressants, then we tapered down. He never refused medication, but I told him to work with the psychologist on medication and decrease them slowly.

He's made progress with regulation of emotion; it's normal to re-gress under stress. His triggers are feeling threatened, he projected what people thought about him and didn't like the way people talk-ed about him and his family. He struggled with victim empathy work, but he did it. He didn't like group therapy. He felt he was different and wasn't interested in gang activity. He perceived that people didn't like him because of his crime. He was hungry for therapy, and we went to a deep place.

Toward the end he was in my office every day, multiple times a day. He handled the transition to the county jail very well, regulating his emotion using coping skills. He never minimized what he did, he took responsibility. He was able to talk about the murders without glorifica-tion or denial.

He's not going to get treatment in the adult criminal justice system. The caseloads are higher and they are focused on severely mentally ill people. He would benefit from working on therapy, social skills, and life skills.

The prosecution then called the behavioral health supervisor who oversaw all the units and who was also assigned to be the family therapist for Ezekiel. He testified.

Ezekiel is polite and respectful toward me. He was standoffish with others. He had a close relationship with one of his peers in the unit and tended to be close with the staff. He wasn't aggressive. He is of average intelligence. He presented himself as mature, respectful, and receptive.

We conducted family therapy from November 2016 through April 2018 to work on communication, conflict resolution, and family history. The family and he were cooperative. Ezekiel made progress. Initially he was reserved and didn't want to talk about the crime. He wanted to talk about the here and now. After a while he would talk about everything. When he talked about the crime, he would show non-verbal stress. His challenge was that there wasn't enough time; he would benefit from more therapy. He did show remorse and is capable of empathy. He would be safe to release with support.

The family was present for all the multidisciplinary team (MDT) meetings, which is not typical. The family was there for everything; they were very engaged in treatment, and other clients don't have that support. Even when Ezekiel was confronted or became uncomfortable, he would continue to participate and didn't shut down. We focused on generational trauma; the family brought difficult trauma into the room and modeled good conflict.

We worked on getting him to look outside of himself and see the reactions of others. Over time he could empathize more. He needs to continue to work on communication skills and expression of his reactions and emotions. For example, he equated crying to being weak. He needs to manage his emotional reaction in a positive way and needs to be more social. Ezekiel's demeanor would change when he would go against a family member or when he would talk about something he experienced growing up.

That was the end of the testimony for the day. Ezekiel's sisters stuck together, and the victims advocate hovered over them. We quickly left the courtroom.

CHAPTER 33

YOUTH DETENTION CENTER STAFF

Day 2: The prosecution called the youth care supervisor for Sandia Cottage.

He used to be the classification officer for Sandia Cottage and conducted most of the MDT meetings we attended. He testified.

I interacted with Ezekiel after I became the supervisor and worked with him Monday through Friday on an 8 to 5 schedule. I got to know Ezekiel very well. When he first came, he was quiet and shy, but as time went on he made friends. He was honest and had a good relationship with the cottage supervisor and with his therapist. There were a couple of the staff he didn't like. Sandia was more structured; the students were age eighteen and up, including violent offenders. The cottage supervisor had strict rules and Ezekiel followed the rules; he liked structure.

I had a feeling he would be assigned to Sandia before he came. I didn't have concerns, but the staff had concerns. They met with the residents ahead of time and they weren't happy when he came; they had issues with his crime. At first they ostracized him, and sometimes they pushed his buttons. He didn't like them much in the beginning, but warmed up to them and in general he got along with his peers. He sought out staff, gravitated toward them intellectually and based on maturity. Ezekiel would stay in my office when he was frustrated; he didn't want to get into trouble. People he didn't like would make fun of his features or talk about his crime. He respected his peers based on their attitude. He didn't like them if they acted dangerous or tough because of gang membership. He didn't think he needed criticism from his peers.

Ezekiel demonstrated racism and superiority. I had him write a paper about it because I was concerned he would spout off and he wouldn't be safe in the community. It got better over time, but Ezekiel said he might pick a community with skinheads. Ezekiel's reasoning for the crime would change. He talked about being in competition with Malachi and that he had to kill his sisters because they were better in heaven. He seemed to look up to his father and had disdain for his mother. He said once that his dad was fired and expressed anger toward Tom's boss.

When he was angry, he would tighten his jaw and crack his knuckles. His coping mechanism was to talk. We were worried that once he got out, he would act out. None of his actions rose to the level of him being restrained; he didn't act out. When he initiated an altercation, they would send him to his room. There was a lot of mutual talking smack between clients that led to altercations. The staff would tease the students.

In general, he was kind to women. He had an issue with one of the female supervisors, staring at her and making comments to other staff. The staff talked to him about how he treated women. He butted heads with Regina and took things better from Leo. We worked with him on trying to see the viewpoint of others. He wasn't realistic about real-life social situations. When he was redirected and felt he wasn't doing anything wrong he would get angry. It was hard to gauge his anger, even if they were just discussing politics.

During plyometrics he attacked a client from behind. Ezekiel would punch himself, for example, when he wasn't performing up to his expectations during exercise. He had no emotion when he talked about performing violent acts, and depending on the act he would get excited. They tracked his progress, and the case workers made entries twice a week and case managers at least once a week. He made progress but he needed more life skills and therapy. Toward the end I responded to more incidents with him. He seemed to regress.

Things he needs to work on are socialization, racism, how he talks to people, and relationships with women. If he is released, I have concerns about how he might respond to everyday situations like being cut off in traffic. I don't believe he can safely be released into society.

On cross-examination, he testified.

My opinion is that the children's court should allow for more time in Ezekiel's case. He's making progress and it's not his fault that they don't have facilities. He was doing tough therapy work, others weren't, and it affected his mood. He thought others were out to get him. He was much better at reading than others, but middle-school level in math. He was raised to be a racist and was triggered by his ancestry report. He had no physical altercations with staff, only peers, and it took a while to calm him down. I am not an expert in trauma or de-escalation. Exercise was a trigger for him because his father forced him to exercise.

The prosecution then called on five other staff members one at a time that worked in Sandia Cottage at some time during Ezekiel's stay. The format of their testimony was the same. They would talk a bit about Ezekiel, talk about incidents where he acted out or when he said racist things, quote things he said in anger, then say they weren't comfortable with him being released. It was very clear that the prosecution coached them to follow that format.

The things they said were similar to what all the witnesses who worked with Ezekiel had said: he's polite, respectful, he liked structure, gravitated to staff, and he worked hard on therapy and at school, and he took both seriously. When they talked about his anger and incidents, they usually numbered about one to five that they witnessed, and they repeated the incidents. When they talked about things, usually threats Ezekiel said in anger, they would also say something like nothing ever came of his threats. They all said his racist remarks were either based on being triggered by being teased or because that behavior was part of the bantering in Sandia Cottage, both with clients and staff. They all said the racist remarks got better over time. None of these witnesses had trauma-informed training, nor did they know how Ezekiel's therapy affected his behavior.

The seventh witness called on Day 2 was a classification officer who worked with Ezekiel for six months. He testified.

We started slow, then were meeting daily toward the end of Ezekiel's stay. His demeanor was guarded. The relationship turned more positive. I have an office on the unit. He was guarded with peers; there was a lot of bullying and a lot of opinions going on. He had a peer he was friends with, and he stuck with that friend.

On cross-examination he testified.

I can administer mental health first aid, and I know de-escalation tactics. Even when Ezekiel was exhausted, he was trying to be a better person. He experienced more anxiety as the end came closer. I helped him manage the anxiety, even after they found out he was going to the county jail. He is ready for community with the necessary support. I am worried more for him because he wants a normal life, but he doesn't necessarily have the skills. I never felt threatened by him, never felt he was going to lash out. Toward the end of his stay he was able to verbalize his emotions more, given he was able to vent.

The next witness called to the stand was the supervisor of Sandia Cottage; someone who we interacted with frequently primarily at MDT meetings and events at the youth detention center. He testified.

Ezekiel was very intelligent, had a strong interest in the military, and was respectful except when he was angry. I had a good relationship with him and I came to care for him. He often regarded his peers beneath him and was aloof. He had difficulties getting along with peers and had physical altercations. Not all were reported. I would deal with things informally with him. He would not mediate well and had issues with race. He didn't get into drugs, and when he was written up it was mostly because of aggression. In his last five months he had five write-ups. He was stressed during that time.

Ezekiel called people hypocrites. Most of his peers learned to leave him alone. He would expect respect from the staff, and based on that he could get angry, go to his room, and cuss under his breath. He was paranoid and thought people were talking about him. His social skills were an issue, but it got better over time. He wasn't tolerant of other people's opinions. I would unpack situations so he could understand them better. Early on he would try to inflict harm on others and wanted to get even.

We worked with a number of staff and family on a transition plan, but it's not guaranteed to succeed. He needs to be in a structured environment that includes therapy for a longer time. He wasn't ready when he turned twenty-one. I would worry about the community.

On cross-examination he testified.

I don't believe Ezekiel is a lost cause; with more work he could be successful. He was paranoid in the beginning, he thought people were out to get him. When he came, people did want to see him fail. Physical activities triggered him; he didn't like team sports and didn't like running. If he goes to prison, he couldn't be in general population, he wouldn't be safe.

CHAPTER 34

THE PROSECUTION'S STAR WITNESS

Day 3: The prosecution called its expert psychiatrist, Dr. Mack. He testified.

Ezekiel was able to describe the crime, why he did it, saying that he killed his mother because he didn't want her as his parent, and his sisters because they were better off dead or in heaven. He wanted to move on with his life. He seemed callous and uncaring. He had minimal medical history. His psychiatric history was that he had hallucinations and anxiety. He had issues with anger, aggression, and violence. Currently he has issues with anxiety and sadness.

Mr. Thomas concluded that he had antisocial personality disorder, which affects the way he interacts with the world. I diagnosed him with antisocial personality disorder. He is uncaring about the rights of others, mean, deceptive, or harmful to others. Personality disorders are regarded as permanent. Psychotherapy is painstaking and takes ten to twenty years. There is no medication for antisocial personality. You can only control the impulsivity or depression. Personality disorders can be properly diagnosed after age eighteen; by age twenty-one you can diagnose with more confidence.

He's currently in county jail. He watches TV and has some interactions with other inmates. He communicates with family and a friend. He reads a lot. He wants to apprentice as an electrician and learn more about financial planning. He is intelligent enough but casts himself as more able than he is. He exhibits grandiosity and bravado. He feels he is smarter than others and won't shy away from a fight, even when he's on the losing end. He is unable to tolerate frustration and actualizes hurt with lack of remorse. For example, killing his sisters. This is part of his personality disorder. His anger is more a reaction to feeling wronged.

His progress is sporadic. He still breaks rules and engages in violence. I do not think he is amenable to treatment.

On cross-examination he confirmed that he had no experience with juvenile justice, hadn't testified at Amenability Hearings, and didn't know anything about the Supreme Court landmark ruling Miller v. Montgomery about sentencing of juvenile offenders. He also confirmed that he made his diagnosis without information from the county jail. He didn't know that the director at the youth detention center said Ezekiel's altercations and write-ups were not extraordinary compared with others; if anything they were on the lower side.

The next witness called was Carla, Ezekiel's half-sister. She testified.

My parents were together until I was three and after that I lived with my mom in Pomona, California. My dad moved to New Mexico when I was thirteen. When I wasn't in school, I would visit my dad and Amy. When I came to visit, I shared a room with Jenny. We would go on trips that were drivable. Amy had the kids in a homeschooling program at Calvary that was state-regulated. Ezekiel wasn't inclined to do the work. Amy was constantly on his case to do his homework. Amy wasn't very structured; she expected Ezekiel to take initiative.

Ezekiel was disrespectful to Amy; he considered her just the woman. Amy came from a hard background. She had to constantly nag him and would say to him, "If you don't cut this out, you're going to end up in prison." She would talk to Tom about it; Ezekiel had more respect for Dad. Jenny and Malachi were more motivated with schoolwork. Amy wasn't physically abusive. She spanked the kids when needed.

I live in California now and I did missionary work, disaster relief logistics, then I was a pastoral assistant; now I'm a stay-at-home mom. After I graduated in 2005, I went to live with my dad and stayed almost three years, attended Bible College, and worked to save money. I also worked at a radio station at Calvary.

My dad's household was normal. While I was in Bible study, the kids would do their schooling. My dad loved Ezekiel. He was very sensitive about his interests and cultivated his interest in music. I never witnessed abuse. I saw him spank him pretty hard. Ezekiel would get pretty angry and cried a lot. He would go to his room and didn't like hanging out with the family. My dad took him on a mission trip not too long before the deaths. It was special because it was just him, not the entire family.

We would do affordable excursions and trips to see the family in California. The home was normal—there was food in the house, sometimes they had to go to the food pantry, and they always had clothing. My dad didn't buy things for himself so he could give extras to the kids. He was always involved at Calvary, food pantry, jail ministry, drug ministry, and others. Those were his people. When God got a hold of his heart, he would give it 100%. He ran groups at church and a Bible study group at home. He ran a God Pod at the county jail and allowed people released from prison to live on his property. He took certain precautions with people living on the property. He watched for issues, was vigilant of sexual abuse stuff. When they came to the door, only Amy or I would answer.

Ezekiel wouldn't do his chores and took things to the extreme, calling it women's work. It was a constant battle with him. He would joke at the expense of others sometimes. He picked on the kids and teased Malachi. He would ridicule our music talent, Jenny and I. Malachi stood up for himself and would leave and go to be with Amy.

There are lots of family in the military; we are proud of their service. My dad didn't run the house like the military. My dad encouraged Ezekiel because he was interested in the military. He was never forced to be a soldier. My dad believed in the Second Amendment. He had guns and taught Ezekiel, Amy, and Malachi to use them. There was an incident where Amy warded off an intruder saying she had a gun. Ezekiel was never forced to stay up or put in a bunker. They ran for exercise as a family and his dad strongly encouraged them all to participate. It was part of the boys' training for wrestling.

My dad couldn't walk me down the aisle when I got married. There are so many experiences that my deceased family will never have with my family. I try to live under the radar.

CHAPTER 35

THE CODE OF JUDICIAL CONDUCT

Day 4: The prosecution called Carla for cross-examination. She testified.

I went to public school in California year-around and attended pre-school. I moved away from living with my dad in 2008, around the time that Ezekiel was eleven. I personally didn't know about all the guns. I wasn't there.

The next witness called was Jenny, Ezekiel's sister. She testified.

This event in my life was very impactful. My dad encouraged me to go into music; now I have a hard time getting back into it. I would like to be like my mom. I miss Malachi, Miriam, and Grace. This thing destroyed the family, especially how close the extended family was. I looked up to my Uncle Leo and I miss him. I live my life scared. I'm sad all the time, trying to rebuild my life. This shattered my world.

The defense called a forensic psychologist, Dr. Ryan. Her credentials were extensive, both medical and law related to juvenile brain development and corrections. She testified.

I train others on trauma. I am well versed in Miller v. Montgomery. I went through an assessment of the various reports. The youth detention center intake psychologist who evaluated Ezekiel over a two- to three-week period considered a diagnosis of conduct disorder and dismissed it. I explored complex trauma and determined there was no personality disorder. I didn't understand why Mr. Thomas did the evaluation in 2017. He used inaccurate and older instruments for evaluation. People who spent time with Ezekiel dismissed the idea of personality disorder. Mr. Thomas failed to consider the environment he grew up in and the environment at the youth detention center. The notes made at the youth detention center on Ezekiel didn't support his evaluation.

Ezekiel's racial remarks reduced over time. Teachers liked him. I was able to talk to Ezekiel. He didn't get the things that most children get as they grow up. Anger was a concern to the staff at the youth detention center. He presents himself as normal, but his ideas when explored are very naïve and he needs to learn the impact of his words. After reviewing all of the behavioral daily progress reports on Ezekiel, he had 82% good days in 2016, 87% in 2017, and 92% in 2018. The vast majority of the days were good before Mr. Thomas decided that he needed to be evaluated.

There were threats to Ezekiel from the beginning; the kids were gunning for him. The reports on him consistently said that he was engaged in individual and family therapy. He was consistently willing to go into hard stuff. He was working on empathy—they never mentioned that he had no empathy. They were helping him to interpret what was going on in the moment. Some corrections officers were sensitive to his difficult work in therapy. Exercise was a trigger; this was acknowledged by the staff, but they never understood why. They missed it as an opportunity for therapeutic intervention. The youth care supervisor reported in December of 2017 that because of therapy his mood fluctuated.

When the relationship with the staff member at the treatment center was reported he was at the youth detention center. In the police notes Ezekiel said he didn't want her to get fired. He didn't understand the whole notion of relationships with people in power. He's not good at judging motives. In my interviews with the staff, the director said his write-ups were on the low side and that he needs life skills. The corrections staff receives suicide training and not trauma training. They made astute observations like, "birthdays and holidays were difficult for Ezekiel, they were gunning for him, he needs structure, more therapy, and life skills." He was irritated with childish behavior because he was being trained as a child soldier. He didn't get to be a child and was mad or envious of children who were acting age appropriate. He was attracted to military people. He didn't have a criminal record or gang mentality. He had fewer scuffles than others.

Ezekiel became more tolerant of people and saw people as people and it created fewer problems. He showed more remorse. He is socially inept, and I fear for him. His family therapist said he routinely came to therapy. He wouldn't be in family therapy unless his therapist thought he had empathy. He got into areas of therapy he didn't initially want to go. His communications skills suffer from what he learned at home, like males don't cry; now he's learning a wider expression of emotions. His therapist said she felt like they were getting places. For example, the impact now of how he grew up. He needs practical application of what he's learned in therapy. He's more able to make judgments about the way he was raised. He doesn't minimize or justify what he did. His interpersonal and sexual development are closer to age nine to eleven years old. He can get there, but we need to take advantage of what he's learned over the last six years.

He made progress, but if developmental trauma were acknowledged, he would have made more. They could teach him about things he should have gotten growing up or that he got incorrectly; repeated over time that changes the brain. Time is of the essence with brain development. He needs doses of good experiences versus negative.

At the county jail he's had one write-up, he's had a job, the corrections staff really like him, and he is in segregation. He had a therapist with a wealth of experience that let him take the driver's seat with the therapy. She said he was engaged in therapy, he wanted to change, and that he understands he doesn't have normal skills. She didn't think he had antisocial personality disorder; she said it was related to trauma. She had to leave the county jail because of medical issues. Ezekiel needs treatment with one central therapist; he needs healthy attachment. Disruption in therapy will stir up attachment issues. He doesn't need a tight lockdown facility. He has a willingness to work on himself. The therapeutic process is one step forward and one step back as new things get uncovered.

Ezekiel understands the trauma from his parents. His mother said she didn't care if he lived or died. His father was his commander and would say ridiculous things like, "Soldiers don't die, they go to hell and regroup." Ezekiel idealized his father as a military man, yet he was in the military for only a short time. What Ezekiel took as normal wasn't normal. When I told him he was brainwashed growing up, he said that it was true. It would have been worse if he denied it.

Tom's natural self was to be a sensitive person, but he learned that his natural self wasn't good enough. There are generational racial issues. Ezekiel had no problem with me as a black woman. Part of his way of dealing with frustration and pushing people away is by making racial comments. Therapy taught him to express himself, but it stirred up feelings of weakness. Exercise took him back to being a grunt.

He hasn't had normal developmental sexual experience. He is awkward with relationships. He had a couple of relationships at the treatment center. These relationships helped him cope with vulnerability. He hasn't had problems at the county jail, and you can get in trouble while in segregation. Ezekiel needs to explore further the family dysfunction. His father wanted to go to war with the government. He wants to be normal, a good person, a good husband, and a good worker.

If he goes to prison, he will be victimized because he is small in stature and young, along with his tendency to allow victimization. In prison there are racial tensions and things divide along rational lines. It will erase the gains he's made on racial awareness. I talked to the director of the Mental Health Co-op as an option. They are very trauma-oriented. He would start out on a ranch, then a farm; they've had success using animals and they provide intensive therapy and a social skills coach.

He has made great strides, he is amenable. He has unmet treatment needs like language, and how trauma makes him vulnerable in relationships. He needs help understanding emotions. He needs help with social skills and learning normative things. It would be better for him to consent to further treatment at a place like The Mental Health Co-op. If he goes to prison it will make him worse. He is not sufficiently treated today to be released.

That was the end of the day. During the testimony, Carla and Jenny told the victims advocate that we were talking too loud, saying things that upset them. The bailiff told us politely to be quieter or use notes. We learned that the prosecution paid to bring Ezekiel's sisters to Albuquerque for every hearing. That struck me as wrong.

On what was to be the last day of the second Amenability Hearing we came early as usual, and the courtroom was filled with people in suits. After asking around, it turned out to be many people from the District Attorney's office and the Attorney General's office. Apparently, the day before when Dr. Ryan went to see Ezekiel in the room behind the courtroom, Judge Baca was exiting the courtroom at the same time. He asked her about a mutual acquaintance, and she responded. It was a short interaction, but the prosecution witnessed it and said he was being partial based on that interaction.

When Judge Baca entered the courtroom he announced, "The Code of Judicial Conduct has been invoked and my impartiality has been questioned. I will follow the procedure and make my decision on recusal."

We were in shock. The prosecution was adversarial the entire week, they took most of the week for their witnesses, and did not abide by the agreements they made with the defense team. They objected repeatedly to the point that it was comical—standing up to object then sitting down again, standing up, sitting down again.

The fact that all those people showed up from the AG and the DA's offices gave us further suspicion that it was an orchestrated effort to send Ezekiel to prison. Everything was in question again and the agony of more time in the courtroom loomed.

PART FIVE
RESOLUTION CAN BE BITTER

CHAPTER 36

REINTEGRATION OPTIONS

We continued to support Ezekiel, who turned twenty-two in March 2019. The State selected a judge from the District Court, an adult court, to replace Judge Baca. Judge Deering would preside for what was essentially a third Amenability Hearing. It was technically the continuation of the second Amenability Hearing, but Judge Deering would be new to the entire case.

Robert said she often favored the prosecution. Judge Deering held an initial hearing to become oriented with the case and determine how things would proceed. She committed to reading all the minutes from the previous Amenability Hearings and all the reports and other evidence submitted during those hearings. It seemed like a huge task for any judge to come in at this point in the case. She had to catch up, but she seemed to be a detail-oriented person and I hoped for the best.

The defense team requested a hearing to petition Judge Deering to allow a therapist visit Ezekiel in the county jail. He hadn't seen a therapist since earlier the previous year. We asked for the same therapist who saw him at the county jail in March 2018. She had since left employment with the county jail. Judge Deering ruled that she couldn't visit, but that the county jail would provide counseling from another counselor. Ezekiel's relationship with the new counselor was helpful; it gave him someone to talk to about issues, but it was not as therapeutic as the sessions he had before.

I began my active journey with gun safety advocacy in January 2019 by participating in work at the New Mexico Legislature with *Moms Demand Action* to enact a law requiring background checks on all gun sales, including private sales. Mark and I had participated passively in *Moms* events before, primarily because the legal case was still pending and I didn't want the visibility or to impact the case in any way. I was now ready to actively participate.

Later in the year I became more active with the *Moms Demand Action* survivor community and took part in a training workshop and gave my first talk at a Gun Sense rally in August 2019, which was an event to increase awareness of gun safety. Mark and I also became active in the *Be SMART* Program within *Moms* and started instructing civic groups and others on the basics of gun safety.

The continuation of the second Amenability Hearing was on April 15-16, 2019. Carla, Julie, and Jenny were there with the victims advocate. Leo, Lily, Mark, and I sat behind Ezekiel.

Day 1: The first witness called by the defense was Dr. Alexander. He testified.

I work with youth who have experienced trauma and the long-term effects of neglect and abuse. I have been working on a model grant program that is community-based for a year. The program's goal is to prevent further incarceration. There are publications on the long-term effects of early trauma. A study of New Mexico juveniles over a year called ACES (Adverse Childhood Experiences-10 Key Experiences) found that based on psychosocial and early childhood data available, there is a remarkable amount of trauma. Trauma that relates to outcomes in the juvenile justice system, relationships, and other aspects of life. This study contributed to trauma-informed care.

The study found that neglect and abuse in early childhood resulted in post-traumatic stress disorder (PTSD). There are also worse long-term effects than PTSD, and the first five years are fundamental. I was aware of Ezekiel at the county detention facility. I was his primary psychiatrist for eight months at the youth detention center. I started with transition planning. Ezekiel made some progress at the treatment center. He was very compromised psychologically when he entered the county detention facility. He was able to tease apart his own thoughts from what had been inculcated.

During his intake at the youth detention center, the multidisciplinary team evaluated him and they discussed the notion of antisocial personality disorder. He did not meet the criteria. It requires consistent violation of others' rights or the rules. He had no prior criminal activity, and his daily behavior over time did not display antisocial personality.

The circumstances surrounding the recent reevaluation by Mr. Thomas were unusual to the point of being unheard of. To do an evaluation at the end of treatment has not been done in the past. The diagnosis of antisocial personality disorder didn't make sense on my visits and evaluation of Ezekiel. A year ago, I looked at Ezekiel's treatment needs. I saw him at the county jail and feel that he needs a supervised and structured transition into community. He benefited from a lot of treatment and education, but he needs practice.

I looked at the letter from the director at the Mental Health Co-op and I think it's remarkable and unique; it's exactly what I would recommend for Ezekiel's reintegration. Abrupt reintegration would not be good. Incarceration would truncate his development, stop his progress, and he is highly impressionable. The adolescent brain mirrors the early periods of sensitive and critical development. It's a period of receptivity.

The clinical and legal definition of amenability is that he has been treated sufficiently to protect society, and that includes within existing available facilities. The clinical definition is the ability or capacity to receive new information and generate new behavior—able to receive care and respond.

Since Ezekiel entered the youth detention center, he was amenable to treatment in the clinical sense. They were able to treat him in terms of danger and we did evaluate the risk. It included the ability to respond to treatment, the original crime, previous risks, substance abuse, and other factors. His risk for violence is quite low. He has no substance abuse, no aggression, and displays adaptive responsiveness. I don't have a concern that he has been treated sufficiently to protect society. The repetition of his type of crime is very rare. There are a number of studies of this kind of violence. He's made progress in every area, including interpersonal responsiveness and social engagement. Every other parameter indicates he is not a danger.

It's usual to the point of being normal that he needs more care. Adolescents lack normal life-rewarding events. They are supervised and educated within a confined setting. You can't give them adequate life experiences which are necessary for every juvenile offender. I worry about the uncertainty of any youth who hasn't had community experience—how they might perform. Many youths continue and have persistent problems, yet none were brought back for a second Amenability Hearing. Ezekiel compares favorably, well ahead of youthful offenders I have seen. Well in the upper quarter for those getting out.

Dr. Mack's evaluation was hasty and rushed; there is not a basis for his diagnosis of antisocial personality disorder. It's not accurate or well supported. Dr. Ryan's evaluation is well supported—very structured. I share her opinion that the least risk exists if he is released to a community-based treatment facility. He needs space to finish growing up. He needs concrete experience, even with inherent risks. Over time, experience can overcome antisocial behavior.

The next witness for the defense was Ezekiel's transition coordinator. She testified.

Transition coordinators are assigned to high-profile cases or particularly troubled clients. We have small caseloads. I was assigned to Ezekiel based on his diagnosis at intake, his high profile, and the fact that he's a youthful offender. I have been assigned to him the whole time. We started preparing his transition plan during monthly MDT team meetings. I began facilitating monthly special meetings as he approached his twentieth birthday. These meetings involved the cabinet secretary for CYFD, his classification officer, his JPO, his individual and family therapist, his aunts and uncles, and me. At times others were invited. We started with New Mexico cities and the conversations evolved because Ezekiel wanted to go out of state.

I reviewed his psychological evaluation to build a foundation of understanding, met with him to see how he presented himself, and helped with transition planning and finding services. The meeting size of the monthly transition meetings was a challenge, as there were so many requirements from different people. It was easier at the MDT meetings. The monthly transition meetings were intimidating for Ezekiel. He had a lot of strong advocates; the family was very vocal which is unusual, and it helped to have family support. I coached him to make sure his voice was heard and part of his future plans. My role is to service the client to come up with a plan that Ezekiel was vested in and that the family and the team thought was sound. I wanted to see him have a life where he could manage on his own.

By process of elimination, we decided on a city in Colorado, because with his name and notoriety we determined he couldn't be successful in New Mexico. The plan covered where he was going to live, how he was going to navigate the community, and how he would get essential documents, services, and employment. I worked with him to create a résumé and on learning how to fill out applications. His classification officer worked on where he would live.

He is very respectful, appropriate—he has an easier time with staff and struggles with peer relationships. Over time he relaxed and became more comfortable and social. I think he's ready to successfully transition based on his support and the detail of the plan, even with struggles. The plan included further treatment, a case manager, and he agreed to go for counseling. I'm not concerned about his anger; I saw him use coping tactics.

The Mental Health Co-op is similar to New Mexico transition centers for juveniles under age twenty-one. They're able to provide gentle support and he's able to put his feet out into the community. I think a place like that would be essential for reintegration, but I'm comfortable with our original plan. Unfortunately, since the beginning I was told he could not go to reintegration, he had to remain locked up until he was twenty-one.

The next witness called was the founder and director of The Mental Health Co-op, a private residence treatment center. He testified.

My approach is to stabilize the client based on their metabolic condition and intervene in behavioral problems like impulse control. My orientation is toward mental health and growth. We address wounding experiences. Most wounding is caused by chaos. I have never received a patient who is presenting at chronological age. After ninety days we will be able to assess a client. We have eight clients under court supervision and provide closer supervision to those who committed murder or attempted murder. We provide both city and farm settings.

Anyone who is placed by the court is assessed by us to determine which unit they would be placed in. The individual would be under twenty-four-hour staff supervision. We provide cognitive treatment, classes, and group treatment. Every sixty to ninety days we send reports to the court on whether they are responding. We could move him after sixty days, but all changes would involve court supervision.

A letter of acceptance and treatment plan for Ezekiel was presented to the court from the Mental Health Co-op. He continued.

We will look at levels of intervention, metabolic and behavioral, and two levels of therapy; how to transition from incarceration to normal living and psychological therapy three times a week. His therapy will assess where he is developmentally, how he has dealt with all of his losses, and discussion about family both dead and alive. All individuals should go back and pick up pieces. He needs life skills, including social relationships and faith relationships—taking the basic parts of self and knowing how to apply himself in relation.

When people are ready, they can be employed two hours a day and will get fifty dollars a week working on the farm. They work with animals or in the kitchen. They can then be employed after training either by us or by seventeen other businesses we have relationships with. I have met with Mark and Regina, and while I'm asking the court to support this option, they have made an initial monetary commitment. I would work with New Mexico if transition back to New Mexico is necessary once they feel safety is not an issue, and I would tell the court if I thought safety was an issue. Alternatively, he can transition to the area where we are located, and we can provide reintegration support.

On cross-examination, he testified.

The facilities are not locked because it is illegal to lock up people in residential treatment facilities, but they are assigned 24/7 monitoring and supervision. Many have ankle monitors. Some of the monitoring staff come from being employed by psych hospitals or prison facilities. Many are trained to take a client down if necessary, including myself. Ezekiel would begin at the ranch or farm. Some residents had a concern about the fact that he killed children, but the staff didn't. There is no certification for mental health, there is oversight by the state. We are an unlicensed assisted living facility.

The next witness called by the defense was the therapist Ezekiel had while he was at the county jail. She testified.

I was asked to work with Ezekiel because of my background in trauma and working with behavioral issues. I had no idea who he was when I took his case and I learned that trauma had a lot to do with what happened. His trauma was self-reported; there were no symptoms displayed while he was in his unit at the county jail that indicated trauma. We collaborated on his treatment. He would bring to the table things he was struggling with, things he was working on, and he worked hard at reconnecting with parts of himself he didn't like. He was very respectful with staff...very respectful with me. I met with him once a week for forty minutes for a total of three months. We started with normal sessions, but later he would reach out to me for therapy.

My theoretic framework is largely trauma-informed; I let the patient bring to the table what they need to work on. I use tools like Cognitive Behavioral Therapy (CBT) and Family Systems Therapy (FST) and work on attaching parts of himself back into the whole. My style, a coffee-house approach, does prove to work. We go deeper faster. It's important for a therapist to provide safety. Ezekiel had more control, and that is very important in trauma work. Ezekiel responded very well. In a supervised environment he could only go so deep, but with him in the driver's seat he worked very hard.

The topics and issues we covered included family dynamics, current and future stressors, and managing jail life. We discussed the event and he was open, expressed regret, remorse, and lots of emotion. He was able to see things from other people's eyes.

He does not have personality disorder, he doesn't have the traits, but he struggles with depressive symptoms. Regarding the traits, people with personality disorder do not recognize the aspects of themself that are problematic, but he recognized when he did something stupid. He didn't use maladaptive behaviors to get what he wanted. Ezekiel did not display sociopathic behavior, either.

His reactions were normal for someone with a trauma background; for example his ambivalent attachment style. He takes steps to achieve something, but then experiences shame and considers himself undeserving. He rejects parts of himself. He was able to self-reflect. Ezekiel responded well to a trauma-informed approach. Our therapeutic alliance was very important. He slowly became comfortable and truly began to engage. We started with easy topics then brought up tougher topics. He was very active in the therapy process and was willing to work on anything to get better and be a contributing member of society.

An ideal transition would be for him to be in a therapeutic environment with the goal of community reintegration. There are no facilities in New Mexico. I like the Mental Health Co-op model because of its step-down program. I like the therapeutic modalities and I like the occupational skills offered. It is very close to what I envisioned for him. He doesn't need to be locked down. An ankle bracelet might be good. His freedom should be progressive.

I'm not concerned about Ezekiel hurting others. I'm more concerned about his safety. He can transition and the community would be safe. He's been treated enough now for the community to be safe, and he would benefit from more treatment. He is amenable to treatment based on his engagement, his ability to self-reflect, his empathy, and his expression of remorse and grief. He has the ability to self-examine, and I didn't see cognitive distortions. He demonstrates the ability to interact with others in a positive way.

CHAPTER 37

THE END OF AMENABILITY

The prosecution closed the State's case by going through the eight amenability factors. For the first four they emphasized how horrible the crime was and that it was premeditated. For the other four they claimed that Ezekiel was making everything up, including his trauma, and that he's deceitful.

The prosecution claimed that the home was more than normal, it was ideal and that the guns were necessary and available for a reason. They cited Carla's testimony several times. They emphasized how terrible the impact of the crime was to the family and law enforcement. They said his sisters live in fear. The prosecution stuck to the diagnosis of personality disorder and that it was hard to treat personality disorders. They argued that many witnesses said that he still needed treatment and that he had anger issues, violent thinking, and limited social and life skills.

The prosecution then went on to quote testimony from witnesses emphasizing the points they made that supported the State's argument and trashed Dr. Alexander. On the last factor they said Ezekiel was a sexual threat, that he had a veracity for telling lies, and that only Carla had firsthand knowledge. The State was worried about all the secondhand knowledge presented. Then they asserted that Ezekiel hadn't changed at all in six years.

The prosecution concluded saying, "All eight factors weigh against amenability for Ezekiel by clear and convincing evidence. The Court of Appeals said that he has to have been adequately treated. We ask the court to find that Ezekiel has not been adequately treated to be released."

The prosecution took a long time and tried to be dramatic about everything and left little time for the defense. It was rude and intentional. I was so annoyed by her demonstration and the audacity of her assertions, in particular that Ezekiel was making everything up and that he hadn't changed at all.

Carla's testimony was a distorted view of reality. She didn't come around much after she left on her mission work. I know because I remember her absence at many big family events like weddings and funerals after 2004-2005, when Ezekiel turned eleven, even when the events were in the summer. She was out of the country for extended periods of time, and she had her adult life to attend to. Her testimony was partly based on when they were all younger. I have photos of that earlier time. Tom was doing well, Ezekiel hadn't hit puberty, and Tom hadn't started treating him like a child soldier. She admitted to not being in the house during the day when she lived with her dad, which is when Amy was supposed to homeschool the children, so she probably didn't know the status of their schooling.

Most obvious was that Jenny didn't testify to what was going on in the house. She was the one who lived there day to day and took care of the children until twenty months before the deaths of the family. She continued to live in Albuquerque after she got married.

She did tell the defense team early on about the abuse, and so did boarders and neighbors.

Robert closed for the defense, saying:

The question before the Court is, "Has Ezekiel been sufficiently treated to be released? "The first four factors were comprehensively addressed by Judge Baca in 2016, and the prosecution got two bites at the apple (the juvenile offender equivalent of double jeopardy, being tried twice for the same crime) with the second Amenability Hearing. Those factors weigh against amenability.

There are three options: 1) Find that Ezekiel has been sufficiently treated. There is evidence to support this, he made a commitment to his family and himself to go to the Mental Health Co-op on his own. 2) Defer the amenability decision for ninety days and allow him to go to the Mental Health Co-op. Conduct a review in ninety days and perhaps give him another ninety days. If he doesn't show progress, the judge can then find him not amenable. 3) Find that he has not been sufficiently treated. I will ask for probation and sentence him to serve the time at the Mental Health Co-op. I filed a motion earlier for option 2 because it is the easiest option for executing the transfer.

On the last four factors, he went through the many inaccuracies in the prosecution's assertions, then said:

The focus today, in 2019, should be, "Has Ezekiel been sufficiently treated?" Ezekiel's maturity was extensively covered in both 2016 and 2019; this factor has remained static. You can't ignore the prevalence of firearms openly accessible. I can't imagine how anyone looking at the progress Ezekiel has made can say that he's not amenable. The burden is on the State to show he's not amenable to treatment.

He walked through all the progress and positive citations of his character made during the first and second Amenability Hearings. He continued.

There are issues of credibility with the State's lone witness; there are other witnesses, the neighbors, boarders, Jenny, and Regina. Carla was at the house on an intermittent basis, Jenny was closer and didn't testify for the State. She reported to Dr. Newman that Ezekiel got hit at least twice a week. The prosecution tried to normalize things when the household was chaotic.

The State made the case that Ezekiel was born racist and sexist. Those attributes were modeled. They assert that the youth detention center is an artificial environment and if he leaves he will go crazy, but at the county jail he's had no trouble. The question is, "What is necessary so that he can be safe in society?" Dr. Alexander and his transition coordinator said Ezekiel was comparable to others released and the biggest concern was with the profile of the case.

The diagnosis of antisocial personality disorder has no validity; not now and not in 2016. Saying he can't be treated flies in the face of reality.

He then compared the psychological experts on the prosecution side to the ones on the defense, and said, "There is no comparison, just like in 2016, in their expertise and the amount of time and effort spent. The Mental Health Co-op can work with him, and they've said that they are willing." He continued.

Dr. Lim conducted a formal risk assessment for the three potential placements: 1) release to the community—moderate risk of violence; 2) prison—high risk for future violence; 3) placement in an intensive treatment facility—lowest risk of violence. The protective factors include family support, no substance abuse issues, and no history of criminality or gang behavior.

This Court must have an open-minded inquiry of available facilities and an open-minded review. No one addressed what would happen if Ezekiel goes to prison. Dr. Berry said in 2016 that it would be "a waste of human life" if he goes to prison. What a waste it would be not only of a human life but of all the treatment he has received, paid for by the State.

That was the end of part two of the second Amenability Hearing for Ezekiel. I was exhausted and so exasperated by the prosecution and the process.

It took until August 9, 2019, for Judge Deering to make her decision on amenability; almost four months after the Amenability Hearing ended and over six and a half years since the deaths of our family. That was the date of our wedding anniversary, and the next day was my birthday. Mark and I were celebrating with my middle daughter, her husband, and her first child, our fourth grandson. We were also celebrating our grandson's first birthday that weekend. I received a Redacted Order Regarding Second Amenability Determination. We knew that the first four factors of amenability would weigh against him since they were concerning the nature of the crime. This is what she concluded about factors 5-8.

Factor 5: The maturity of the child as determined by consideration of the child's home, environmental situation, social and emotional health, pattern of living, brain development, trauma history, and disability: Given the number of years of exposure to profoundly negative influences and the pervasive nature and extent of those negative influences on Child's development, and considering the amount of therapeutic effort required to reverse the impact of these influences, this factor weighs in favor of a finding that Child is not amenable to treatment and rehabilitation as a child in available facilities.

Factor 6: The record and previous history of the child: This factor weighs in favor of a finding that Child is amenable to treatment and rehabilitation as a child in available facilities.

Factor 7: The prospects for adequate protection of the public and the likelihood of reasonable rehabilitation of the child by the use of procedures, services, and facilities currently available: This factor weighs in favor of a finding that Child is not amenable to treatment and rehabilitation as a child in available facilities.

Factor 8: Any other relevant factor, provided that factor is stated on the record: This factor neither weighs for or against a finding that Child is not amenable to treatment and rehabilitation as a child in available facilities under the current posture of this case. The arguments raised by Child under this factor are more appropriately made at sentencing.

She then concluded with her order.

WHEREAS, six of the eight factors outlined...weigh against a finding of amenability, one factor weighs in favor of amenability, and one factor has no weight for or against amenability. This Court hereby finds the State has shown by clear and convincing evidence that:

1. Child is not amenable to treatment or rehabilitation as a child in available facilities.
2. Child is not eligible for commitment to an institution for children with developmental disabilities or mental disorders.

IT IS HEREBY ORDERED that Child shall be sentenced as an adult.

I was devastated and so angry at the process and the system. My daughter tried hard to console me. It took me a day or so, and time with my grandson, before I could block it from my mind. Again, compartmentalizing so I could be present with my family and celebrate my grandson's first birthday.

CHAPTER 38

THE FINAL SENTENCING

Leo, Lily, Mark, Ezekiel, and I worked intensely with the defense attorney preparing for the Sentencing Hearing scheduled for mid-October 2019, two months after the amenability decision. We prepared statements and provided feedback on each other's statements. We searched for options on where Ezekiel could go for treatment. Mark and I took a trip to the Mental Health Co-op to visit the staff. The defense obtained a letter stating they would accept Ezekiel.

After extensive planning and preparing, we went to the Sentencing Hearing on October 15, 2019. It was scheduled to start at 9:00 a.m. Carla, Jenny, Julie, and the cousin from Calvary were there, and each was going to speak.

The prosecution opened, saying that Ezekiel should get the maximum sentence, which was three consecutive life sentences for the children and two consecutive sentences of fifteen years for Ezekiel's parents. A life sentence in New Mexico is thirty years, so they were asking for a sentence of 120 years. They said that Ezekiel hasn't changed. Miller v. Alabama stated that the nature and circumstances of the crime must be considered, and a central point is irreparable corruption. They then went over the event again, detailing every murder, and said he lacked remorse and showed some of the video of his confession.

The prosecution had people read statements prepared against Ezekiel being released. Here are some highlights:

Carla said, "The abuse was made up by the defense team. I believe Ezekiel has a mental disorder and I hope he gets more therapy." She recounted the loss and the impact on her. She said, "Five people, three of whom were very young children who he knew and professed to love, were not safe around him. The question must be asked, then who is?"

Jenny got up and talked about the three kids and how she misses them, then talked about her mother and father.

Julie got up next saying, "I miss my father. Hate is not the way to live your life. I forgive Ezekiel, even though he didn't have empathy. You can't teach empathy or remorse."

A friend of Tom's from Calvary who spoke at the first Amenability Hearing got up and said, "I knew Tom as a Chaplin, he did pioneer work in the jail. He was a mentor for me. You must make sure Ezekiel is not a danger to society. Working on redemption of prisoners was Tom's ministry. I hope Ezekiel finds redemption."

The cousin from Calvary spoke, saying she missed Tom and how he mentored her children. The two detectives who testified got up and talked about the impact on their lives. They spoke of what lingered with them from the night they went into Tom's house after the murders.

The lawyer then read letters. The first was Janice's, which said, "I urge you to listen to my nieces, they are closer to the situation. I hope Ezekiel will get help. The family impact was devastating." She then read a letter from another of Ezekiel's half-sisters and from a friend of Jenny's who attended Calvary.

The prosecution then summarized saying, "Ezekiel committed crimes outside the norms; he is irreparably corrupt. He hides and blames, and he has not changed. He deserves the highest penalty."

Robert got up and said, "The Court should look at this through the lens of Miller v. Alabama," and cited an article by Thomas Grisso: "When it comes to heinous crime, the crime itself should not be the only thing to consider for children."

He discounted the testimony of the prosecution's expert witness, Dr. Mack, based on his lack of experience with adolescents and said, "Ezekiel has overwhelmingly shown he can be rehabilitated, contrary to the State's argument." He referred to a court brief that states how vulnerable teenagers are to peer influence and said, "No doubt that we wouldn't be here had it not been for the influence of the young lady. There is greater influence for reform of teenagers as they go into their twenties. Recidivism is unlikely in cases like Ezekiel's." He referred to a current inmate and said, "The prison system is desperately lacking therapeutic support. This man, despite many obstacles, aged out of criminal behavior. He received two life sentences, he struggles between hopelessness and having hope. We need to come up with a creative solution for Ezekiel."

In the process, he entered a number of exhibits including letters, legal briefings, and articles to include memos of the interviews of neighbors, boarders, Carla, and Jenny done by the defense team early in the case. He said, "A neighbor said that the household was dysfunctional and chaotic. A boarder described things in very dark terms. The dependency factors and rehabilitation potential must be considered before sentencing."

He called Dr. Alexander to speak before the Court. He said:

I know Ezekiel's case well, I've seen snapshots over the last six years and I got to see the transformation. At the time of the crime he lost touch with reality, he was psychotic, not due to neuropsychology but due to trauma. He shared his psychosis with his family; ferocious, paranoia, racist, authoritarian. I've seen many abused kids. Ezekiel presents as abused, he has a fragmented personality. This is not about his father, but about his father's actions. At the youth detention center there was significant hostility toward Ezekiel, yet he formed relationships, presented as a normal adolescent, and dealt with unrealistic stuff like racism that he had been taught growing up.

There is lots of culpability in what happened that night; CYFD, the neighbors. There was a report we got at the youth detention center that mentioned all the missed signals; that night was preventable. Is he damaged forever? The answer is self-evident. He won't be completely unmarked, but it doesn't mean he is dangerous. Ezekiel was at the top of the class at the youth detention center. To complete his rehabilitation he needs a greater degree of freedom, a safe setting, consistent with the defense's proposal.

In the majority opinion of Graham vs. Florida, "Children are more capable of rehabilitation and children should not be deprived of maturity."

Dr. Lim spoke next; he is an expert in forensic psychology who did the risk assessment on Ezekiel. He said:

I was called to evaluate if Ezekiel was a psychopath; he is not. I was called back for a risk assessment by Dr. Ryan. I reviewed all written reports from psychological experts, all records from the county detention facility, the treatment center, the youth detention center, and the county jail. I talked to the director of the Mental Health Co-op about the programs offered and safety measures.

He then discussed the Miller v. Alabama decisional factors, and continued, saying:

Ezekiel was developmentally delayed; he suffered a TBI because he was slugged in the face. He had low intellectual level, and functioned three to five years younger. This relates to texting a twelve-year-old girl-friend, and he is much more vulnerable to peer influence. They found him to have a learning disability and he was behind for his age. There was the presence of psychosis based on trauma or incredible stress. Based on testing he was not malingering. He demonstrates self-control by following the rules. At the youth detention center his treatment gen-erated loss of control, and at the county jail there were no behavioral concerns. He was able to delay gratification as demonstrated by the fact that he got a high school diploma.

Another dependency factor was his home environment. He lived in a world where he had very little control over his life. His ability to express himself was severely restricted. It was a bizarre home. He was taught that firearms were to be used against people. Tom abused animals and modeled preemptive violence. Ezekiel couldn't just leave; he was controlled very tightly. He couldn't go see friends. In these cases, there is usually an external person who helps. Ezekiel couldn't have that. His mother was abused herself and was utterly obedient to Tom. She inflicted psychologic abuse, which leaves the child looking around for someone to love. His situation was so narrow, it was a prison; he couldn't go to a teacher or anyone.

He was trained to be a soldier. His greatest goal was to go to the New Mexico Military Institute (NMMI). He patrolled the compound; there was a chain of command. His abuse of animals, small innocent creatures, is a sign that a child needs intervention. His first intense rela-tionship was with a twelve-year-old. The texts were sent two or three at a time at the same time the auditory hallucinations were encouraging him to do the crime. This reduces his culpability; there were factors outside his power, and it bodes well for rehabilitation. Ezekiel never learned to solve problems. He was socially inept and had no clue how to relate to females; he needs treatment for that.

Based on the research I did, the potential for violence if he is imme-diately released is not likely. If you evaluate him under the curve with other children the signs are very positive. He works toward goals, he works in psychotherapy because of a bond with the therapist, and he has done this in multiple settings. Personality forms into the early twenties. We used to think that if an adolescent does a really bad crime, they should be locked up. These days there are buckets of studies that show there is very little recidivism. The notion that he has a personality disorder, first of all he's too young; second, people with personality disorders are always trying to pull one over on others.

If we're going to do the best job, his treatment has to be targeted, a program that can treat him in a sophisticated way. Prison is a bad idea because adolescents will be rearrested within three years after release. They can't be vulnerable in prison—they have to be paranoid. It is highly likely that he will be victimized in prison. He will be a target. He will probably need to be put in protective custody. In a highly structured environment, he can learn autonomy. He needs to be socialized; he is functionally twelve to thirteen years old. In prison he will be socialized into a gang, which is an authoritarian family structure. His mental health status will deteriorate, and he will end up in segregation.

The prosecution took the floor again and discussed what the expert in the first Amenability Hearing said about predatory violence. She then went on to repeat many things she said before and refuted what Dr. Alexander and Dr. Lim had just said. She said Ezekiel would be OK in prison. She took significant time that was allotted to the defense. It was 4:10 p.m. by the time the statements for the defense were able to be read.

Lily and Leo read their statements; each were about fifteen minutes. Leo talked through the timeline with the family since the incident, citing statements and petitions we made united as a family and said:

Unfortunately, the family unity that we shared in the first two years after this tragedy fell apart. Some of those who said they would support a juvenile sentence and stand by Ezekiel changed their minds. Encouraged by the prosecution and joined by some others who have not been involved in the case or Ezekiel's treatment, they launched an aggressive campaign to appeal Judge Baca's decision and to ask the Court to sentence Ezekiel as an adult.

Over the past few years I have often felt like we were pawns in a larger legal and political battle between prosecutors, the media, the former governor, Calvary's attempt to protect their image, and the broken judicial and social welfare systems. It is something no family should have to endure on top of such a tragic loss.

Unfortunately, I believe politics and PR more than science, fairness, or public safety have driven this case. After Judge Baca ruled that he was amenable to treatment, the former governor directly intervened to make sure Ezekiel's behavior was under a microscope at the youth detention center. Politics drove the governor's decision to take the unprecedented move to have her CYFD cabinet secretary and legal counsel directly involved in Ezekiel's transition meetings. Three of the governor's appointees to the Appeals Court, who were up for election at the time, then made an unexpected and unprecedented ruling overturning Judge Baca's decision. Even though he is considered one of the most respected and experienced Children's Court judges on the bench, they questioned his decision. Then the prosecution and their public relations staff used every legal maneuver and PR tactic they could think of to win, even questioning Judge Baca's ethics based on an innocuous conversation he had with a defense expert to get him to remove himself from the case. The prosecution and their PR staff (working with Calvary officials) have done everything in their power to make sure the deck was stacked against Ezekiel.

Along the way, the Victims Advocate office, rather than trying to represent all the victims and bringing the family together to reach a fair decision for all, has fueled division and acrimony among the family. Unfortunately, the Public Defender's office does not have an "advocate," much less public relations staff like the prosecution, whose job it is to actively push their narrative with the media. They used Calvary, the state police, and others to orchestrate testimony and manipulate the media all so that the prosecution—not our family—could claim victory. Your honor, there's no victory for our family. We lost five family members already. Now we will lose another if they get their way.

He went on to ask Judge Deering not to sentence Ezekiel to prison where he might die, but to opt for treatment instead.

Lily talked about how she supported Leo through the six-and -a-half-years and how big an impact it made in her life, but she believes in Ezekiel.

I went next and Mark, who would go after me, went up with me. I felt pressure to read my statement quickly. Judge Deering wanted to end by 5:30 p.m. and Ezekiel was still going to speak. I covered the timeline of my experience with Ezekiel since the very beginning. Because I was speaking too fast and trying to summarize on the fly, I did a horrible job. Mark, on the other hand, decided that the people speaking on behalf of Ezekiel had been robbed of our time and he was going to take the time allotted to him.

In his statement, he reviewed all the obstacles that Ezekiel had to overcome, starting with his home environment. He talked about his experience as a Court Appointed Special Advocate (CASA) volunteer, where he learned what to look for and how to report when visiting families' homes. He said, "I cannot speak of direct child abuse as I never witnessed any. I can without a doubt report to you the harmful neglect of the Pacheco children. ...There were signs of inadequate food, educational neglect, medical neglect, unsanitary conditions, unsafe household hazards, and an unsecured firearm arsenal." He went on to describe what he saw.

Mark then went on from there to discuss the many times when Ezekiel could have given up but didn't. He ended with how well Ezekiel did after they reversed Judge Baca's decision for his release and sent him to the county jail.

Ezekiel spoke for the first time in public. He was soft-spoken. He turned to his sisters and apologized, saying, "I'm sorry for taking our parents and our sibs, I wish I could take it back, but the reality is that I can't." He went on, "I want no retaliation. I love you guys, and I want to see the best for ya'll, whatever you may do, and I do pray for you guys to have healing, the way I'm having healing." Then he turned to Leo, Lily, Mark, and me saying, "After it happened, I thought I would be all by myself. You've shown me what forgiveness is when I expected retaliation and abandonment. Nobody has showed me that kind of mercy and that kind of compassion the way you guys have, and I am so damn grateful to you guys." He then addressed us individually, talking about the relationship and thanking each of us, saying, "One thing you guys have given me more than anything else is hope. Hope in a better future, hope in a better self."

When he said to Mark, "You've basically been a second father to me. You're the father I wish I had," Carla started crying and got up and stormed out of the court. Ezekiel glanced at her but continued. He ended asking Judge Deering to give him a chance.

I knew how hard that was for him. He had worked on what he was going to say and practiced for weeks before.

CHAPTER 39

THE JUDGE'S ALTERNATIVES

We received the Redacted Sentencing Memorandum and Decision on November 1, 2019, two-and-a-half weeks later, by e-mail. The sentencing memorandum gave the background, context, rationale, and ended with her sentence in a lengthy conclusion.

Conclusion

Defense's presentation highlights the likelihood that the Department of Corrections has limited ability to provide appropriate rehabilitation for Defendant's needs. Additionally, lengthy incarceration in an adult facility is likely to result in negative behavioral and mental health consequences for Defendant that would essentially unravel the work accomplished while Defendant was treated in the juvenile system. ...

What is needed to balance both what is best for the community and what is best for Defendant does not currently exist as a resource for the Court to consider today. If such a resource does exist, it has not been presented by the parties. The Court would favor the ability to impose a suspended sentence that provides for a term that ranges in the number of years and allows for further rehabilitative efforts specific to Defendant's needs in a locked treatment facility. ...

But what the Court lacks is the ability to impose a sentence upon a youthful offender resulting in placement in a locked treatment setting beyond age twenty-one, even in situations where the offender has shown motivation to rehabilitate and progress. Without this option, what remains is the distressing result of Defendant's incarceration with the most serious adult offenders, exposure to violence, and all the negative influences Defendant and the professionals within the juvenile system worked to counteract.

Given the options presented, the Court essentially has no choice but to protect society at the expense of Defendant's continued trauma-informed treatment since such targeted, sophisticated treatment is not available in the Department of Corrections. A sentence that addresses punishment and provides for the immediate protection of society, based on Defendant's current level of rehabilitation, will likely undo the work accomplished through the juvenile system and place the public at greater risk in the future. The Court recognizes the failings created by the sentencing option of incarceration and would much prefer a different alternative that would allow for continued treatment in a locked setting, if one existed. ...

Therefore, in a case such as this, a parole review is necessary as protection to ensure release only at a point when the public will not be subjected to an unreasonable risk of violence. Consequently, Defendant's sentence will include a life sentence with the possibility of parole. Under such a sentencing scheme, Defendant may obtain parole release based on a demonstration of maturity and rehabilitation. When serving a life sentence, Defendant must serve at least thirty years imprisonment before the possibility of parole and without good time credit eligibility. ...

A sentence of seven years is imposed on the charge of second degree murder as charged in Count One. ...

A sentence of seven years is imposed on the charge of second degree murder as charged in Count Two. ...

A sentence of life imprisonment with the possibility of parole is imposed on the charge of intentional child abuse resulting in death of a child under twelve years of age as charged in Count Six. ...

A sentence of life imprisonment with the possibility of parole is imposed on the charge of intentional child abuse resulting in death of a child under twelve years of age as charged in Count Seven. ...

A sentence of life imprisonment with the possibility of parole is imposed on the charge of intentional child abuse resulting in death of a child under twelve years of age as charged in Count Eight. ...

The sentences on Count One and Count Two shall run concurrent to one another. The sentences on Count Six, Count Seven, and Count Eight shall run concurrent to one another and consecutive to the sentences on Count One and Count Two. Defendant shall serve the sentences on Count One and Count Two before earning credit for the sentences on Count Six, Count Seven, and Count Eight. Defendant shall be awarded 2,476 days of pre-sentence confinement credit, from the date of arrest, January 19, 2013, until the date of sentencing on November 1, 2019, and post-sentence confinement credit from November 2, 2019, until delivery to the Department of Corrections. Defendant shall not have any contact with his siblings, unless the sibling initiates and welcomes the contact.

It was a heartbreaking sentence, two seven-year sentences for the deaths of his parents served concurrently and the opportunity to use time served, plus three lifetime sentences served concurrently with the possibility of parole only after he served the full thirty years. This meant they would not even consider him for parole until age fifty-two.

Her logic in the sentencing was that since the defense presented evidence that the greatest risk of Ezekiel reoffending is if they incarcerate him in an adult prison, and we have nowhere else to put him since he's a juvenile offender over age twenty-one, then we must keep him in prison for a life sentence. She made the choice to throw him away even when offered an alternative at a public adult treatment center that we were willing to pay for and that accepted Ezekiel. She maintained that it had to be a locked facility, even with extensive testimony that a locked facility wasn't required, an ankle bracelet would be adequate, especially since he would be secluded on a farm.

I was beside myself. I wrote a letter to my best friend Gwen. I also sent a version of it to many people close who were interested in my journey with Ezekiel.

November 7, 2019
Dearest Gwen,

It is with great sadness that I write this letter. About a week ago we received the sentencing order for Ezekiel from Judge Deering. She has opted to give him a total prison sentence of thirty-seven years, but he gets credit for time served so he will serve thirty years from the date of January 19, 2020, and in 2050 he will go before a parole board and basically undergo another trial. He will be fifty-two, almost fifty-three years old at that time and there is no guarantee of release.

Judge Deering wrote that since he had made good progress with his therapy over six years, she would have preferred an option of a locked facility where he could continue trauma-informed treatment. The only option the defense was able to provide was an unlocked facility with 24/7 supervision and an ankle monitor. She wanted an option that carried zero risk to society, and there is no such thing for juvenile offenders once they reach the age of twenty-one in New Mexico. Somehow the bureaucracy of the corrections custody process did not facilitate using another state with juvenile facilities that provide treatment until age twenty-five. If that had been an option, perhaps it could have been combined with the option the defense provided at the Mental Health Co-op.

The only hope at this stage is a movement in New Mexico to pass a law in the state legislature either in 2020 or 2021 that requires a review of all prison sentences for people who committed crimes as minors once they reach age thirty. While I will support this effort, it feels like a long shot because first, the law must pass, second, Ezekiel would have to survive (not get killed) in prison for another seven and half years, and third, the review would likely be very similar to what we just went through and would require that he remain squeaky clean in prison until that time. Our fears are that he is likely going to be a target in prison based on his crimes and his physical size and attributes, and that prison is a very hard and hardening environment. He is unlikely to receive any treatment or counseling there. A small consolation is that he did receive six years of therapy over the last almost seven years, he graduated high school and reads a lot, and he is now twenty-two years old. It would have been much worse if they sent him to prison as a minor or at age eighteen.

I cannot express the level of sorrow and despair I feel about this outcome. It feels like a death. It feels like a continuation of a story I have been living since Tom and I were kids. I witnessed many of Tom's struggles, humiliations, abuse, and his reactions to those, including joining the gangs in Los Angeles after going AWOL from the Army 82nd Airborne. I tried desperately to help him in high school and college. When he ultimately joined the gangs and was drinking and doing drugs, I feared that I would get a call at any moment that he was dead. I feel as though I am in that place again with Ezekiel going to prison.

While Tom ultimately "gave his life over to Christ" and became a minister, it was clear that he never really healed his own trauma. I pray that I can remain hopeful that the story will turn out different for Ezekiel and that prison won't damage him too much, and that he will get out.

This whole tragedy was a perfect storm, and I am angry at the system. Many systems failed leading up to what happened that fateful night when we lost five family members.

I am deeply disappointed and disheartened with our society, especially family members, who have such backward and retributive notions of justice, especially for children who commit crimes. What they advocate for amounts to "an eye for an eye," revenge, and vengeance, some in the name of "Christianity." What happened to restorative justice or rehabilitation? It is such a sad indictment of our country. I still carry the grief of losing Tom, Amy, and three precious little ones in such an unimaginable and tragic circumstance. With everything else going on in this country, the world, and to our planet, I find myself weeping and I struggle to find breath sometimes, let alone hope.

I am struggling to integrate my love and commitment to Ezekiel (and Tom) with the rest of my life. He still needs an advocate, someone in his corner. I feel as though I must compartmentalize it because I do not want it to become my identity and mood, and I don't want it to contaminate my relationships with Mark, our children, our grandchildren, friends, and others.

I know that this does not define me, but it feels so big right now. I know I will hopefully gain perspective, but I fear it will leave a deleterious effect on me. I relate to the quote in the movie Lord of the Rings, Return of the King at the end when Frodo said, "How do you pick up the threads of an old life? How do you move on when in your heart you begin to understand there is no going back? There are some things that time cannot mend, some hurts that go too deep—that have taken hold."

Please pray for Ezekiel, please pray for the family, and please pray for me.

I love you, Regina

I received several heartfelt responses based on my sharing. Gwen e-mailed me back.

Dear Regina,

I just finished reading the letter that you sent about Ezekiel and the court ruling. My heart is very heavy and filled with great sorrow from this news, and for you and for your family, for Ezekiel, and for the whole wretched system. All the things you brought up are so valid. There is much to think about and much to process.

I am truly sorry to get this news. I was very hopeful that things could turn out better. I am going to just have to sit with this for a little while before I can figure out any kind of reaction.

Love you back my dearest, hugs, Gwen

CHAPTER 40

MANY SYSTEMS FAILED

There are so many ways that systems fail and betray children. What happened to my family was a perfect storm; a case of multiple systems failing in a way that manifested a tragic and unimaginable outcome. It highlights how society takes for granted the systems they rely on to operate at a nominal level so that families and society will be OK even if there are a few bumps along the way.

What are the systems that we depend on that failed in this case? Starting with the smallest system and working outward from there. Ezekiel experienced a mental breakdown; his brain failed. He experienced abuse, neglect, and isolation that resulted in a psychotic break. He grew up in a family and community who regarded psychology and psychotherapy as a cult. He was afraid to say anything to his parents about his visual and auditory hallucinations. Because of his isolation, there were no teachers or counselors who might have caught signs of his abuse and brain illness. Every adult needs to recognize the signs of brain illness, especially parents. Rudimentary training should be offered to parents, teachers, clergy, law enforcement, and any community members who play a role in the lives of children so they recognize the symptoms of a potential problem with a child's mental well-being. It shouldn't be stigmatized.

The next layer is the family system, including the nuclear family, the extended family, and his church family of which Ezekiel was a part. Tom's family was exhibiting signs of struggle. He didn't reach out for help that I know of, but there were signs. In his nuclear family, he was able to exert his will on Amy and establish a normality that was detrimental to the health of the children; it wasn't a functional family. This is enabled by our culture of rugged individualism. As part of his extended family, I overlooked signs and hoped things would be OK. Partly because I was just so relieved that my brother was no longer in a gang in Los Angeles and that he seemed to be making a life for himself through ministry. Tom and the family spent significant time at Calvary, and they ended up firing him. I often wonder what they observed about Tom and the family, and made the choice not to intervene in a constructive way. What was the real basis for them firing Tom?

The next system that failed as we move to larger and larger systems was the social safety net offered by our city and state. CYFD and Animal Control were called to intervene in the family about four to five times, and allowed themselves to be chased away by Tom without visiting the home or talking to the children. One call to CYFD was because someone at church noticed that Miriam's teeth were rotting. Another call to Animal Control was because of animals that weren't being cared for, including horses that ate the bark of trees in the yard as far as they could reach. In this case they disregarded policy that called for them to visit the household.

Ezekiel shared that he felt he had no way out of what he lived with. In the article "Tragedy in the Family: When kids murder their parents," Kathleen Heide lists characteristics of kids who kill, including evidence of family violence, attempts to run away or commit suicide, isolation from peers, increasingly intolerable family situations, children feeling helpless to change the home situation, inability to cope with what is happening, no criminal record, and a gun available in the home. There are several articles about kids killing parents or family members, and the characteristics are similar. Part of the state and local social safety net should be one way, or multiple ways, for kids to get help when they are in bad situations or feel desperate. I asked Ezekiel if he had a way to anonymously report what was happening, if he would have done that. He said, "Yes, probably. If my dad didn't know, because he would probably kill me."

Part of this larger system in our state is the New Mexico Department of Education, which allows families to simply declare they are homeschooling and there is no follow-up or accountability. This needs to change with laws passed in our legislature. The Coalition for Responsible Education (CRHE) was founded in 2013 to address a problem: the use of homeschooling to isolate or abuse children. There are many children who will become adults without proper education, and potentially suffer abuse and isolation as Ezekiel did, and it will go undetected. I have friends who do homeschooling well, and they would gladly submit to any requirements associated with accountability.

Crossing the boundary of the state and national systems, our justice system failed beginning the night that they arrested Ezekiel. Jenny was in the police station and yet she was not invited to talk with her brother. The deputies didn't contact any of the family even though Jenny gave them my number. There were no social workers or legal representatives called the night of his arrest before they isolated him in a room with at least two adult deputies. They knew that Ezekiel had not slept for two days. There is no evidence that the detectives were trained in mental illness. It was obvious to me when

I first saw Ezekiel that he had undergone some kind of psychological break. Ezekiel was a minor, fifteen years old, he weighed 100 pounds, and yet they eagerly interrogated him and got a confession with no family member, no attorney, no one who might have recognized his state of mind, or any adult representation present. This can change with laws intended to reform law enforcement practice. There should always be a social worker available to a minor when they are arrested.

Additionally, the juvenile justice system provided two choices in this very complicated case; he stays in the juvenile system until age twenty-one and receives treatment or he spends his life in prison. The juvenile justice system in our state and many other states is broken. It does not serve our children, as demonstrated by Ezekiel's case. We were very grateful that Ezekiel got into the treatment center where he was treated with therapy and got a proper education. Both the county detention facility and the youth detention center were problematic.

The county detention facility did the bare minimum. The youth detention center was hostile, and Ezekiel's therapy essentially worked against him because the State was both treating him and trying to get him sent to prison. There is a conflict of interest, especially when you factor in the role that the Victims Advocate office played in dividing our family. They didn't advocate for the family, they essentially advocated sending Ezekiel to prison. The fact that the DA so easily got his therapy notes takes that conflict of interest to a whole new level. Very few corrections officers have trauma-informed training, and yet most juveniles who are at the youth detention center have experienced trauma, as the Adverse Childhood Experiences (ACEs) study that Dr. Alexander discussed in court concluded. The Victims Advocate office must be independent from both the DA and the Defense; they should not bias the outcome of criminal cases. The civil rights of children in custody must be sacrosanct and subject to criminal penalties.

After Ezekiel's incarceration, Leo, Lilly, Mark, and I advocated hard for him. We put in countless hours making sure he got his needs met, including making up for years of neglect, and helping with his legal situation. We invested our own social and political capital for his wellness and future. Doctors, attorneys, therapists, and staff at the facilities mentioned multiple times how involved we were, and how unusual that was. Yet the facilities were often difficult to engage with and sometimes outwardly hostile. We were persistent. Many families are discouraged by the level of effort and hostility they are met with at these facilities. These State facilities should encourage and welcome engagement of parents and family; they need to be accommodating and open to that involvement. Imagine all the children that do not have sufficient advocacy and support; they just fall through the cracks.

The fact that we have a juvenile justice system in our state, and many others, which is so out of date with scientific understanding, is inexcusable, especially since we have a premiere Brain Research Center in New Mexico. The first clinical Magnetic Resonance Imaging (MRI) scanners were installed for clinical use in the early 1980s. I was a systems engineer at a company that built MRI systems in the early 1990s. We have done detailed brain scans for forty years now. We have learned so much about the brain in that time, and one of the things we've learned is that it takes a while for the brain to mature, for most until their mid-twenties. We've also learned that chronic trauma, malnourishment, and head trauma delays brain development. Yet we have a system in many states where juveniles can only stay in the system as a juvenile and get treatment until they're age twenty-one. The only other option provided after age twenty-one is adult prison, where there are virtually no services for them and rehabilitation is no longer their goal. New Mexico has considered offering current juvenile facilities to youthful offenders up to age twenty-five for years, especially in these types of complicated cases. This needs to be made the law, perhaps by court order.

Next is our state and national safety system related to firearms, which is incredibly complicated in this country and pivotal to what happened the night when Ezekiel had a psychotic break. My brother had an arsenal of weapons that he acquired through private sales, including two AR-15 weapons and fifteen thousand rounds of ammunition, all unsecured and stored with ammunition. Ezekiel would go with him to purchase these firearms. Ezekiel reported that Malachi pulled a handgun on him sometime in 2012 when he got angry. It is utterly irresponsible to have those firearms readily available when there are four children in the home, and one is a teenage male.

According to Everytown for Gun Safety, "Annually, more than 3,000 children and teens (ages zero to nineteen) are shot and killed, and 15,000 are shot and wounded—that's an average of 51 American young people every day." The impact of this extends far beyond the deaths and injuries. Ezekiel is an example. It affects the immediate family, the extended family, and the community. It is exceedingly expensive as well; consider all the costs in the aftermath of what happened, the police investigation and prosecution, the legal and other services Ezekiel received, and the costs of incarceration. Passing simple laws like requiring and enforcing background checks on all firearm purchases, red flag laws, and safe storage laws nationwide would dramatically deter gun tragedies, especially involving children. These laws have been proven to work in a number of states. Our nation's unregulated gun epidemic is a catastrophic failure in our nation's safety systems and a betrayal of our children.

Two more intractable national problems include the media (including social media) and the militarism that is part of our culture. The sensationalized and often myopic media, especially in New Mexico, but also across our nation, seems to be focused on keeping people watching or reading in order to sell advertising. In mainstream media today, in many cases, there is little journalism, unbalanced analysis, and sparse critical thinking. Their goal is often to get some kind of story out that targets the amygdala, the part of the human brain that processes fearful and threatening stimuli. The impact to individuals, families, or the long-term consequence to society is rarely considered in the race for more viewers and more sponsors.

In our nation, the military is revered and glorified more than in most other advanced democracies. Patriotism justifies militarism, and this fealty to our military is how many families are socialized; especially many poor and minority families. This is evident when you consider the number of law enforcement who are ex-military and the number of radical militia groups composed of ex-military, and sadly the number of mass shooters who have military ties. Protecting our nation is one thing, evolving into a militaristic society is another and we are seeing the result of this national obsession.

Many will see Ezekiel's case as an anomaly or say something like, "Tom or Ezekiel are completely responsible for what happened." While they were the main actors in this tragedy and Ezekiel committed a horrific act, the entire tragedy could have been avoided or the pain and loss didn't have to be as great. Social systems are complex systems, which means there are so many variables that predicting an outcome with any degree of certainty isn't possible. Families are social systems; society is a social system. My brother walked a different path and made different choices than I did. He was faced with different environmental pressures than I was. I believe this is true for boys and young men in general. I would never say, "I did it, why couldn't he?" Anyone who says things like, "others were abused, and they didn't kill anyone," or, "my parents kept guns and I used them freely and we did fine," are ignorant, naive, or very lucky. We have drilled in the Gulf hundreds of times, why did the Gulf oil spill happen? Because both families and oil drilling operations are complex systems, and both involve people.

I started the journey to support Ezekiel out of love for my brother and the belief that something went terribly wrong with Ezekiel's brain. That's the only way I could explain why this kid I knew and loved had done such a horrific thing. He needed help, and I felt called to help him. I had no idea where it would lead. It has been a painful journey full of discoveries, tears, sadness, betrayal, and heart-wrenching grief. I do not wish it on anyone. I learned of the good and the bad that my brother passed on to Ezekiel. I learned that my brother had not healed from what was passed on to him, and that so shaped his soul and ability to be a father.

Tom was a good person; he did a great deal of good in his life, especially with his prison work. I celebrated with him in his work, including attending dinners for the *Light and Liberty* ministry, going to prison ministry breakfasts, and attending the very first Spanish speaking service at Calvary where he presided. He was the officiant at our wedding and best man at Leo's wedding. Tom did a lot of good and loved his children **and** he made poor choices as a parent; **both** are true. The person he portrayed outside his home was distinct from the person he was inside the home. The difference was largely because he had not transformed his own childhood pain.

Frederick Douglass said, "It is easier to build strong children than to repair broken men." It is a spiritual truth that if pain is not transformed it will only be transmitted. Hurt people hurt people; traumatized people pass on the trauma. This transforming work is hard and painful in its own right. Ask anyone who has been through a twelve-step program or recovery. Our family and community went through enormous pain because of this tragedy. Transforming rather than transmitting this pain should be the legacy of Tom and Amy.

Both Amy and Tom were deeply wounded by their own struggles growing up. Their own pain was transmitted to their children. This was not out of lack of love. It is tempting and common to deny or hide family secrets, but exposing them and admitting them is part of the hard work of healing our society. We must stop transmitting this generational pain. That is the vow I made to myself back in 1986 when I was pregnant with my third child and began attending Adult Children of Alcoholics (ACA). In our work with Ezekiel at the treatment center he made the same vow: "This stops with me!"

EPILOGUE

I have turned my attention to gun sense and youth justice advocacy, hoping that some good will come out of my family's tragedy. I am currently a Survivor Fellow of Everytown for Gun Safety and an active member of the New Mexico Chapter of Moms Demand Action. We work with our legislators on gun sense bills like safe storage laws to keep guns out of the hands of children. We also work to educate the public on gun safety and safe storage.

I am also a member of the New Mexico Coalition for the Fair Sentencing of Youth (NMCFSY), which is affiliated with the Campaign for the Fair Sentencing of Youth (CFSY), a nonprofit based in Washington, DC. We are working on fairer sentencing of youth. One of the bills that we hope to pass soon is a bill that will allow people serving crimes in an adult prison, who committed their crimes as children, to get a parole hearing within ten to fifteen years after they enter the adult prison. Children change tremendously from the time when they are fifteen to twenty-one years old when they are put in adult prison until they are twenty-seven to thirty. Their brains mature, they are completely different; think about yourself when you were between the ages of fifteen and twenty-one.

I spent time recovering from the disillusionment and finality of Judge Deering's decision and what felt like a death for Ezekiel, because he might never be able to live free. He will likely end up incarcerated his entire life; first by his father, then by the juvenile justice system, and now in an adult prison, which by all accounts is a cruel place, particularly to people like Ezekiel who are both brown and poor. As I sit with this *death*, I realize there was a death of something in me. Perhaps it goes back to the notion that I couldn't *save* my brother, nor could I *save* his son.

I decided to take relationships with extended family one day at a time and focus most of my energy on my immediate family, including my children and grandchildren. Desmond and Myho Tutu's book, *Book on Forgiveness*, says first to decide who you want to keep in your life; which relationships matter. This is a time of reconciling and integrating all that happened in the journey after the family tragedy, especially my love for both my brother and the son who killed him. It is a time to tell my exceedingly difficult story, knowing that I was called to walk the journey with Ezekiel.

Following the notions that families hand down from generation to generation by example without questioning what is being passed preserves dysfunction and ignorance. I have always believed that those who really love me will love me no matter what, whether they participate in my life or not. I know my intentions and actions were good, even if a bit halting and awkward at times. One does not get to practice for such unimaginable tragedies.

I continue to support and advocate for Ezekiel, though I am not able to see him much. We write to each other and talk on the phone. He is serving time now in North Carolina until he gets a parole hearing in 2050. Ironically, he couldn't be transferred to another state as a juvenile, but now he's in North Carolina. Ezekiel will be two months from turning fifty-three at that point, and I will be eighty-nine years old, and there is no guarantee he'll get out.

The North Carolina prison is a very harsh place. He is not getting any mental health or educational services. The prison that he's in is very racist and it is a survival situation for him. There is a large population of black inmates and several factions within that population. There are a good number of white inmates. The black are against the white and the white are against the black, and both are against the brown. There are now only two in the brown population in his unit. He has been stabbed eight times and has had a couple of severe fights. He doesn't sleep well because he's on guard, even in his cell. He has had health issues and an abscessed tooth that have gone untreated. It's not clear why he was sent so far away, two thousand miles from New Mexico, to one of the harshest systems in our nation. I assume it was deliberate.

I remain a mentor and touchstone for Ezekiel. Talking with him regularly on the phone I ask, "How far did you get with the book on Russia?"

And his response: "About a quarter of the way."

We send him books regularly; this book was a college textbook on Russia that he requested. He is a history buff and I like to probe his interest, knowing he needs someone genuinely interested in him.

"Did you get your exercise in today?" I ask.

"I'm going for rec this afternoon," he replies.

"That's good," I say and then give him the normal motherly spiel about how keeping himself busy creates a positive spiral.

I mostly listen for Ezekiel's mood and emotion and try to help him navigate the torrents of frustration, hopelessness, and anger, and always ask him to be the best version of himself possible in any moment.

I have come to terms that he is still very much alive, living in a bubble that I can't imagine and will never completely understand. There are some places the people you love go that you cannot follow, including into an operating room, into their addiction, to jail, and death. I guess it would have been similar had he joined the Army as a *grunt* like his father and he had planned. I still hold out hope; who knows what the future holds? Where there is life there is hope. I still argue with him about his politics. I get impatient when his racism shows itself. When the racism is at its worst, I can tell that's when he's in a bad place. But it's hard for him since he's swimming in racism, our country's original sin.

I love Ezekiel and I can't let go of him; he is a tether for me to Tom, my deeply sensitive brother. I hope that what happened to our family is a wakeup call for other families and a call to action for our communities, state, and nation. I remember what my best friend told me when I talked to her on the phone after Judge Deering's final sentence, telling her that it was like a *death*. "But Regina, it is going to be his life even if it isn't the life we live or the life we would wish for him."

NOTES

TIMELINE OF EVENTS

Date: Description

2012 Nov: Family Thanksgiving

2013 Jan: Shooting

2013 Jan: Ezekiel is incarcerated at county juvenile detention facility

2013 Oct: Carla ends contact with Ezekiel

2014 Feb: Jenny ends contact with Ezekiel

2014 Apr: Visit from maternal aunt

2014 May: Ezekiel transferred to treatment center

2015 Oct: Plea hearing

2016 Jan: 1st Amenability Hearing (included in Prologue)

2016 Feb: 1st Amenability Hearing continued

2016 Mar: Disposition Hearing and Ezekiel is transferred to youth detention center

2016 Apr: DA files notice of appeal

2018 Jan: Sham investigation

2018 Mar: Appellate court reverses Judge Baca's decision

2018 Mar: Ezekiel is transferred to adult county jail

2018 Dec: 2nd Amenability Hearing and Judge Baca recuses himself

2019 Mar: Ezekiel turns twenty-two

2019 Apr: 2nd Amenability Hearing Part 2

2019 Aug: Final Amenability Ruling

2019 Oct: Sentencing Hearing

2019 Nov: Sentencing Decision

2020 Jan: Moved to NM Adult Prison

2020 Mar: Ezekiel turns twenty-three

2020 Sep: Moved to NC Adult Prison

FAMILY TREE

This reflects only those family members discussed in the book.

Vincent (maternal half-brother) and
Amalia

|

[9 years between]

|

Janice and
John

|

[2 years between]

|

Regina and
Mark

|

[1 year between]

|

Tom and ---- (Tom's children) ----> - Eldest son
Amy*   - Eldest daughter
| - Carla
[4 years between]   - Daughter
| - Julie
Leo and   - Jenny*
Lily   - Ezekiel*
| - Malachi*
[4 years between]   - Miriam*
| - Grace*
Paternal half-brother
and his wife

ACKNOWLEDGEMENTS

I am grateful to my husband, Mark, who after only five years of knowing me was plunged into the hell of this family tragedy. He jumped in with both feet and supported me as I walked the perilous journey, often being my life-support system. He has also read various pieces of the manuscript and listened to me read it to him. His suggestions were always helpful. After we first met attending a drumming circle at The Center for Action and Contemplation (CAC) Retreat we began e-mailing each other and became "spiritual pen pals" after he received a message from the Spirit that we should "carry each other's burdens." Little did we know. Mark remains the most beautiful man I know.

I'd like to acknowledge the teachings of Father Richard Rohr and the Center for Action and Contemplation (CAC) for providing a spiritual foundation that helped us through this tragedy. Their teaching of taking action from the place of contemplation, grounded in the Divine, enabled us to take action in love without knowing the outcome. Mark and I did this when we first met and throughout our continued journey with Ezekiel. We remain eternally grateful to Richard for our own spiritual transformation.

Our children were there and felt the impact of the tragedy and its impact on us. I love each of you so very much, thank you for always being a part of our lives and for loving us. This work is for the generations.

I am grateful to my brother Leo and his wife, Lily. I have known his heart since the day he was born and he is one of the most compassionate and remarkable people I know. I depended on his partnership as we navigated the waters to support Ezekiel. He has worked his whole life to try to change the system for the poor, underserved, and families. Born of his own experience and pain, he wears his heart on his sleeve and he is treasured by many. Lily is the sparkle and light that has supported his flame and keeps him grounded.

To the first readers of my book, starting with my best friend, Gwen who is a most avid reader and has the consummate curiosity and joy of a child. She supported me through this and has been my advisor, cheerleader, and comforter since we met in 1988. She is my soul sister.

Thanks to Tom Tenorio, Annie Pausback, Rebecca Dakota, Allison Jaramillo, Lorian Kostranchuk, and Patricia Maisch for reading the manuscript and providing extensive feedback that made this story much better. I also want to thank all the people in my Moms Demand Action and New Mexico Coalition for the Fair Sentencing of Youth (NMCFSY) spheres. They encouraged me to tell my story. My thanks also to Marjorie St. Clair, a writing coach that I met months after the tragedy who coached me to write along with many other women in writing groups over the years.

Thanks to the professionals including all the people at Steve Harrison's Get Published Now group (GPN), especially my two coaches Suzette Webb and Debra Englander. Thanks to the editors, Valerie Costa at Costa Creative Services who did the final editing; thanks also to the editors I had early on: Diane Stockwell and Jaime Grechika. Rachel Shuster did an exceptional job at proofreading, thanks also to her. Thanks to Christy Day at Constellation Book Services for the design and production of this memoir.

I am extremely grateful for all the professionals who cared for and defended Ezekiel and all those that testified and advocated for him. These people are advocates for our children and tirelessly spend their life's energy for our children.

ABOUT THE AUTHOR

After retiring from a distinguished career as an engineer, Regina is now a coach, author, and speaker. Regina was born and raised in New Mexico and her Hispanic roots go back 400 years. She is married with six children in a blended family and has seven grandchildren. Regina has coached and mentored many young people as a professor, senior engineer, and leadership coach. She is an active member of organizations that support gun safety and juvenile justice. Regina is a Georgetown trained coach and a Fellow of the INCOSE, the largest International Systems Engineering Professional Organization. She holds a PhD, MS, and BS in Electrical and Computer Engineering and an MS in Computer Science.

Transcending-Futures.com
Facebook.com/TranscendingFutures
Instagram: @transcendingfutures

Made in the USA
Coppell, TX
22 July 2022

80329848R00193